Fifty More Hikes in New Hampshire

Fifty More Hikes in New Hampshire

Day Hikes and
Backpacking Trips from
the Coast to
Coos County

Daniel Doan

Photographs by
Jacqueline Donegan

SECOND REVISED EDITION

Backcountry Publications
Woodstock,
Vermont

Climbing Blue Job

An Invitation to the Reader

If you find that conditions have changed
along these trails, please let the author and
publisher know so that corrections may be
made in future editions. Address all
correspondence:
Editor, *50 More Hikes*
Backcountry Publications, Inc.
P.O. Box 175
Woodstock, VT 05091

Photo Credits

Cover photograph by Fred Bavendam.

Photographs on page 34 by John Ballentine;
pages 15, 37, 99, 104, and 193 by Daniel Doan;
pages 13, 58, and 199 by Nancy-Jane Jackson;
pages 84 and 123 by Lawrence S. Millard; page
45 by Sandy Tosi; and page 47 by W. Roots,
Crotched Mountain Rehabilitation Center. All
other photographs by Jacqueline Donegan.

Text and cover design by Wladislaw Finne

Library of Congress Cataloging in Publication Data

Doan, Daniel, 1914-
    Fifty more hikes in New Hampshire.

    1. Hiking—New Hampshire—Guide-
books.   2. Back-
packing—New Hampshire—Guide-books.   3.
New Hampshire—Description and
travel—1951—
Guide-books.   I. Title.
GV199.42.N4D6   1983   917.42   82-20665
ISBN O-942440-06-4

Second edition: third printing 1988, updated.

Acknowledgments

I am indebted to many hiking friends,
old and new, for their experience and
companionship on these trails. Particularly I want to express my appreciation to members of the New Hampshire
Chapter of the Appalachian Mountain
Club. My admirable wife extended her
patience to include my many absences.
For Frank Donegan's valuable
assistance I'm again grateful. Jacki
Donegan, the photographer, contributed
immensely.

D.D.

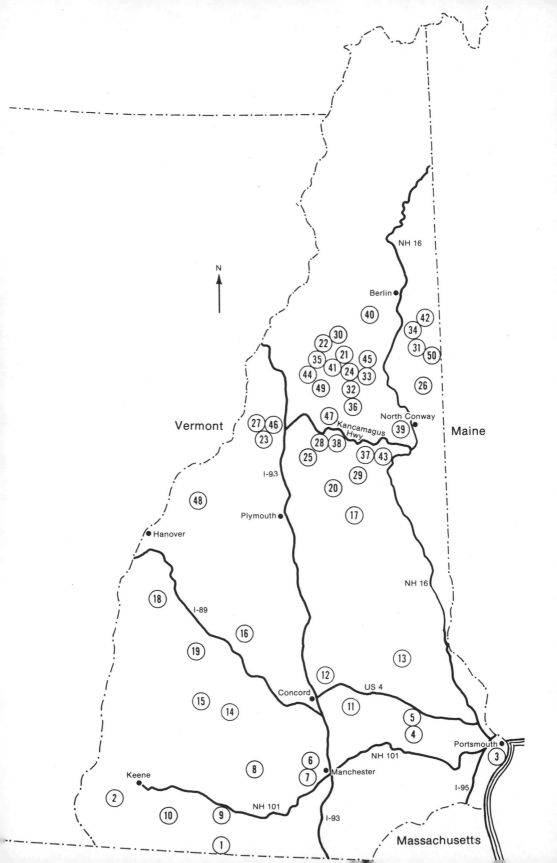

Contents

Backpacking Hikes

Introduction

These day hikes, walks, and backpacks cover the territory from Mount Adams in the White Mountains to trails near the Massachusetts border. I have divided the book into three geographical sections: Southern New Hampshire, Central New Hampshire, and the White Mountains. In the fourth section, Backpacking, all but one of the hikes are in the White Mountains, and that one, Smarts Mountain, is in the southwestern foothills of the higher ranges. Each section begins with the easier walks and climbs. Because of the natural contours of the state, the hikes in the southern and central sections take you to lower elevations or on simple woods walks.

I've included summits and places less known than those in my first book, *50 Hikes in the White Mountains of New Hampshire*. There is no duplication (other than about ten miles on overlapping trails mentioned in the earlier book).

A word about maps. The diagrammatic maps for each hike are meant to provide a general guide to and along the route. As on most maps, the top is north. For a thorough understanding of the hikes and the country they pass through, you should consider buying the maps put out by the United States Geological Survey (USGS) and by the Appalachian Mountain Club (AMC). The excellent AMC maps cover the White Mountains and Mount Monadnock. For central and other southern sections of the state, use the USGS maps. The USGS maps will also give you more topographical details than the AMC maps. The relevant maps have been listed along with the other basic data at the beginning of each hike.

In using the USGS maps, you should realize that those in the 15 minute series may be seriously out of date because some of the surveys were made in the 1930s or earlier. The topography is reliable, but houses are gone; roads, railroads, and trails have been abandoned, and new ones do not appear. Many fire towers have been taken down but still show on the maps. Also still shown are trails in the National Forest constructed by the Civilian Conservation Corps. Some, of course, have remained in use since those days of Franklin D. Roosevelt, while others were never reopened after the hurricane of 1938 and World War II. The partially completed 7.5 minute USGS series — much larger and more detailed than the

15 minute series — is accurate for the trails I have checked, although recent Forest Service roads do not appear; unfortunately 7.5 minute maps are not yet available for more than half the hikes in this book. Problems also arise when a hike requires maps from both series, which don't match; you'll find that for a time you're walking across an unmapped gap. Watch trail signs, blazes, and cairns carefully.

The age of the USGS maps for New Hampshire is the main reason I have chosen to continue using diagram maps in this book, even though several other volumes in the "Fifty Hikes" series (covering regions with more up-to-date USGS maps) now use topographical maps based on the USGS maps.

Two pamphlets put out by the USGS are also helpful. From the "Index to Topographic Maps of New Hampshire and Vermont" you learn which maps (called quadrangles) you'll need for different hikes. To learn the symbols and use of maps, get "Topographic Maps — Silent Guides for the Outdoorsman" and the sheet illustrating and explaining symbols. The pamphlets are free; the maps cost $2.50. Both can be obtained at outfitters, bookstores, and sporting goods stores, or you can send to the USGS.

One of my aims in this book has been to describe some remote territory for both the beginning hiker and the experienced climber. Many of the hikes avoid the more popular trails where overuse is a problem. In the White Mountain National Forest the U.S. Forest Service and the AMC are trying to deal with this increasing traffic — and are succeeding, too, in protecting and conserving the forest and trails.

This overuse, although bad for some of the more popular trails, is an indication of the joys of hiking and backpacking. Of course every hiker wants to see the famous peaks. But an infinite number of enjoyable, more remote hikes warrant your attention.

The ultimate end of a program aimed at avoiding busy trails and campsites is hiking on no trails at all. That's commonly called *bushwhacking.* I've included in the backpacking section a simple bushwhack route to a remote beaver pond: Cheney Brook. To show you the contrast between overused trails and forest solitude I also put together the Redrock Brook backpack. There are miles and miles of New Hampshire forest without trails. Try them. I advise first that you follow streams and go with companions experienced in the use of maps and compass. You'll discover another world.

The hiking season on southern and central trails runs from March to December. In the White Mountains it's shorter: May to October. These arbitrary dates vary from year to year depending on the arrival and melting of snow. On higher elevations, especially in the White Mountains, you can expect snow on the ground through May and storms of sleet and snow in any month.

Snowshoes can make you a winter hiker, and they extend the season year-round. Cross-country skiing is also a great way to span the winters between hiking seasons. For either sport (when you have learned to travel on snowshoes and skis and have the proper winter gear, clothing, and experience) I suggest you try Croydon Turnpike, Fox Forest, Bear Brook State Park, Pisgah State Park — to name only a few almost level routes.

Except for the bushwhacks, the hikes follow maintained trails, paths, or old roads. In the White Mountains the majority of the trails are maintained by the forest service and the AMC, although some are kept up by smaller clubs. To the south various clubs, conservation groups, and public organizations look after the trails. In state parks the New Hampshire Division of Parks and Recreation does the job.

Old logging roads appear often in the hike descriptions, because many trails follow these routes, which were once used to sled out timber. They usually lead to rougher mountain trails farther up steeper slopes. Of similar vintage are the abandoned old logging railroads. The tracks are gone but the grades make for good walking. You may encounter logging operations south of the White Mountains, but in the national forest the forest service supervises the cutting to leave wide bands of trees on either side of the trails.

Many of the trails are on private property to reach the national forest. The forest service posts little yellow signs at the boundaries where trails cross from privately owned land. Through private property you hike on sufferance. Needless to say, behavior should be that of a considerate guest. Otherwise there'll be closed trails and NO TRESPASSING signs.

The trails change from year to year because of natural causes such as erosion, landslides, beavers flooding low ground along streams, and wind storms blowing down trees. Yet many have remained virtually unchanged for generations.

Distance, Walking Time, and Vertical Rise

Each hike description begins with gauges by which you can decide the hike you want, depending on the time and amount of energy you have to expend and your physical fitness. The distances are for a round trip unless otherwise noted.

The times are based on moderate climbing speed — the pace at which a moderately fit hiker can walk and still talk to his companion without gasping for breath. This is the only sensible pace to use. The times do not include stops for snacks, observing nature, eating lunch, or viewing scenery.

The vertical rise is the actual amount of upward climbing. If you start at a 1,000-foot elevation and climb to a 2,500-foot summit, no matter how far you walk or for how long, you'll climb an equivalent of 1,500 feet straight up. In general, if the climb contains only 750 feet of vertical rise, it is half as difficult as one with 1,500 feet of vertical rise. I must add that this is not always so. If the 750 feet go up difficult boulders, ledges, gullies, and rock slides, they may be more of a challenge than 1,500 feet on a gradual trail. There are too many variables for a useful rating system, and I've not included one.

The White Mountain National Forest

Because more than half of these hikes — twenty-eight to be exact —are partially or completely within the White Mountain National Forest, you should know a bit about its history. Many of these 752,648 acres had not been logged until the 1880s and 1890s when railroads built by lumber barons such as J.E. Henry of Lincoln penetrated the rugged valleys. By 1905 the spruce and pine had largely fallen to axe and saw. Logging continued through World War I, with pulpwood for paper and hardwood for veneer a large part of operations as late as the 1930s. During the peak years of logging and immediately after, fire consumed thousands of acres. When lightning struck in tinder-dry branches left by loggers, the remains of the forest exploded like a giant torch. Sparks from wood-burning locomotives also were a danger. So were careless smokers and campers who touched off some devastating fires.

Concern by conservationists resulted in the founding in 1901 of the Society for the Protection of New Hampshire Forests. To this day it is active and effective in the state. The society led the fight to save the mountains and succeeded with the Weeks Act of 1911. The federal government began to purchase land for a national forest in the White Mountains the next year.

The national forest is managed by the forest service. Its directives are based on a "multiple-use policy," which provides for timber production, watershed protection, recreational development, and wildlife protection. Nine scenic areas and four wilderness areas protect for posterity the wild environment of thousands of acres within the national forest.

Trees and Animals

Since about 1850 the New Hampshire forests cut down by the early settlers have been growing back. In the southern and central sections mile after mile of fields and hilltop pastures returned to woods as families migrated west, as men never returned from the Civil War, and as young people sought wages in city mills. This natural reforestation is continuing.

The forest is composed of diversified conifers and deciduous trees. The evergreens populate the high elevations and the swamps, the leafy trees fill in between, and mixtures of both varieties are common everywhere depending on soil and exposure. Of course some

peaks like Monadnock still remain bare after more than a hundred years since early fires denuded their slopes.

In the White Mountains proper the division of tree types is more marked. Beech, maple, yellow birch, and white birch took over after the cutting of the original spruce on the lower slopes. From an elevation of about 3,000 feet up to treeline, evergreens — red spruce, black spruce, and balsam fir — are better adapted; they cover the mountainside and many summits. (The alpine zone, treeless, at about 5,000 feet and up, cannot support trees because of the elevation's climate, which resembles that of Labrador and Greenland.) White birch is often dominant on burned land. The evergreen hemlocks and white pines blend with the deciduous forests. Twisted white birches and small mountain ash trees commonly grow with the highest spruce and fir.

Scrub spruce at treeline deserves special mention because it closes in the trails with impenetrable thickets. Don't try to travel in this scrub.

New Hampshire animals are almost invariably shy or nocturnal or both. Red squirrels, chipmunks, and gray squirrels are exceptions. I haven't seen a black bear for over ten years. I never saw a bobcat. There are no problems with poisonous snakes. Each year a rattlesnake is reported in the southern and central sections usually in a newspaper account, but I have yet to meet anyone who laid eyes on one.

Like all mice, the New Hampshire woods resident, known as the white-footed mouse or deer mouse, will chew your pack if you leave it on the ground. Raccoons will raid food containers you leave unattended for the night. Sleeping

Cinnamon Fern Fruiting

with your pack next to you usually settles this problem.

Porcupines aren't dangerous, but don't fool with one; their quilled tails move faster than lightning. If your dog attacks one he'll learn the error of aggression.

One dangerous species is *Homo sapiens*. Ironically the "wild" woods and mountains seem to have a civilizing effect on most people. Trail heads and parked cars, however, do invite theft and vandalism. Don't leave anything you value in your car. A locked trunk can be an inducement to force it open on the theory that you've used it for a strong box.

Of the larger animals, you'll see white-tailed deer in the evening or morning; most moving hikers make too much noise to see deer along trails. Deer stay off the high peaks. Moose are becoming more common, but you'll probably see only their oxlike tracks. Stillness is important, if you would see animals. If you remain silent as you step out on a pond's shore you might see a moose belly deep feeding on roots of water lilies. In recent years coyotes have moved into the northern half of the state.

Skunks, foxes, hares, and small rodents such as mice forage mostly at night. Beavers are also active then. In daylight sometimes a beaver will swim about his pond apparently checking on the water level and the dam. Fishers are as scarce as bobcats, and both have been protected from trapping. Mink and otter frequent ponds and streams.

Clothing and Equipment

Start with comfortable underwear, a long-sleeved shirt of cotton-polyester blend, and fully cut walking pants of the same material. (I think blue jeans are an abomination in the woods. They are cold when wet, take forever to dry, and are cut like tights. You have to be a contortionist to get into the pockets, from which you lose valuables when you lie down. Besides, they remind me of work.)

Boots should be leather, ankle high, and need weigh no more than three pounds per pair. Rubber lug soles are best. For hiking in the early spring or in the first fall snow, leather-topped rubbers with an innersole keep your feet drier than leather boots. Sneakers inevitably turn out to be fine for easy woods walks and encourage you to wear them on trails too rough and rocky for them to protect your feet. I've tried the lug-sole sneakers, ankle high — again, good woods footgear.

After the above conservative advice, however, I will add a more up-to-date suggestion. Modern lightweight hiking boots, which incorporate designs and materials from jogging shoes, may be right for your purposes and feet. During a long hike, such boots, compared to some of the monstrosities on the market, can save you from lifting literally tons. I use a pair that weighs two pounds but would not recommend them for backpacking unless your feet are tougher than mine.

Inside your hiking boots wear a light inner sock of wool and nylon and an outer all-wool (or nearly so) heavy sock. Hikers favor the ragg-knit type.

Rain or shine, a hat is a necessity. It stops insects from crawling through your hair and protects you from both rain and sun. The brim shades your eyes.

What about the knapsack or rucksack and its size, style, and contents? If you buy a small one you'll want a bigger one. Mine is made of waterproofed nylon. It's fourteen by eighteen inches, with side pockets and a pocket in the flap. I use it year-round.

Carry in your rucksack a heavy wool shirt, sweater, or insulated jacket and a poncho or rain suit with hood. A nylon parka or "shell" is a must above treeline and a comfort for hiking the lowlands on cool windy days. Over a wool shirt it's better hiking garb in showers than a rain suit in which your own sweat and condensed vapor wet you as much as rain would. Wool is still the simple answer to hiking in the rain; it's warm even when it's wet. Pack ex-

tra wool socks. If you don't wear them on your feet they'll be welcome as mittens some cold, wet day.

You should consider a parka made of a laminated material that is microporous, making it both breathable and waterproof. Many equipment companies produce such parkas for a wide choice of styles and conditions. There are also rain pants. Recently boots utilize it for uppers in lightweight hiking footwear. Expensive, this material could, however, eliminate your other rain gear for active use, but don't expect a miracle of total sweat evaporation. Such

The author on the trail

a parka will at times substitute for a windproof shell.

You might include a fishnet undershirt. Get the kind with cloth shoulders to protect where your pack straps rub. These undershirts trap air next to your skin for insulation under a T-shirt or jersey. They prevent mosquitos from piercing through to you. I like the way they cushion my back under my pack.

Besides suitable clothing you should have matches and firestarter in waterproof containers within your rucksack's side pockets. Compass, map, and guidebook should be there also. I pack a flashlight but seldom use it.

Here are pants and shirt pocket items: matches in a waterproof holder; pocketknife with can opener and screwdriver; sunglasses; insect repellent in a small squeeze bottle. I carry a collapsible cup for filling water containers at small springs.

The rucksack should contain your spare water and extra food. You should have a quart of water in a canteen or plastic bottles. Besides the day's lunch and whatever trail snacks you like to munch on, carry spare food for two meals. A simple first-aid kit and elastic bandage for sprained ankles or knees should be in a waterproof bag.

Backpackers will need a tent, sleeping bag, foam pad to sleep on, and cooking equipment. Freeze-dried food is excellent, and there are less expensive dehydrated and dried foods at supermarkets. Of course you'll need a large pack to put all this in.

Such a sketchy summary of equipment is only an introduction to vast and varied choices. I suggest you read a book on the subject, study catalogs, visit outfitting stores, and talk to other hikers. Renting from outfitters is a good way to avoid making mistakes in permanent purchases. Equipment should be simple, lightweight, and practical. Try it

out before you go on an extended day hike or backpack. This last piece of advice applies particularly to new boots. They should be well broken-in. To accomplish this in a hurry, stand in a tub of water with the boots over your two pairs of socks, and then walk the boots dry. That'll fix 'em. Watch the tongues while you pause during your walk and make sure they stay centered. The position of the tongues when broken-in remains for the life of the boots. Broken-in or not, your boots can give you blisters. Carry moleskin in your first aid kit.

Rules and Regulations

In general, sensible behavior keeps you within most rules and regulations. There are certain specifics, however. If you are hiking on private property, no wood or charcoal fires may be built without the landowner's permission and a fire permit from the district fire chief. Use a portable stove; it's a simpler solution. Furthermore, there's no overnight camping allowed on private property without the landowner's permission. Carry out all your empty containers, wrappers, and other trash. Don't litter. Don't cut trees or boughs; don't destroy plants. Park your car completely off traveled roads. Don't park in any opening into the woods, any gateway, or any logging road. A state law prohibits obstruction of a right-of-way.

For the White Mountain National Forest the long-standing requirement of fire permits was discontinued in 1985. There are, however, special regulations about camping and fires. You should get the latest seasonal information from the office of the Forest Supervisor in Laconia, or from district ranger stations in Conway, Gorham, Plymouth, Bethlehem, and Bethel, Maine. The forest service also maintains information centers located near I-93 at Campton and Lincoln and on the Kancamagus Highway at Passaconaway.

The AMC offers information at Pinkham Notch Camp, at Lafayette Place in Franconia Notch, and at the former depot near the Crawford House site just north of Crawford Notch.

New Hampshire State Parks, Reservations, and Forests have other rules and regulations. In general no camping or wood or charcoal fires are allowed outside designated campgrounds. Regulations are posted. The N.H. Division of Parks and Recreation provides a brochure, "N.H. Camping Guide."

Although in the White Mountain National Forest no fire permits are required, this does not reduce the danger nor your responsibility. You must obtain and abide by a map and rules entitled "Restricted Use Area Information, White Mountain National Forest." The map of the national forest provides an excellent overall perspective of the mountains and shows in color specific areas (RUAs) where camping and fires are prohibited. In these places overuse has compacted the soil, damaged plants, trees, and water. Natural recovery is encouraged by RUAs, and future harm is prevented. The other side of the map deals with descriptions of the RUAs, how to build and cook with your campfire, camping and hiking ethics, safety, and even dog etiquette. The forest service also offers helpful brochures on recreational opportunities in the mountains.

Here are some examples of RUAs. No camping is allowed above treeline, which has been set at the altitude where trees are less than eight feet high. Similar restrictions apply to land within 200 feet of certain trails, and within ¼ mile along some roads and around various huts, shelters, tent platforms, and lakes.

The RUA map shows the four wilderness areas, namely, Great Gulf, Presidential-Dry River, and the recently designated Pemigewasset River's East Branch drainage, and Sandwich Range. Only in the Great Gulf are camping permits and reservations required, issued by the district ranger in Gorham. All four areas are open to day hikes. I should point out that in the two new areas various structures and shelters may be removed in accordance with the policy set forth in the Wilderness Act. Check when you get your RUA Information sheet.

Only one hike in this book, #49, Redrock Brook, penetrates a designated wilderness area, the Pemigewasset. To avoid confusion, you should know that this drainage of the East Branch has been known since about 1880 as the Pemigewasset Wilderness, or to the numerous hikers who enjoy it, "The Pemi."

Huts and Shelters

In the White Mountains the forest service and the AMC provide shelters and accommodations of various sorts. The AMC's eight mountain huts have bunkrooms and serve meals. Make reservations at the Pinkham Notch Camp, which is the center for the AMC trail system. Log or board shelters, whose open fronts face stone fireplaces, are maintained by the forest service, AMC, and several other clubs. At some AMC shelters and campsites, tent platforms for backpacking tents have been built. A caretaker supervises the site and collects a modest fee per night per person.

Safety

Surely you've seen the annual headlines about some hiker dying on the trail. Storms above treeline can be fiercer than you believed possible when you were down in the forest, and they can be sudden. When you reach treeline make a judgement of the weather: if clouds or winds foretell a storm, turn back. Indeed, if the forecasts have indicated possible bad weather, don't go to treeline at all. If you must hike regardless of weather (and when you're hooked as I am you sometimes feel that way), hike on a forest trail to a pond or a low wooded mountain.

Storms above treeline always get worse. Fog and winds will shove you, semiblinded, from rock to rock in a dangerous teetering gait. Don't try it. Turn back into the trees.

You should hike with a companion. Loners invite trouble (and cause it for their rescuers) if they twist an ankle or move off the trail and fall.

Before a hike, study your maps and guide books. Estimate the time needed to get back before dark. Carry a compass and learn how to use it. Carry enough emergency clothing and food so you can spend a night in the woods if you have to.

Getting lost happens to even the best hikers. The standard advice is to sit down and think about your predicament. It *does* work. Very likely you will remember where you missed the trail or took a wrong turn. Study your map and orient it with your compass. Distances out to the roads are not great in most of New Hampshire. When you are really confused, follow a stream. If injured, build a fire (assuming you can). Throw on ferns and leaves to make a smudge that will signal above the trees. Someone will spot it and come looking for the fire if not for you. Even if you can't build a fire, someone will come looking — if you have left your itinerary with a responsible person and have adhered to it. Leave word at home and with

rangers or other officials. Even a note under the windshield wiper of your car will do.

It's best to have an alternate hike for unpredictable bad weather and to leave word of this. Go to one or the other. You'll probably never need to worry about being searched for, but it's a good feeling to know you'll be found if something happens. Cares have no place on hikes. Leave them all behind; enjoy the forests and the mountains.

Addresses

Appalachian Mountain Club
5 Joy Street
Boston, Massachusetts 02108
or
Pinkham Notch Camp
Gorham, New Hampshire 03581

United States Forest Service
719 Main Street
Laconia, New Hampshire 03246

New Hampshire Department of Resources and Economic Development
Concord, New Hampshire 03301

New Hampshire Division of Parks and Recreation
Concord, New Hampshire 03301

Society for the Protection of New Hampshire Forests
54 Portsmouth Street
Concord, New Hampshire 03301

United States Geological Survey
Washington, D.C. 20242

For USGS maps by mail, order from:
**Branch Distribution,
U.S. Geological Survey**
Box 25286, Denver Federal Center
Denver CO 80225

Southern
New Hampshire

1

Barrett Mountain

Distance: 6½ miles
Walking time: 4½ hours
Vertical rise: 795 feet
Map: USGS 15' Peterborough

Blueberries in June? Sometimes they ripen then on Middle Barrett Mountain, whose name on the USGS map (Peterborough Quadrangle) is New Ipswich Mountain. To a man from central New Hampshire, June is early for blueberries. Although later he's accustomed to extending the season by going farther north and upward in the mountains, he thinks finding blueberries during the strawberry season is too much luck for his own good. Nevertheless, I ate blueberries on Middle Barrett one recent June 22 and at home the same day picked strawberries for supper.

The route of this hike is simple. It's a section of the Wapack Trail. Your destination can vary. I have chosen to approach from the north and pick up the Wapack Trail off NH 123. (In this area NH 123 and NH 124 coincide.) The hike follows the trail to and from an arbitrary point of no return and lunch spot at the lookoff ledges on the north side of Middle Barrett Mountain.

The Wapack Trail's twenty-one miles extend over Watatic Mountain in Massachusetts and into New Hampshire

Witches broom

for Barrett Mountain, Kidder, Temple, and Pack Monadnock. The trail crosses NH 123 north of Barrett Mountain, 6.75 miles south of NH 101 out of Peterborough.

The landmark to watch for on NH 123 appears .5 mile after the junction with NH 124. It is a large, gray, dilapidated building on the right, once known as Wapack Lodge. It no longer serves vacationers and hikers. The section of the Wapack Trail leading south over Barrett Mountain begins at a sign (or a triangular blaze) on a big oak tree. You'll find it near the corner where the driveway past the lodge turns left to another house. Park off the highway shoulder.

The trail immediately angles uphill and to the left until you reach level ground beyond a house on the far right. Continue across a woods road, where the trail enters spruces and avoids a narrow clearing on the left. The Wapack Trail blaze, a yellow triangle, marks the way. Soon you come to a sharp left turn; straight ahead a ski trail marked "expert" drops off steeply. The Wapack Trail remains on high ground, and about ten minutes from the start you step out on a lookoff ledge that opens toward

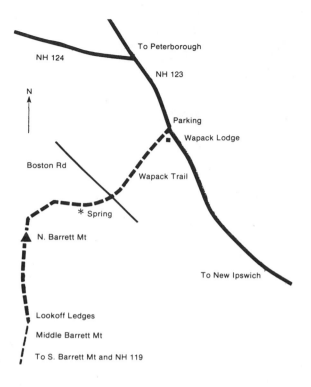

the long ridge's four summits. Far away to the left you may discern the Binney Ponds.

The mountain is all forested except for rocks similar to those found at this viewpoint. As on most mountains of southern New Hampshire, trees have taken over the old pastures, which once provided summer grass for cattle and sheep. The cattle were often driven up from Massachusetts farms.

Descending, the trail levels and crosses a stone wall past a junction with the White Trail coming in on the right. Several trails intersect the Wapack Trail along here. These are primarily ski touring trails that originate at Windblown cross-country skiing center to the north. Junctions are marked, and reasonable care will keep you on the Wapack Trail. Its yellow

blazes are distinctive, and the path is much more worn.

The Wapack Trail slabs through older woods, ascends a slight grade under hemlocks, crosses the Green Trail, and dips into a narrow ravine. The damp shade favors the lichens and moss growing on the rocks that stud the opposite steep mountainside. The ravine is the route of the Green Trail, which you cross again here. The upper branches of tall maples and beeches provide a perfect home for that patient, unobtrusive flycatcher, the wood peewee, whose plaintive notes are also his name. The ravine in 1753 became a route for the "Boston Road" several years after New Ipswich was settled.

The trail bears right to cross the ravine and faces up the mountain for your first steep climb. An ascent of a few yards brings you to a rocky trickle at your left, which in late summer may be a line of dry rocks. You climb to its source in a shallow basin. On one June hike I drank two cups of this spring water and saved my water bottle for lunch.

Climbing on you soon top out on Barrett's north shoulder. An opening to the right invites you to look for views. You find mostly gray birches and spruces surrounding a flat ledge and a boulder just right for sitting upon. You may notice paint marks northward where the ledge extends through grassy turf. They lead to more Windblown trails.

The Wapack Trail heads south, to the left, without actually entering the open area. You walk into a young spruce forest. Meadowsweet, the high bush similar to hardtack but with a white flower spike instead of pink, borders the trail. It obviously can survive for a time in woods after its chosen habitat, a sunny pasture, is gone. Open rocks contain enough soil to support northern bush honeysuckle. Fifteen minutes beyond the north shoulder a sign on a spruce to the left announces: BARRETT MOUNTAIN 1,853 FEET.

In the next ¾-mile section the trail crosses two stone walls, surmounts two minor knobs, and takes shade in two declivities before rising toward the daylight shining over a crude wall and through a cluster of mountain ash trees. The open ledge, which turns out to be the light source, offers no striking view but invites you to return in autumn to admire the red berry bunches.

Proceeding higher, the trail winds to partially wooded rock, where extensive vistas spread north and west as far as Pack Monadnock and Grand Monad-nock. The tower you see rises from the south summit of Pack Monadnock. (The two peaks are known to hikers as South Pack and North Pack.) To the west Grand Monadnock's pyramid rises into the sky alone and is unforgettable.

Directly ahead of you to the north, Barrett's summit presents a green, bosomy contour. To the right and more in the distance, Kidder Mountain and then Temple Mountain show you the terrain that the Wapack Trail traverses north of NH 123 beyond your car.

Although you are at a pleasant lunch spot, continue along the trail, ascending gradually, for another twenty minutes (about ½ mile) to this ridge's true summit, Middle Barrett, and wider views from open ledges.

Now turn your back on the mountains and exchange the views for the blueberries I mentioned earlier. Wander off the trail into the small patches of low bushes. After sandwiches, the tart-sweet little morsels make a delicious dessert.

I like to pick a handful instead of eating them one at a time. This procedure satisfies my need for a little (very little) postponed gratification, which doubtless I inherited from Puritan ancestors. Better still, I like to have a companion more avid to pick them than I am and also generous. I've decided there's no comfortable blueberry-picking position, except maybe kneeling, and in time that gives me a crick in the back. Besides, it stains the knees of my pants. Still, the berries are worth any inconvenience. If I can't wangle a gift of a half cup I'll pick my own quick enough.

The return retraces the morning hike.

Pisgah State Park

Distance: 10 miles
Walking time: 6 hours
Vertical rise: 1,640 feet
Maps: USGS 15' Keene; Winter Trails
Map: Pisgah State Park

This forested state park spreads southwest of Keene across 13,000 acres of low ridges, ponds, and marshes. The ponds and streams drain south to the Ashuelot River, and Broad Brook, in the eastern section, runs through a valley once cleared for farms. This inviting spot could well have been the Promised Land for a pioneer arriving with his axe and Bible; naming the overlook Mount Pisgah would have been natural.

In the park's northwest section, where this loop hike is set, there are no remnants of earlier farming. These steep ridges were probably better suited for logging and pasturing. The American Box Company once logged the area extensively, but the forest has renewed itself, and the land is rough and wild.

While the USGS Keene Quadrangle includes the area of your hike, it omits several of the dirt roads, snowmobile trails, former logging tracks, and foot trails you will encounter. Consequently, you should supplement the USGS map with the "Winter Trails Map: Pisgah State Park," a diagrammatic map that depicts your route and gives the numbers of various junctions. You will find this map in the *New Hampshire*

Snowmobiler's Guide, which you can obtain from the Bureau of Off-Highway Vehicles, Christian Mutual Building, 6 Loudon Road, P.O. Box 856, Concord, NH 03301. The guide is also available at information booths, including those at rest areas on I-89 and I-93. A mailbox near the parking area for this hike may contain individual copies of the map.

To arrive at the parking area, turn east off NH 63 at Chesterfield. You can't miss the stone church, town hall, and post office. The way to the park begins with the Old Chesterfield Road opposite the post office. After driving a short distance, turn right onto Horseshoe Road, which soon becomes gravel and winds up and down through the woods. About 1.75 miles from the village you reach the parking area at the memorial to Chief Justice Harlan F. Stone. Nearby is the granite foundation of the house where he was born.

From a field east and south of the road you have a sweeping view across the park's wooded ridges. The panorama begins to take on meaning when you get out your maps and orient them. Mount Pisgah lies 2½ miles to the south and slightly west. Out of sight behind the ridge is the trail you will de-

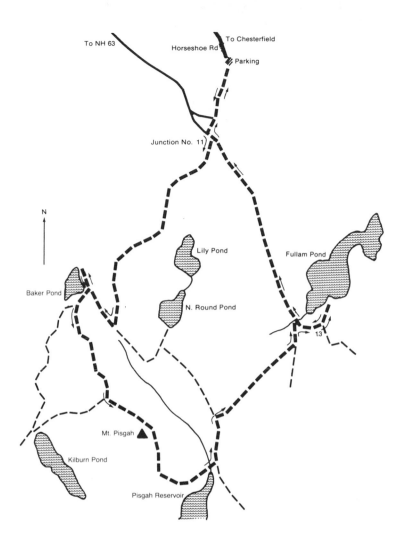

scend to the northern arm of Pisgah Reservoir (the name "Round Pond" appearing on the "Winter Trails Map" refers to the shape of that part of the reservoir before a dam created the present elongated body of water). Also hidden from view is Fullam Pond, but you should get a general picture of the country you'll be walking through.

Before you start your hike, make sure you have plenty of water. Ponds are boggy, and many of the brooks are seasonal.

Set out down the continuation of Horseshoe Road. At the bottom of the hill bear left across an overgrown field (Horseshoe Road bends right here for its return back to NH 63). Beyond the old field you pass above a little swamp on your right and join a dirt road branching southeast from Horseshoe Road. Turn left downhill. Almost at once you come to a fork and a numbered sign on a tree for junction 11, your first location on the "Winter Trails Map," and the point at which you will complete your loop.

Keep to the right uphill. As you climb you pass two forks on your left and one on your right. Some of these roads do not appear on either of your maps, so pay close attention and make notes about junctions, forks, and bearings. With these observations, this hike can be a base for later explorations of the park.

As the road begins to level, it brings you to an opening cut in the tall oaks and maples to your left. You are about forty minutes from your car. Eastward the green forested ridges running north and south set off a distant view of Mount Monadnock.

Now the way is downhill past laurel and other shrubs under the trees to junction 8 on your "Winter Trails Map." Leave the road here and turn right onto a snowmobile trail which crosses a bridge over a seasonal brook. The trail winds up in S-curves into hemlocks. After fifteen minutes you see a glimmer of Baker Pond ahead. Notice a wide trail forking left. You will take this to the Pisgah Mountain Trail, but first you should continue straight ahead to see Baker Pond.

There is a path to the shore about midway on the east side. Beside it, sprouts of chestnut trees may attain a height of fifteen feet before the blight kills them. Another stranger to the northern woods is the black birch, here quite at home. A variety of water brush lines the shore, and out in the pond a rounded rock "island" gives root-holds to bushes.

After a rest, and perhaps a snack, return to the fork at the wide trail you passed earlier. This is a snowmobile trail leading to Kilburn Pond. Follow this trail for about ten minutes until you come to a sign reading "To Pisgah Mt. Tr." A few steps beyond it you turn left off the snowmobile trail onto this traverse of the long ridge. A big sign

forbids snowmobile use. A series of black dash lines indicates the trail on your "Winter Trails Map."

Orange tapes frequently encircle trees (paint blazes are in the future). Remember, this wide trail is new, and although the stubs of trees have been sawed off close to the ground, a number of years must pass before they rot and cease to be a hazard for hikers. Bracken and other ferns hide them along this stretch. In the more shaded open woods, ferns don't thrive and you can see the stubs.

You climb out of these woods to the first rocky outlook along this ridge trail. Beyond it you descend into a ledgy ravine where the trail keeps parallel with the jumbled rocks that suggest dens for porcupines, bobcats, and fishers. You climb out of this craggy glen to the left, over a ridge, and down to a trail junction and signs. You are about forty minutes from the start of this trail, if you walk as I do, to enjoy the scenery.

The signs orient you. To the right (west) a trail leads to Kilburn Pond. To the left (east) the Pisgah Mountain Trail continues. A sign points behind you to Baker Pond.

Turn left. After a short descent, you climb uphill to a rock summit. Views east and west have been opened to Monadnock and the Connecticut River valley. Keep straight south between these two outlooks, staying on the rocks and then entering the woods where the trees are again plainly marked with orange tapes. You descend and climb two more knolls before reaching the crest of Mount Pisgah.

Again the bedrock forms an outlook to your left, although the trail stays along the top at the edge of the woods. Directly ahead and not far from the

Along Pisgah Trail

cliff, which drops off more than 300 feet, a beaver dam forms a pond in Pisgah Brook. Monadnock continues to dominate the horizon in that direction. To the south you see an arm of Pisgah ᵎ Reservoir extending toward you.

You pass one more outlook, then descend past an enormous boulder on the right. In a little valley a brookbed may contain water. Turn left along it to an old logging road, which you follow down to a boggy pond. Here the trail swings left and is once more newly cut through the woods. As you follow the pond's shoreline, watch for ducks and herons. Checking the "Winter Trails Map," you can see that you are on a hook-like curve and heading northeast.

A footbridge takes you across Pisgah Brook. On the far side a sign marks the way behind you as "Pisgah Mt. Tr." Walk a few yards to a junction with a snowmobile trail. It's the end of the black dash line on the "Winter Trails Map." Turn left onto the snowmobile trail, and you are following a red line on the map, heading toward junction 17.

Fifteen minutes from the bridge you pass a beaver pond on your left. You saw it an hour earlier from Mount Pisgah, and there far above you is the rounded rock cliff where you stood.

The trail bears right from the beaver pond. Five minutes in fine hemlock woods brings you to the trail forking right toward Fullam Pond. At last report a sign marked the start of this trail, but Park authorities caution that signs are sometimes stolen. In any case, orange tape marks a large tree at the start, and other tapes lead you over a low ridge and into a young forest of white birches. Your map shows this trail as another black dash line leading northeast to a red snowmobile trail and junction 10.

Beyond a low ridge you descend to an old logging road, and to an unmarked junction with the snowmobile trail. Turn left, and soon you are at junction 10. You have been walking about forty-five minutes since the beaver pond.

On your left at junction 10 the road crosses a bridge over an inlet to Fullam Pond. Turn right, and stride along this dirt road above swampy ground for five minutes to junction 13. Go left past a big pine tree for another five minutes to Fullam Pond.

Like all woodland ponds, Fullam is a fine habitat for ducks, herons, and the insectivorous birds who feast on some of the pests you've warded off with bug repellent. Beavers have built a lodge on the far shore. There are no "improvements" here; Fullam remains unspoiled.

For the return to your car, allow for an hour's walk northwest on the dirt road from junction 13. You pass junction 10, cross the bridge, and start uphill. You'll be climbing steadily most of the way as you pass junction 14 to complete the loop at junction 11. Turn right and continue uphill on Horseshoe Road to the parking area.

Odiorne Point

Distance: 2 miles
Walking time: 1½ hours
Vertical rise: 60 feet
Map: USGS 7½' Kittery

This is a seashore state park. Waves and tides reach across the stony shore toward marsh grass and bayberry bushes; the everlasting fascination of the ocean holds you. Even when you wander in woods of oaks and pines, the mewing gulls coasting overhead and the smell of seaweed remind you that salt water is near. I have outlined a walk to many attractions. Anyone choosing to alter the route will not get lost and will be equally rewarded.

Odiorne Point State Park extends along NH 1A in Rye for about two miles. It takes in the shoreline from Odiorne Point on the south to the salt marshes of Witch Creek on the north. The park had been a military reservation for coastal artillery. Fort Dearborn, as it was then named, guarded the entrance to Portsmouth harbor and navy yard. The government dismantled it after World War II but concrete casemates still remain as reminders of the park's wartime function. They look out over picnic tables, trees, shrubbery, marshes, rocky shores, and sea as far as the Isles of Shoals. I suppose I'm pointing out the obvious (I can't resist the irony of the park's origin) by stating that a world war, in effect, preserved

this unique bit of New Hampshire's exploited coastline. Shut behind its chain-link fence for many years, the land became a state park in 1972.

Unlike nearby Wallis Sands or Hampton Beach, this is not a park for sandy lolling or saltwater bathing, although there is sand at low tide off the northern rocks that form Frost Point. The park is primarily a place to enjoy the ocean setting and study the related ecology. The Audubon Society of New Hampshire conducts walks and classes from the nature center.

There are various ways of picking up NH 1A and driving to the park. You may follow the coast north from Hampton through Rye. Driving south from Portsmouth on US 1, take Elwyn Road east just beyond Yokum's Restaurant. Drive 1.4 miles to NH 1A and follow that route south 2 miles to the hanging sign, on the left, at the gate in the chain-link fence.

For a base from which to hike, I have chosen the central parking area beyond and to the right of the gatehouse, where someone collects a small fee. The gate opens at 10 A.M. and closes at 6 P.M.

The smell of the sea comes to you from beyond the brushy flat. A cool

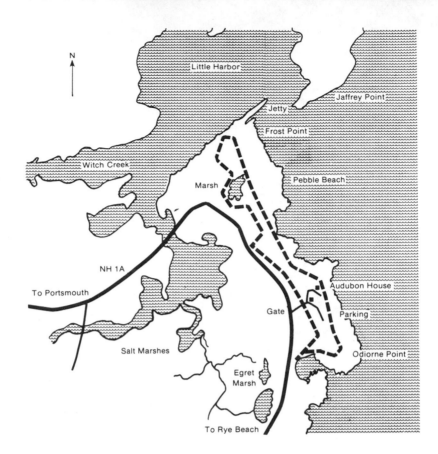

breeze sweeps out of the sunny spaciousness, which extends over the water to the horizon. The adventurous English landed here in the spring of 1623. They built a stone manor house, smithy, cooperage, fort, and racks for drying fish.

The route of this hike shows you first the southern area of the park including Odiorne Point. From the parking area, walk south, keeping west of the rest rooms; continue past a fine grove of Scotch pines on the left to a stony beach and a tremendous view of the ocean.

At the cove beyond the point the wave-lapped shingle rises to heaped seaweed deposited by the highest tides.

Beach peas extend their vines over the pebbles, and the common nightshade thrives in the unpromising habitat. Poison ivy in places will probably keep you from taking closeup color photos of the *Rosa rugosa* bushes and their dark pink blossoms.

Above the shingle, where there's enough soil, tansy grows. It's common all over the park. When you walk through it, the pungent odor, suggesting thyme to me, draws into your nose.

This cove marks the southern end of your walk. Before returning along the shore, however, climb onto the jumbled rocks and look over the road to the marshes and ponds. The large white birds, snowy egrets, which you are likely to see, once faced extermination by plume hunters throughout their range, until they were saved by the Audubon Society.

Retrace your route back to the Scotch pines on Odiorne Point. Then bear right along the shore past a round concrete foundation on the left. Look for the ledges extending beyond the scattered rocks and pools. At low tide you can walk out to the metamorphic bedrock of the ledge. A basal-like trap dike forms a grayish black band through the pressure-folded sandstone.

Keeping to the upper shore for easier walking, you pass picnic tables and the Audubon nature center. All along here gulls sail over the bayberry bushes and the *Rosa rugosa* or they slant gracefully out to sea. At your feet, close to the coarse sand, three-toothed cinquefoil, often seen on barren mountaintops, displays white flowers and the notched leaf that gives the name. Back from the shore, arrowwood blooms white in June. This shrub's straight sprouts provided arrow shafts for the Indians who camped near here and lived well in summer on fish, clams, crabs, and sea birds.

As you approach Pebble Beach, groups of rocks favored by gulls for sunning and dozing catch waves offshore on windy days. One of the rocks, black and at times awash with waves breaking starkly white, is a basalt erratic that the glacier dropped. It's about the size of a Volkswagen bug. Sometimes a black-backed gull roosts on it: black feathers above black stone. Our largest gull, the black-backed, is much bigger than the gray-backed herring gull.

Daisies and dusty miller plants colonize the shore as you clamber up the back of elongated, flattened, smooth stones of the storm dike called Pebble Beach. The crescent of shapely stones extends to Frost Point. When the waves roll up Pebble Beach, you can hear the stones grinding back and forth under the water.

Inland from Pebble Beach a marsh spreads out to the base of the largest casemate. You look for shore birds under the scowl of the concrete watchroom that caps the forty-foot knoll. A smaller casemate to the south also commands views of the marsh and its winged inhabitants: red-winged blackbirds in the cattails; killdeer nesting on the hot sand; swallows skimming above blue-flag clusters; kingbirds on guard against crows and hawks; and in the brush, yellow-throats calling "witchery, witchery, witchery."

Pebble Beach ends at a field with a view toward boats moored in Little Harbor, the great old Hotel Wentworth, and New Castle Island. In calm weather the granite jetty accommodates fishermen. Farther at sea you look across into Maine beyond the entrance to Portsmouth harbor. Near at hand the shore's ledges include a pegmatite dike extruded through the metamorphic layers and containing large crystals of glinting mica and gray-yellow feldspar. The rock is worn and scratched by the glacier.

For a lunch spot climb to the high point of the park—the top of the casemate west of the field. A path leads up the steep slope. Green grass on the flat top contrasts with gray concrete walls. I suggest lying in the fragrant tansy. Then sit up and watch ships at sea, observe the buildings and lighthouse on the Isles of Shoals, and admire white gulls gliding and black cormorants skimming the waves. Binoculars are helpful.

Your return walk is inland. Take the path down the west slope of the casemate through bittersweet vines and under oaks and pine trees. You'll probably hear mockingbirds. They have recently expanded their range into New Hampshire. The lavishness of their songs (in a Southern accent) distinguishes them from our catbirds, as do the white feathers edging their tails in flight.

When you reach level ground, follow the mowed path that curves left to a junction with a path coming from Pebble Beach. Turn right past spirea bushes, which mix with native shrubs such as winterberry. During the park's military era many alien species of shrubs and trees, such as the spirea, were planted.

The grassy path leads to a dirt road. Keep left on this along low ground. The tangled alders are as suited to the moist earth as the brush-loving yellow warblers and yellow-throats. The clouds in the blue sky seem hardly to clear the alders.

The dirt road takes you to the shore near the big rocks favored by gulls. Here you turn right onto another dirt road between stone walls half hidden in poplars, cherries, and arrowwood. The walls mark this land as having once been a "saltwater farm."

You emerge in a field shaded on the west by oaks near the chain-link fence and NH 1A. To the east is massed shrubbery below small trees, including sumac, where cedar waxwings hunt the berry bushes for fruit and insects. Keep walking south, to the left, through the field, passing east of an old barracks.

The field continues to be your thoroughfare. Orange and yellow hawkweed add dashes of brighter color to the green grass and weeds. Bear left at the gatehouse, crossing the road and keeping right of a pine-clad casemate. Your car is in the rank facing the seashore, the *Rosa rugosa,* and the wide sky.

4

Pawtuckaway: The Tower

Distance: ¾ mile
Walking time: ¾ hour
Vertical rise: 370 feet
Map: USGS 15' Mt. Pawtuckaway

Among the rolling hills of southeastern New Hampshire, a wooded park shelters wilderness as it might have looked not long after human beings first penetrated it. Yet the 5,501 acres of Pawtuckaway State Park were cultivated and pastured for more than a century. Now oak, pine, and hemlock have reclaimed the hills and valleys.

The stone walls that border beaver ponds and narrow dirt roads are about the only remainders of man's presence. You pass no fancy camping areas or developed picnic grounds with elaborate grills and benches. You can find solitude and forested isolation among marshes, ponds, and high cliffs that rise above immense boulders.

All this awaits you near creeping megalopolis (represented by Manchester and Concord to the west, Durham and Portsmouth to the east). From the fire tower atop South Peak you can see—on clear days—from Mount Washington to the sea.

The road into the park heads eastward from NH 107 between Deerfield and Raymond. Approaching from the north, look for it on your left just 2.7 miles south of Deerfield. From the south it is on the right, 4 miles north of Ray-

mond (3.2 miles past the NH 107-NH 101 junction). The park road turns from asphalt to gravel after .9 mile. Continue from this point, bearing right onto the south half of the loop road through the park. You'll pass a cemetery on the right, 2 miles from NH 107. Proceed .5 mile farther until you find yourself at an apparent dead end in the midst of marshes and old beaver ponds; turn left (the woods road on your right is unlikely to entice you).

For .7 mile beyond this corner the road winds up and down through the forest. Then it curves to the right up a longer hill, passing an abandoned cellar hole and grassy plateau on the left. Park just beyond here on the right.

A well-blazed snowmobile trail is at the lower end of this parking area, but you will take the wide path to the tower which begins near the upper right-hand corner. Under pine boughs you climb quite steeply over exposed pine roots. The aisles between the trees open to vistas where oven birds sing with ascending emphasis, "teacher, TEAcher, TEACHER!"

Farther on the left the mountainside exposes its foundation of imposing, rounded bedrock. The small cliff supports fine growths of rock tripe, a leathery, large, gray-green lichen.

Rock tripe is edible if boiled long enough, but consult books and lichen experts first. It was the famine food of Indians. Ernest Thompson Seton, the naturalist-artist-writer whose books I pored over as a boy, advises drying rock tripe to prevent its purging effect, and then boiling it for three hours to produce a sticky liquid that's slightly sweet and tastes of licorice. Thus encouraged, although wary of eating rock tripe for years, I've recently discovered he's right. His report is somewhat exaggerated about the licorice, but the glutinous porridge is indeed as he says in his *Book of Woodcraft:* "far from unpalatable at any time, and to a starving man, no doubt, a boon from heaven." I admit to avoiding a full meal.

The plants near the ledges, growing not on harsh stone but in soft forest duff, include the fringed polygala, which blooms in May showing tiny pink flowers with fringed "tongues" among the ferns

Nearing the tower

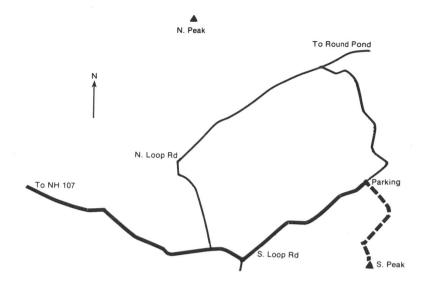

and lady's slippers' leaves. Conscientious hikers these days regard picking as a form of vandalism.

The ledges take on the smooth shapes typical of the Pawtuckaway Mountains. They look like grazing elephants. The level stretch below the rock changes to a curve left uphill. You pass a stoned-up well overflowing into the path from your left. The tower appears ahead. Oaks and maples continue to shade the trail until you climb to the open rock.

The nearby water to the east, indented with bays, divided by peninsulas, and dotted with islands, is Lake Pawtuckaway. (There the park, off NH 156, offers swimming, camping, fishing, and picnicking.) Your distant views of sea and northern mountains are most likely to appear on a clear fall day.

Smog from the Manchester area may obscure Mount Monadnock off to the southwest. Smog from other cities to the south—Nashua, Salem, Haverhill, Lawrence, Newburyport, Boston—won't improve visibility. But here at least are trees, skies, birds, and primeval verities that existed long before population centers.

Unless you seek out the Indian Steps, fifteen-odd shelves in an igneous rock dike northwest of the summit, you'll need only twenty minutes for the descent to your car.

The return to NH 107 may be made by the north loop road. Stay in low gear from the parking area to the top of the hill, and then keep on the winding section for .75 mile to the left turn onto the north loop road. In 2.25 miles the narrow gravel lane traverses the low ground and marshes. These separate the park's center ridge from its northern heights. Now you realize that the Pawtuckaway Mountains consist of three parallel ridges extending east and west.

From the low ground you reach drier woods and rejoin the entrance road at the south-loop junction. Keep right for NH 107 and a return to Our World.

Pawtuckaway: Rainy-Day Hike

Distance: 3½ miles
Walking time: 3 hours
Vertical rise: 530 feet
Map: USGS 15' Mt. Pawtuckaway

Every hiker should set aside a forest for a rainy-day hike. Sometimes you feel you must get out, get away, take off, yet the heavens open upon you for a week, and the weatherman sees only clouds and rain ahead. Then your rainy-day hike saves you from utter frustration.

I specify the forest because it shelters you. For this purpose I like Pawtuckaway State Park and North Peak. As well as release, you'll find that the ridge can provide practice in bushwhacking with compass and map. The map in this area is USGS Mt. Pawtuckaway Quadrangle. This map, a compass, and the ability to use them are essential in rain and fog. Otherwise you could end up lost in this wild section of the park.

The tall oaks, pines, and hemlocks along the lower section of trail filter the raindrops into a fine mist. If the wind shakes down big splashes of rainwater, ponchos easily shed them or you can wear wool and get wet but stay warm. On top, you will come to no harm if you stay off the wet and slippery rocks.

The entrance road to the park leaves east off NH 107, 2.7 miles south of Deerfield. At 1.2 miles from NH 107

bear right into the park. The ranger's trailer is just within the boundary. Drive slowly and watch out for rocks and ruts. In spring mud season you'll have to pull off the road, if your car might drag, and park on solid ground, and start walking. This could add a mile or more to the hike.

The access road continues past an old cemetery on the right. At a left fork, keep right onto the south half of the park's loop road. In a swampy area take the next left. A steep hill at 3.2 miles from NH 107 leads up past the trail to South Peak's tower. Continue over the hill. Drive past the left fork, which is the north half of the loop. Follow the right fork east into a valley for .5 mile, and drive over a little bridge between two stone guard walls.

The road rises and swings to the right. Park off the road. Your trail begins on the left, north side. Fallen trees at first confuse the way. Avoid a path to the left. Your trail bears to the right, aimed down at massive boulders out of sight in the woods.

The trail becomes plain as it slants down to a seasonal brook, while a ridge to the right hides the road. The first of the enormous boulders appears after

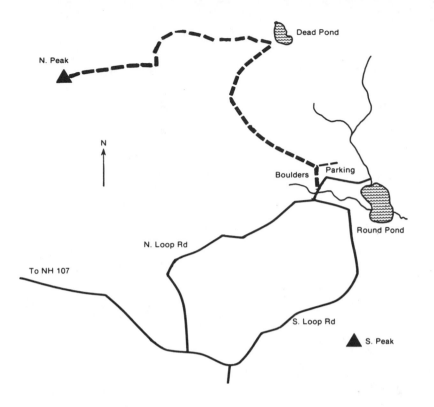

five or six minutes. On your right among tall pines and hemlocks, its top rises thirty feet into green boughs. A split in the rock has heaped pieces into a cave tunnel through which you can crouch and step toward the light.

Nearby are similar rocks of almost equal size. You may find your attention divided between the extraordinary boulders and the curious (to me) nutshells on the ground. Shagbark hickories, parents of the nuts, are not common farther north where I do most of my hiking. Long strips of bark flake from the mature trunks.

A few yards north of the boulders a sign on a tree points left to the trail for Dead Pond, which is midway on your hike to North Peak. The graded path rises slightly among pines and hemlocks and more hickories. White blazes on the big trees mark your way. Another scat-

tering of huge boulders appears to the left below a wooded cliff. About twenty minutes from the first group of boulders the gleam of Dead Pond lightens the shadowy, wet woods. The trail turns left just before the pond.

If you approach the pond you will see that the boggy water extends out of sight into areas of brush and marsh. The low shore is host to sphagnum moss, goldthread, young hemlocks, and leatherleaf bushes. Where the rootless sphagnum moss extends into the bog it supports cranberries. The plants with spear-shaped leaves and single white "petals" are water-arum or wild calla. They grow in open water. Pitcher plant and sundew prey on insects, as do the swallows overhead.

Rejoin the trail to the left of the pond. After a brief descent it abruptly becomes a mountain trail. You scramble over rocks and past big pines, some of which display old white blazes and one or two arrow signs. You can grasp striped maples and note that their broad leaves suggest webbed feet of giant geese. Black birches are common.

As you approach the cliff on your left you see the jumble of rocks called the Devil's Den. The trail bears to the right. To the left is a faint path, which I now judge to have been worn by rock climbers with proper equipment. Don't take that path. I once did and found myself in mist and rain on a slippery shelf, peering down at treetops. I managed a retreat back into the gully and discovered the real trail bearing to the right, and up steeply. It takes you to a flat ledge overlooking Dead Pond, all misty below you. Face about and head up the slope. The trail becomes obscure, but keep upward.

You naturally, however, will bypass the rocky ascent to your left and climb in a curve around and above that ledged obstacle, where you have no business on a rainy day. You enter an open growth of leverwood trees, or hop hornbeam, as the climb gradually levels at the top of this east shoulder of North Peak.

Here you should consult your watch, compass, and map. In rain and fog if you are uncertain how to proceed with the map and compass, or have neither, turn around and go back. Don't rely on a few indications of a trail. Occasional stretches of trodden leaves, sometimes called a "herd path," do exist; a few yellow blazes, red ribbons, and cairns mark the ridge top. You may see scattered blue blazes but pay no attention to them. Depend on your map and compass.

Start west along the ridge. The open woods change to gloomy hemlocks as you descend into a col. You soon face a sudden height of jagged ledges contrasting with soft duff from fallen hemlock needles.

Bear right and slab this rugged height under the hemlocks. There's a faint path to lead you upward in a north circle under the crest on your left. It leads to a clearing and a scaffolding of steel girders set on concrete piers. The frame supports a flimsy, khaki-colored wallboard construction and faces in the general direction of Pease Air Force Base.

At a rainy-day pace you require half an hour or three-quarters to get here from the east shoulder above the cliffs. Now turn right and climb higher into the clouds and rain. Entering open woods again, you'll see the herd path with occasional blazes and cairns. Keep your compass bearing in mind, however, and your compass often in hand to check. It's good experience for the day when you get caught in a mountain storm. Keep to the crest of the ridge through oak woods and across another shoulder among rock outcroppings, still west to the final little rise.

North Peak's topmost ledges once supported a small, dilapidated wooden tower for a view toward Concord and the capitol's golden dome. Fortunately the dangers of that flimsy lookoff are gone, but unfortunately now the trees increasingly hide the view.

You're about a half hour from the clearing with the scaffolding and one hour from the first shoulder above the cliffs. Elevation is 1,011 feet.

Lunchtime has arrived. On a rainy day a backpacker's gas stove is great for hot soup.

The simplest return to Dead Pond is by the same route you took up, remembering to bear left above the cliffs. At the pond keep to the right along the trail through those fine woods. A right turn at the boulders soon takes you out to your car.

The Uncanoonucs: North Peak

Distance: 1½ miles
Walking time: 1¼ hours
Vertical rise: 730 feet
Map: USGS 7½' Pinardville

On the North Peak of the Uncanoonucs nature is busy reforesting an old pasture. On the South Peak man asserts himself with relay towers and auto road. The consequent environments on these twin hills west of Manchester provide complete contrast for the hiker; yet from a distance their rounded contours present the same silhouettes. The close physical resemblance no doubt provided the Indian name Uncanoonucs, which is said to mean "The Woman's Breasts." Preserving the vastly different zones on the two summits, no trail connects them.

Both can be climbed in a long afternoon. I suggest choosing North Peak first, to prepare yourself spiritually for the exploitation you'll see later on South Peak. Other hikers may prefer to climb South Peak first and recover faith in the future on North Peak.

Mountain Road runs south from NH 114 at Goffstown toward North Peak. At .2 miles from NH 114 and a traffic island, you pass the Wee Care Center on your right. At the next fork, .7 mile farther along, turn left. You soon pass a farmhouse and large barn on the right. Just beyond, begin to watch for a stone,

also on the right, displaying a painted white circle. This marks the start of the White Circle Trail. The stone and the circle, which are small, are found part way up a wooded hill, 1.6 miles from NH 114. Park clear of the asphalt on the road's shoulder.

The White Circle Trail climbs immediately under hemlocks. You cross a woods road. White circles appear on trees, as do white dots. The trail stays clear of logging slash to the north. The steep grade gives you the feeling that on this miniature mountain you'll reach the summit quickly. But you'll use the better part of an hour.

Time passes easily, however, as you ascend the varied slope. Leafy trees and bushes have taken root among the ledges, where frisky lambs probably once gamboled on the greensward. Hemlocks spread their green branches to the sun. They shade their seedlings, which thrive in this protection. Due to this affinity for shade, hemlocks may in time take over the land of the leafy trees—except for beeches, whose seedlings also love shade.

After eight or ten minutes you reach a lookoff rock. Goffstown is down there, and to the north, Mount Kearsarge.

Ahead you'll find better views free of treetops.

The trail bears left and then right. You climb steadily to a remarkable rock overhang, which forms a cave in which you can almost stand upright. Part of the overhang has been closed by a neat wall of laid-up stones. The cave reminded me recently that phoebes in their natural habitat attach their nests under sheltering rocks. One forgets that there were phoebes in New Hampshire before house eaves or bridges came along to shelter their nests.

The outside rock holds lichens, mosses, and ferns. They are rapidly (geologically speaking) breaking down the rock in combination with weather and making earth for trees to grow upon.

The trail swings above the cave in a left curve that takes you to a ledge slanting upward and wooded just enough, on its several shelves, to suit pink lady's slippers. I stopped there one May 27 and quickly counted sixteen flowers. (No one seems to call them moccasin flowers any more.)

This rock outcropping leads up to more open outlooks, including a very satisfactory view of Mount Kearsarge, and on clear days, of the White Mountains. Oaks and other trees will take root here in a few years until eventually their branches close off all but views of clouds in the sky.

Among other trees on North Peak black birch thrives here, although it cannot do so fifty or sixty miles north. Along with the black birch, whose dark brown bark resembles that of black cherry, striped maple and hornbeam appear. These two varieties of trees also occur farther up North Peak; trees of the latter variety form a grove through which the trail winds to the 1,329-foot summit.

There oaks shade flat rocks, blueberry bushes, grass, moss, ferns, and junipers. A frame of green leaves

View north to Goffstown

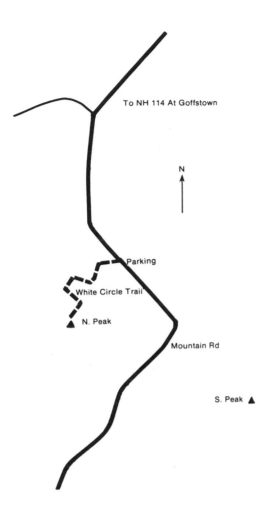

To NH 114 At Goffstown

N

Parking

White Circle Trail

▲ N. Peak

Mountain Rd

S. Peak ▲

sets off South Peak and causes the distance to seem greater than the mile it is. Above South Peak's rounded summit and scanty trees, openwork steel needles bristle and relay cones gleam.

For a view of Mount Monadnock you must go southwest through open oak woods, where Canada mayflowers form a mosaic in hues of green. The twin leaves are cleft like hearts at the stem and taper to points. Flowers resemble tufts of white foam; later they yield white-spotted berries that turn red in the fall. You descend the gradual slope, and then hemlocks seem to block all views. But they open up a few yards beyond their first branches. There's Monadnock, and a breezy spot for lunch as well.

To the south you'll see the slope of Joe English Mountain, shaped like a bulldozed gravel pile. Eight miles or so beyond, the Souhegan River cuts east and west through the town of Milford. The wooded flat land is dotted with ponds. You can look across miles and miles of countryside. The scene may not be as dramatic as it is on other mountains, but it's a quiet pleasure that should not be underrated.

Descend to your car by the same White Circle Trail. Paint marks are scarce on the summit. If you have wandered far enough to be uncertain of the summit, look for the rock fireplaces drawn together by picnickers for their hot-dog roasts near the top ledges. The trail leads down from the northern corner of the clearing.

7

The Uncanoonucs: South Peak

Distance: 2 miles
Walking time: 1¼ hours
Vertical rise: 660 feet
Map: USGS 7½' Pinardville

Of the twin Uncanoonucs, the South Peak for its view overlooks the city of Manchester. This seems fitting because the summit bears the effects of civilization and progress. I've mentioned the towers and auto road in the hike to North Peak (see hike 6). I should say again that South Peak's contour and elevation (1,321 feet) bestow on it a startling similarity to North Peak. But the ambiance is totally different when you climb them. On North Peak it's natural forest regrowth. On South Peak it's careless commercialism, although important to our radios, and for all I know, to our phones and TV sets.

The removal of the fire tower has done away with views of all southern New Hampshire and Mount Monadnock. North to Mount Washington is no longer possible, and sad to say in recent years haze and smog have often hidden the White Mountains altogether. Communication towers and a chainlink fence have replaced the 62-foot fire tower and cab. The easterly terrace, however, still opens wide over the city and surrounding countryside. To the south on a clear day you can see the silhouettes of tall buildings in Boston. On the horizon to the east several summits are the Paw-

tuckaway Mountains, which you can explore by hikes 4 and 5.

One true improvement does not exploit the mountain. The Goffstown Conservation Commission has marked a nature trail to the summit. A pamphlet describes interesting facts about habitat and history at seven stations. Included is the story of the mountain's unique cable cars, two of which operated on a trestle and rails from 1904 to 1938. The downward weight of one car helped the ascent of the other. A hotel on the summit was an added attraction. If you have heard about the "snow trains" out of Boston in the 1930s, you may imagine skiers swooping down trails from the summit, the experts demonstrating the Arlberg technique—stem-christie turns and a crouch for rough bumps.

To reach the South Peak trail, turn off NH 114 south about .5 mile east of Goffstown onto Wallace Road. You are still within the town's residential district. Just after the turn onto Wallace Road you will see a right fork. Don't take it. Bear left along Wallace Road and keep driving 1.4 miles. Turn right onto Mountain Base Road. This takes you after 1 mile through a neighborhood of small houses and trailers to the south side of

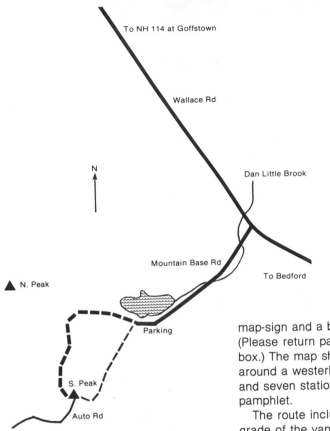

To NH 114 at Goffstown

Wallace Rd

N

Dan Little Brook

Mountain Base Rd

To Bedford

N. Peak

Parking

S. Peak

Auto Rd

Uncanoonuc Lake at a beach. The mountain rises to your left.

There's parking between the beach and mountain. Don't drive farther on this dirt road. Watch for a sign on a tree directing you toward the nature trail, ahead along the road. First face toward the mountain. A concrete foundation partially hidden in bushes is visible between a house up on the slope to the left and a cottage in the trees on your right. This was the lower base for the cable cars. A crude footbridge and steep path up the old grade can be a descent route from the summit. More about this soon.

Follow the dirt road around the edge of the lake. At the woods a sign notifies you of the nature trail. About forty yards farther into the hemlocks you come to a map-sign and a box for the pamphlets. (Please return pamphlets at the summit box.) The map shows the trail swinging around a westerly arc to the summit and seven stations keyed to the pamphlet.

The route includes descent by the grade of the vanished trestle and rails. I seriously advise against it. From the summit to reach the grade you may not be a trespasser on property adjacent to the houses below, but warning signs and barking dogs make it a concern. Aside from this, the steep grade is littered with ankle-threatening rocks the sizes of jagged baseballs and angular golf balls. A more pleasant and less dangerous descent is a return by the trail you climb, and this is the directive here.

But now walk up from the sign, bearing left from a driveway to a cottage. The path is wide enough for two-abreast walking. You'll also find tracks of four-wheel drive vehicles and trail bikes. The southern auto road offers no challenge to owners of off-road vehicles. These erosion machines can destroy trails. As I mentioned, modern technology has taken over the mountain. For the present, at least, the trail absorbs the punishment.

About five minutes from the sign the trail forks. The way to the summit is left uphill (The right fork is a spur leading to hemlock woods and a marsh described in the pamphlet—well worth a visit and return to this junction, but the time and distance are not included in this hike.)

Now you climb up steadily along a curving trail in a forest of trees that become larger as you ascend. A snowmobile trail joins from the right, with several red poster arrows on trees. You'll notice that beech trees begin to predominate. Their smooth, pewter-colored bark glows when the western sun flashes under green branches. Thrushes proclaim a peaceful afternoon. Oven birds stridently declare they own a patch of forest. After a shower, red salamanders appear like magic from beneath stones and bark. Terrestrial for a year or more, they return in their older age to water as the familiar olive-green newts you find in ponds.

A great hemlock, left of the trail, remains as a memento of an earlier forest. It is so large that an arm hug—six feet, let's say—reaches only halfway around the rough bark. Beyond the hemlock the trail tops the steepest rise and passes among more hemlocks and again into open woods. You are walking under the summit's western slope. On your left you get glimpses through the trees of steel girders forming one of the various towers. Leveling eastward among oaks, ledges, and bracken, the trail soon takes you to the asphalt auto road.

Here is another sign for the nature trail and a box for pamphlets. A smaller sign directs you to the "Inclined RR." (As I've said, I think this inadvisable and best disregarded.) Turn left up the auto road a few yards, then leave it by a dirt road to the right before you come to a cluster of towers and service buildings on the left. The dirt road circles the summit, but first takes you past more towers inside a chainlink fence to the eastern terrace and view of Manchester about five miles away.

Binoculars bring details closer. The city's bridges span the Merrimack River. A brick mill with many windows extends along the falls of the river. Waterpower built Manchester. Amoskeag Mills, now divided into various businesses, once were among the world's greatest spinners and weavers of cotton goods. Throughout the city church spires pointedly contrast with square commercial structures and modern highrise buildings and the cubes of houses with angled roofs. The flat land outside the city extends southward to Massachusetts and east to the coast.

Nearby in front of you and below a section of asphalt you can see rooftops. To the left was the upper terminal for the cable cars.

Returning to the nature trail you may retrace your steps along the dirt road or complete its circle of the summit. Off the auto road turn to your right past the sign for the nature trail. The unspoiled forest seems to surround you with nature's beneficence. Don't let the mood lead you down the snowmobile trail. Keep to the right at the red arrows on trees, as the nature trail curves north and east, to the lower signs and your car.

You have come down from one of New Hampshire's most interesting unwild summits, and perhaps have decided to help preserve others, still wild, from a similar fate.

Crotched Mountain

Distance: 4 miles
Walking time: 2¾ hours
Vertical rise: 755 feet
Map: USGS 15' Peterborough

Crotched Mountain is typical of many New Hampshire blueberry ridges. The southern approach to the summit treats you to wide views long before you reach the topmost ledges. Spread out behind you lies all the country between Pack Monadnock on the east and Mount Monadnock on the west. During a summer day the heat distills fragrances from the open turf, bushes, and seedling pines. Sparrows and towhees flit close to the ground or sing from gray birches. Hawks sail the windswept skies.

The access road to the Greenfield Trail up Crotched Mountain branches northeast from NH 31 one mile north of Greenfield and 4¼ miles south of Bennington. A large sign identifies this road to the Crotched Mountain Rehabilitation Center for handicapped children. Drive past the Greenfield swimming beach and up the winding asphalt for 1.75 miles. You pass Verney Drive which leads to the Center's hospital on the right. Then at the top of the hill watch on the left for a locked gate. This blocks access only to vehicles, not to people. Park off the road near the gate. There may not be a trail sign.

Beginning as a gravel road to the

blueberry ridge, the trail takes a left fork almost at once and soon another. These are service roads for the blueberry harvest. (The second right fork leads to the center's camp buildings.) A reasonable grade lifts you to wide views. Ahead the summit and its abandoned tower, partially hidden by spruces, appear remote, and the hike to them is adventurous despite a civilized beginning on a gravel road. Look behind you often. In the southwest the light and shade on Mount Monadnock change each time you turn your head.

The service road becomes a grassy jeep track curving through the blueberry bushes. One of the fragrances the heat brings out originates in a knee-high shrub called sweet fern. Its misleading name refers to leaves that resemble— but are not—fern fronds. Their aromatic odor may suggest bayberry, which is a member of the same family.

At the top of the ridge your route turns left from the jeep track and becomes a trail. An arrow on a tree points the way downhill through spruce and birch woods. The wide, firm path leads into a little valley where a 150-yard spur trail branches left to a seasonal brook and then to a boxed spring with pipe and faucet.

Soon the main trail crosses the upper reaches of the brook on a crude bridge laid across the muck and trickles. Then upward you go, through a gap in a stone wall and out of the woods into thick junipers and scattered trees. If you wear shorts and brush against the junipers carelessly, you'll learn that their evergreen needles can prickle. The purple berries help flavor gin. Another pasture pest, steeplebush, blossoms in August. The pink cones or spires exhibit the reason for the name. The derivation of its other common name, hardhack, must go back to the first farmer who attempted to stop with a scythe its invasion of his pasture. The stems are woody and tough.

Now the trail curves more steeply to the left. You climb out on a ledge for a lookoff at Pack Monadnock, Temple Mountain, and Barrett Mountain in a diminishing series. To the southwest Monadnock lives up to its old name, Grand Monadnock.

The trail beyond the ledge winds into spruces and approaches the final climb to the summit in a wide S-turn. The way is much eroded. Tree roots seem to grip the rocks with tenacity. They are mostly red spruce, which support trunks that frame the tower.

The tower rises from a north-south ledge. The first flight of steps has been removed. To the east the rock sheltered the warden's cabin, which is now gone. A relay tower beyond aims two big convex discs off the mountain. Power-line poles drop down out of sight toward the valley and Francestown. The summit, at 2,055 feet, is the center of the trio of heights that form Crotched Mountain. The "crotched" or twinned silhouette I have been able to make out only from Mount Monadnock.

View of Crotched Mountain

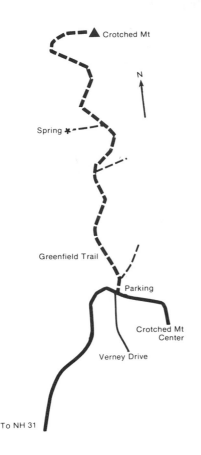

For views, now that the tower is closed, turn south and descend over several ledges. Keep on through a bushy little ravine. You emerge at rocks forming a massive wall. This is a good lunch spot.

The last time I was on Crotched Mountain a thunderstorm chased us away from those rocks and into the safety of the spruces. My companion and I had been watching a storm pass over Mount Monadnock and deliver a shower to Pack Monadnock. Dark clouds, seething and rising, had formed spectacular anvil shapes. We were so occupied with the fine show of weather (and our sandwiches) that we didn't notice a threatening black cloud sneaking up behind us. It let go with a flash of lightning. We grabbed rucksacks and lit out for the spruces. I think the next bolt bounced off the rocks.

The sheltering spruces and rain gear were necessary for only twenty minutes. We walked down the mountain admiring another weather display. This time sunlight in long shafts illuminated distant woods and fields, as though celestial spotlights had been switched on through holes in the clouds.

There's a nice thing about returning down Crotched Mountain: you face the panorama all the way, except for the short time when you pass through the little valley of the spring. You don't have to turn around to see the mountains and the rolling countryside.

Pack Monadnock Mountain

Distance: 6 miles
Walking time: 4 hours
Vertical rise: 1,480 feet
Map: USGS 15' Peterborough

This high ridge east of Peterborough has two summits: civilized, 2,300-foot South Pack, and wild, 2,278-foot North Pack. There is no resemblance to Grand Monadnock, although the meaning of *pack* is said to be "little" in Indian language. An auto road up South Pack leads to a fire tower, relay towers, a stone shelter, picnic tables, and a northern viewpoint, from which North Pack's barren crags urge you to get away from it all.

To visit both summits requires either an across-and-return trek (7¾ miles) or two cars. This hike description is for two cars. Pack Monadnock, traversed by a northern section of the Wapack Trail (see hike 1), should be hiked from south to north so your final impression is of an unspoiled mountain. This means leaving a spare car at the northern end of the trail.

To do this, drive two cars from the blinker in Greenfield east on NH 31 for 2.8 miles to the Russell Station Road on the right. There is a small street sign and an A-frame house to the left as you turn onto the Russell Station Road. You soon cross railroad tracks. At .5 mile from NH 31 you pass a dirt road on the right and a cream-yellow house in the

corner. Stay on the Russell Station Road for .8 mile from NH 31. Here an asphalt road branches to the right uphill. It is identified by a yellow house on the right and a brown house at the opposite corner. This is the Old Mountain Road. The board sign to your left on a tree is nearly illegible.

Check your mileage. You are 1.9 miles from the trail head. Turn right onto the Old Mountain Road. At 1.5 miles the asphalt changes to gravel, but the road is graded. Watch the woods to your left. The trail's first few yards up a slope have been paved with large stones. There's supposed to be a "Wapack Trail" sign, but it is often missing. Two hundred feet up the trail a tree displays the triangular Wapack blaze. A great hemlock on the right helps locate the spot and shades your car parked on the road shoulder. This will be the end point of your hike.

After you've left off your pick-up car here, drive the second car west, straight ahead, toward Peterborough. (This road is sometimes called the Peterborough-Russell Road.) At 1.4 miles from where you left your first car turn sharply left onto East Mountain Road. There's a steel post topped by a

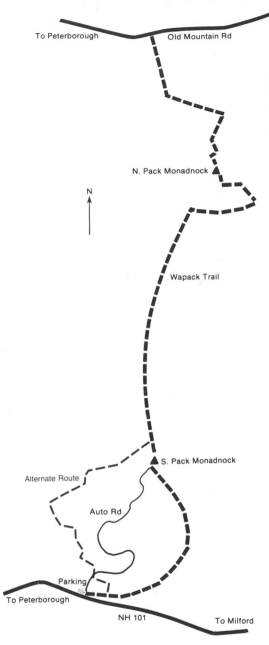

long grade, and in .6 mile delivers you to NH 101. Turn left uphill on NH 101 for .3 mile to the sign on the left for Miller State Park. Turn left into the extensive parking at the base of the auto road up South Pack.

Confused by the multiplicity of roads? I was. Maybe you should search out the route before the actual date of the hike.

So now you have your two cars arranged and your party gathered at the parking area. To reach the start of the Wapack Trail, walk to the east corner of the parking area and a sign, "Foot Trails". Entering the woods, you soon come to a trail junction, where the Wapack Trail forks. You have a choice of the old route with its blue blazes or a new, more challenging trail to the left, identified by a "Wapack Trail" sign.

This new trail crosses the auto road and ascends over rough ledges, which require use of hands as well as feet, and agility. Atop the ledges, it bears northerly along the cliffs and then heads up through the woods west of the auto road. It joins the old Wapack Trail on open ledges 200 yards north of the summit tower on South Pack Monadnock. With this summary of the new trail, I am not suggesting that you take it. I advise you to bear right at the junction near the parking area and follow the blue blazes of the older, easier route.

After a stone wall and birches, the trail curves steeply left up past huge rocks and under large red oaks. You walk down into a little ravine among spruces and then into the light of leafy trees. You climb once more. You cross another stone wall. You are alternately slabbing the mountainside and climbing abruptly. This is the trail's method of ascent for the hour or so required to

street sign. Drive the hilly road for 2.8 miles to a fork. Turn left. (A street sign identifies the right fork as "Cunningham Pond Road.") Your left turn leads up a

Shelter atop South Peak

reach South Pack's upper rock slabs, a three-legged tower, a small brown shed, the summit spruces, the auto road, and two relay towers. Turn right onto the auto road for the three-minute hike to the summit's fire tower.

From that high vantage point southern New Hampshire spreads out all around you. Grand Monadnock's unique, shouldered pyramid dominates the west. The popularity of South Pack, however, does nothing to encourage lingering. Auto fumes, families of sightseers, and noise are sufficient incentive to take up the trail again. But first, inspect the shelter. A solid structure of mortared flat stones, open-front, based against a ledge, it faces a large fireplace.

To the left of the shelter, as you're heading north, the Wapack Trail continues by slanting into a little depression among spruces. It leads to lookoff rocks.

Here the new trail joins from the left. Looking off this shoulder, which drops sharply, you can see North Pack and a massive cliff to the right of the summit. Spruces grow along the ridge. The topmost ledges are barren. Although twenty-two feet lower than South Pack, they seem on a greater mountain. An obvious spruce-grown knob about midway between you and North Pack is 1,942 feet. I should add that the descent from South Pack to the col is more than 500 feet. The traverse of Pack Monadnock is no ridgepole walk.

Falling away steeply from South Pack's ledges, the Wapack Trail enters spruce woods. At a rock with both yellow and blue arrows, keep left with the yellow arrow. (The blue arrow points the way a short distance to a good view.) After larger spruce trees, where roots crisscross the rocky trail, you encounter small-scale deciduous woods. You are entering an area of former pastures. Trees have slowly but surely taken over heights cleared by settlers with axe and fire. These same tough pioneers and their descendants also laid up the unbelievable distances of stone walls.

The trail over the middle knob crosses ledges where you may want to stop for lunch and sunning, although the view is limited. Then continue walking toward North Pack. You should watch for a sign painted on a rock: "Cliff Trail". Turn right onto this bypass of the old route. The Wapack Trail here formerly went directly ahead to the summit of North Pack. That section is still sometimes used.

The Cliff Trail takes you into a little hollow watered by an upper spring. Follow the orange blazes toward the base of the cliffs. As you climb around the shoulder, perhaps ravens will entertain you with their barking calls and seemingly playful use of wind currents. Achieving the ridge, you swing left above the cliffs through open spruce woods growing to the edge of the cliffs.

Thence the trail bears westerly over several rocky outcrops with occasional orange blazes. These lead to open ledges as you approach the bare summit and its cairn.

Directly ahead, north across the valley and past the town of Greenfield, you see Crotched Mountain rising as a three-summit ridge. Beyond, if the day is blessed with crystal atmosphere, you see the distant White Mountains. South, the towered summit you first climbed seems far away, perhaps because, except for Monadnock on the west, flat countryside stretches all around it.

North Pack's summit drops off abruptly from ledges on the west. A rocky perch near the cairn is a great place to watch storms out of the west in the making. Exploration of the summit eastward reveals an interesting little bog surrounded by scrub spruces, blueberry bushes, and brush much frequented by warblers and sparrows.

The Wapack Trail departs the summit northward from the cairn. It leads across several rocky outcrops before curving down to the left into a stand of spruces.

Two sections of trail keep to the west of eroded gullies along the old route. They rejoin it after short loops and are marked with orange blazes.

There's a spring about midway along the 1½ miles of descent, during which you go through brushland of birches, rhodora, bracken, and highbush blueberries. Then hemlocks shade you for the final yards to the road and your car.

10

Mount Monadnock

Distance: 9 miles
Walking time: 7 hours
Vertical rise: 2,670 feet
Map: USGS 15' Monadnock

Traditionally known as Grand Monadnock, and rising from the mists of the past as it now rises from the morning mists in southwestern New Hampshire, Monadnock's rocky crest entices or challenges 100,000 hikers a year. Although a small mountain, 3,165 feet, Monadnock is everlastingly impressive.

The first recorded ascent was on July 31, 1725. A party of rangers from Lancaster, Massachusetts, scouting and hunting Indians under the command of Captain Samuel Willard, camped on top. It was then forested, but as now, it stood alone, which is the meaning of its Indian name.

The earliest date chiseled into the rocks is 1801. Between that year and 1815, forest fires laid waste the slopes and summit.

Climbing to the newly barren crags became more popular. During the summer of 1815 several parties made their way to the top. There came to be a path. Famous men felt the spell of the mountain. The sage of Concord, Massachusetts, Ralph Waldo Emerson, wrote a poem about his experience, and his eccentric friend Henry David Thoreau made camp below the upper rocks.

As popular interest in the mountain grew, so did a concern for its preservation. Now the area includes a reservation of some 5,000 acres under the cooperative guardianship of the New Hampshire Parks Division, the town of Jaffrey, the Association to Protect Mount Monadnock, and the Society for the Protection of New Hampshire Forests. The latter has been a prime mover for years in Monadnock conservation.

The town of Jaffrey has long been the southern takeoff to many trails. On that side are the state park and nature center. I think, however, you'll enjoy a lesser-known, northern, and longer route — the Pumpelly Trail.

To reach the Pumpelly Trail, drive on NH 101 to the east end of Dublin Lake and turn south on the Lake Road. You follow it less than .5 mile. As soon as you come to the lakeshore on your right, watch for the trail. It's a woods road and bridle path opposite a shorefront log cabin. There may not be a sign. Park off the shoulder of the road farther along.

Take plenty of food and water. The hike is long and dry. Prepare for above-treeline weather by carrying suitable

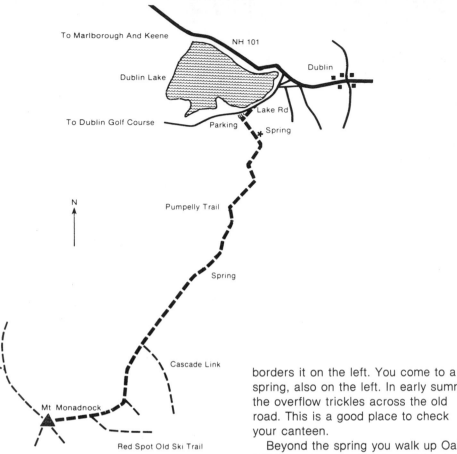

To Marlborough And Keene

NH 101

Dublin

Dublin Lake

To Dublin Golf Course

Lake Rd

Parking

Spring

N

Pumpelly Trail

Spring

Cascade Link

Mt Monadnock

Red Spot Old Ski Trail

clothing and equipment in your knapsack. Take along the AMC Monadnock map.

You walk up a wide path into the woods. Move quietly and with respect for the people in two houses set back among the trees. This is private land.

About 350 feet from the Lake Road your route leaves the path at a sharp right turn onto a trail; a sign points the way. Passing through a stone wall at a narrow break, the trail curves left under ancient pines, hemlocks, and oaks.

You shortly come to another woods road about five minutes from the Lake Road. Turn left uphill. This is an abandoned farm road. A stone wall

borders it on the left. You come to a spring, also on the left. In early summer the overflow trickles across the old road. This is a good place to check your canteen.

Beyond the spring you walk up Oak Hill through a growth of small hardwoods, and down to a little valley. Climb out of the valley and watch for a right turn onto a true trail. Piled brush blocks the old farm road, which continues straight on between the trees that have grown up in the fields.

Now you're on a winding footpath and really headed for the mountain. The trail is named for its originator, the geologist and conservationist Ralph Pumpelly, a summer resident of Dublin. He laid out the route in 1884.

About three-quarters of an hour from the Lake Road you pass another spring on the left. It dries up during a drought. It's the last possible water, not counting stagnant pools and bogs near the summit.

Now you begin the serious climb. No

longer following a woods path, you're at last on a mountain trail. Part of the enjoyment and interest comes from noting the changes in vegetation and the season as you climb beyond the 2,000-foot elevation. By the second week in June blueberry bushes may be past blooming below but up here they will be displaying massed, creamy flowers.

Several lookout ledges on spur trails to the left give views of Crotched Mountain's saddled ridge, Mount Kearsarge farther north, and the Uncanoonucs on the northeast horizon. Pack Monadnock arises to the east, identifiable by north and south summits with a low ridge between.

On the main trail you come to a slanting ledge with scattered evergreens. Keep to the crest and you'll find the cairns marking the way. A westerly view opens and shows you a sharp triangle of a mountain over in

Vermont. That's Mount Ascutney.

Then there's the summit ahead, but far away. It's attached to your Dublin Ridge by a long eastern shoulder. The trail continues upward and southwest among rocks and evergreens. Yellow paint marks Cascade Link Trail on your left among spruces. (Cascade Link drops to the state park via the White Dot Trail.) A dome of rock on your left turns the trail west around its base.

Here as you cross the Dublin town line into Jaffrey, mountain cranberry puts on a vivid display if you happen to be climbing in mid-June. The modest, dark pink flowers on the creeping vines somehow manage to be spectacular.

Time for lunch. The rounded knob on your left gives wide outlooks.

After your repast the way along the trail for twenty minutes traverses open ledges alternating with corridors through scrub spruce. Watch for the cairns as you cross the bare rock. You reach the

Monadnock in winter

top of Dublin Ridge. The trail bears left and descends into woods, then turns right, up into cranberry territory again. The Spellman Trail, identified by white letters and blazes on the rock, forks to your left. (The Spellman Trail is a steep route down to Cascade Link.)

At the Spellman Trail junction, your Pumpelly Trail turns abruptly right and dips into a little wooded ravine. Climbing out of this you approach a rectangular rock left by the glacier. Named the Sarcophagus, and also called the Boat, it makes me think of a whale.

A few minutes beyond the Sarcophagus (you've swung westward toward the summit now) there's a large cairn surmounting a high ledge. The Red Spot-Old Ski Trail is marked with paint to the left of the ledge. (The Red Spot-Old Ski Trail descends to Cascade Link.) From beside the cairn you have an excellent view of the summit, which is still ¾ mile away by trail.

Blossoming mountain sandwort grows at the foot of the ledge. White flowers on leafy stems cluster above shorter clumps of leaves and decorate the shallow soil from mid-June till frost. From here on you'll be watching for cairns, which are far apart. You'll see at the same time the low plants of goldthread and three-toothed cinquefoil. In bogs surrounding two pools are plant communities that include sheep laurel and cotton grass.

You at last approach the topmost rocks and begin the final climb. The smooth, billowed schist shows glacial striations here and there, which stones imbedded in ice scratched thirty thousand years ago. Man-made marks consist of names, initials, and dates. Tapping hammers and clinking chisels annoyed Henry Thoreau when he camped on the mountain.

Although you may be in fine physical condition and not winded at all on the summit rocks, you'll catch your breath I'm sure. The whole of New England extends around you, or so it seems. The distant mountains fade into the afternoon haze, and your stand on the summit seems remote — despite the company of many other hikers. That's the magic of Monadnock.

Beginning the descent you can easily miss the way unless you locate the large white letters "PUMPELLY TRAIL" and an arrow painted on the rocks. Then you must make certain you pass the first cairn and several more to insure your picking up the trail. After about twenty minutes you reach the Red Spot-Old Ski Trail and the big cairn atop the ledge. You are well on your way to the upper end of Dublin Ridge. The trail winding past the Sarcophagus and through the little ravine could almost be new as seen from these return angles. There's the Spellman Trail, the knob where you ate lunch, and Cascade Link. You are on the narrow ridge heading down into the woods. But first, face about for a last look to the summit. Yes, you were indeed there an hour and a half ago.

Central
New Hampshire

11

Bear Brook State Park

Distance: 3½ miles
Walking time: 1½ hours
Vertical rise: 280 feet
Maps: USGS 7½' Gossville; USGS 7½' Suncook;
　　　USGS 7½' Candia

For a day of hiking, nature study, and swimming, visit Bear Brook State Park. In the evening you can end up with a cookout.

The park access road branches east from NH 28 just 5.5 miles south of the Epsom traffic circle on US 202 east of Concord. One mile from NH 28 you come to the park office and admission booth; the small fee that you pay here includes admission to the state-operated Nature Center.

Driving on across a neck of Catamount Pond, you pass the swimming beach and bathhouse to your left and then picnic areas on both sides of the road. A little farther along the pine groves open up as a road branches to the right. A sign on the corner is a map of the park.

Continue to the nature center by turning right just past the map. Drive a short distance and park near the building on the left surrounded by pines. Beyond on the right are the maintenance garages and shops.

You could spend several afternoons at the nature center and not exhaust its resources. The nature library alone

The edible Oyster Mushroom

could occupy you for many long rainy days. I was impressed by the fine exhibitions of live and mounted plants and animals. I learned that the "apple" galls on oaks are caused by a hornet propagating its kind. The bees in the glass "hive" are busy, all right. The exhibition depicting the stages in the formation of dirt is a lot more interesting than it sounds. The wetlands exhibit increases your appreciation of real swamps and marshes.

The nature center is open from late June through Labor Day, 10:00 A.M. to 5:00 P.M. It is closed Wednesdays and Thursdays. There are three self-guiding nature trails. These require little time compared to the enjoyment and future pleasure the information will give you for other hikes.

The nature center is also the place to obtain free park maps. For this hike get the winter trails map. It is for snowmobilers but the prominently numbered signs at trail and road junctions, keyed to the map, show you where you are during the hike. I propose a walk along a woods road leading past Bear Hill Pond, from number 8 to number 12 and return. For this you first drive to Podunk Road shown on the

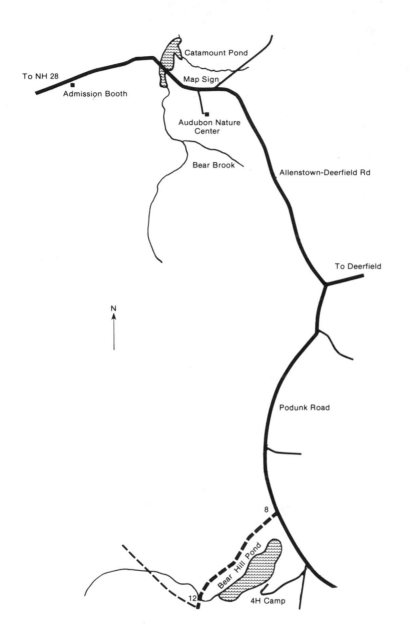

Catamount Pond

To NH 28

Admission Booth

Map Sign

Audubon Nature
Center

Bear Brook

Allenstown-Deerfield Rd

To Deerfield

N

Podunk Road

8

Bear Hill Pond

12

4H Camp

map. The park's access road is also the Allenstown-Deerfield Road. Drive past a left fork and then up a hill and past a right fork leading to trailers on a gore of land not part of the park. Continue on the Allenstown-Deerfield Road for 1.75 miles beyond the map corner. Beyond a cemetery, on the right, a road is marked by a Bear Brook State Park sign. This is Podunk Road.

It dips into a little valley and up again. You pass the manager's house to your left and a road to campgrounds. Podunk Road is tarred gravel, and climbs through deciduous woods. You pass the left-branching road to Spruce Pond. At 2.4 miles from the Allenstown-Deerfield Road you come to a woods road on the right. A sign attached to a tree identifies this junction as number 8. Park off the shoulder.

The woods road, a wide wintertime route for snowmobiles, makes easy summer walking. After a short upward slope it swings downward gradually toward the west shore of Bear Hill Pond. A left fork leads to a good picnic ledge beside the pond.

The trees here are mostly oaks, and acorns begin dropping onto the road by late summer. Sassafras grows to bush size under the oaks. Its three shapes of leaves give it an unfinished look.

Another tree you may not recognize so easily is the chestnut. Its leaves resemble those of a relative, the beech, but they are narrower and longer, and the leaf lobes have definite points.

Japanese chestnut bark disease destroyed all the magnificent chestnut forests. It continues to kill young trees as they approach twenty feet in height. But they persist in trying, growing mainly as sprouts from old stumps, and there is some hope that they will eventually develop immunity. Both sassafras and chestnut appear in New Hampshire from the central area south.

In Bear Hill Pond, off to the left, large rocks stand out of shallow water. The shore is host to a thick growth of leather-leaf bushes and other water brush. Across on the far shore you see the beach and buildings for the 4-H summer camp. Past the pond the woods road descends into low ground crossing little bridges built of timbers laid on railroad rails. Big pines and hemlocks join leafy trees in the forest, and there's cool quiet at corner number 12.

Returning along the same route, you realize from leg muscles and lungs that you walked downhill more than you thought. Another day, when you are better acquainted with the park, you may want to explore a complete loop.

12

Oak Hill

Distance: 2 miles
Walking time: 1¼ hours
Vertical rise: 400 feet
Maps: USGS 15' Gilmanton;
      USGS 15' Penacook

Like most of middle New Hampshire, the forested land sloping up Oak Hill in Loudon and Concord was once field and pasture. Now the jeep road to the fire tower is bordered by a recently logged forest of white oaks, red oaks, and maples. The road begins as a farm lane leading about a half-mile to the cellar, still containing fallen timbers, and shown on the 1927 USGS map as a house at the end of the lane. No fire tower then existed on top of Oak Hill from which to survey the rolling forest.

Take NH 106 north out of Loudon village. Cross the bridge over the Soucook River. Beyond the bridge a street forks left at a sign for the Oak Hill tower. You leave NH 106 on this west-branching street. Note your mileage. Drive past a school on the left to a four-corner intersection. Turn left onto Oak Hill Road. You leave the residential section. (This street becomes the road leading to NH 3B at East Concord.) Going uphill for 1 mile or so, then leveling, the road takes you past farms, woods, and houses. Watch your mileage and drive slowly, because no landmark identifies the fire warden's jeep road up Oak Hill.

Climbing the right bank, 1.5 miles

from NH 106, the gated jeep road rises steeply as Oak Hill Road makes a wide right turn downhill. The small sign and jeep road are midway in this turn. Park off the highway shoulder away from the curve.

As a grade for walking, the road allows effortless observation and enjoyment of the woods. The fields were first taken over by deciduous trees, but white pines are already thriving. White pines are the climax forest in this area. The pines form a green line suggestive of a thick hedge beyond the stone walls.

In a dead stub you may see annual nest holes — one above the other — of pileated woodpeckers. The red crested, black and white birds as big as crows will use the same stub for several years, but will chisel out new nest holes with their powerful bills. The nest holes are round, whereas the holes chiseled in search of grubs are elongated and wide open.

At the cellar the tremendous, hand-split granite slabs for the foundation appear as the tower road forks left, but an

Stone wall through the woods

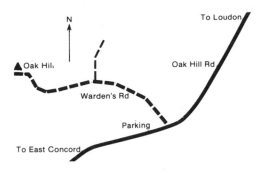

older, less used way continues uphill beyond.

Stay on the jeep road. The earth becomes dryer at a slight upward pitch near a pile of stones cleared from fields and dumped on a ledge. Low blueberries line the road. Canada mayflowers, also called wild lilies-of-the-valley, grow so thickly that you can squint your eyes and blend the little leaves into a green rug. Along here you'll see the slash of extensive logging.

The tower, silvery from aluminum paint, gleams through the remaining pines. Steep stairs zigzagging up from landing to landing may discourage anyone troubled by heights, but the railings will steady the most timorous hiker. From the glassed-in room you are rewarded with a view of New Hamp-shire's historic central countryside and its scattered mountains. The twin Uncanoonucs near Manchester stand out prominently to the south. Farther away and to the west you see Pack Monadnock and Crotched Mountain. To the southwest you can't miss the crags of Monadnock. Directly west, Sunapee Mountain extends a long shoulder from the summit. To the northwest there's Mount Kearsarge. Next comes a ridge, which is Ragged Mountain.

A scant five miles to the southwest the state capitol's dome glistens golden in the sunlight. Below it at certain times and in certain years, New Hampshire's General Court, as our legislature is known, meets in Concord, if not in concord.

On Oak Hill an about-face from the capitol ought to show you another distinctive New Hampshire sight: one of the world's windiest mountains, Mount Washington. I have yet to see it from Oak Hill. Clouds through the seventy miles have always intervened.

This reminds me — haze reduces the effectiveness of the panorama from the tower. Visibility is usually better in the morning. Oak Hill requires distant vision to be entirely successful. Perhaps it should be an early morning hike.

Blue Job Mountain

Distance: 1 mile
Walking time: ¾ hour
Vertical rise: 356 feet
Map: USGS 15' Alton

Pronounce it *Job,* as in " the patience of . . . . "

How can a 1,356-foot hill open up the vastest views for the least effort in New Hampshire? The isolated location helps. So does the fire tower on top. Blue Job's elevation is much higher than the surrounding countryside in the east-central townships of Farmington, Barnstead, and Strafford. As for the effort, you drive to an elevation of 1,000 feet before you begin the climb.

How vast is the view? To the north you see Mount Washington and other White Mountain peaks cutting the horizon. To the south your binoculars may pick out Boston's John Hancock Tower. East beyond Portsmouth the Atlantic Ocean encircles the Isles of Shoals. To the west you look into Vermont.

Save little Blue Job for a day when the weather forecaster predicts visibility limited only by the earth's curve. Otherwise you'll be disappointed. I suggest May or October. At either time Mount Washington could be capped with shining snow. The John Hancock Tower will gleam on the southern skyline. On the ocean you may see a freighter making

its way into Portsmouth harbor.

Take NH 202A west out of Rochester to Crown Point Road 2 miles beyond Meaderboro Corner, which you can identify by the Four Corners Antique Store. Crown Point Road forks right, as NH 202A bears left toward Center Strafford and Northwood. Note your mileage. You have 5.5 miles to go on Crown Point Road. After .5 mile you reach Strafford Corner, where you pass Crown Point Grange Hall on the left and then a church on the right. The asphalt road then runs straight for several miles through farmland and woods. You'll see the rounded knob on your right that's Blue Job topped by its tower. Opposite a farmhouse on your left, turn to park before a locked gate leading into a blueberry field. There are no trail signs. You'll see a service line strung on poles above the bushes and extending up into Blue Job's oak forest. The tower is hidden by the slope.

Look for the trail to the east from the gate — that is, to your right as you face the mountain. The well-worn trail leads directly toward the hillside. Behind you the scenery is open woodland and trees growing into old fields. A large

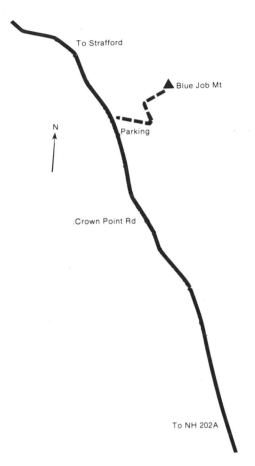

To Strafford

Blue Job Mt

N

Parking

Crown Point Rd

To NH 202A

marsh farther in that direction collects meandering streams at the source of Big River.

You enter the oak woods. The trail seems to bear left, but this is a route for blueberry pickers. Keep to the right and walk up a slanting ledge. From here to the top the trail is plain enough. Stone steps ease your climb here and there as you follow the gradually ascending path. It circles east, so the steeper slopes are on your left.

An open ledge gives the first views. Soon the oaks blend with spruces and pines. You climb left and emerge upon a grassy clearing with scattered trees, the tower ahead, picnic tables and fireplaces beyond it, the warden's cabin on your right. (Check with him about using his well, or better still, carry your own fluid supplies.)

Approach the tower's stairs with caution. A steel crossbeam is set at the correct height to deliver a blow on your head — if you're 5'10'' as I am.

In addition to the points of interest already mentioned, others will claim your attention — Pease Air Force Base, the University of New Hampshire with its heating plant chimney, a radar tower at Andover, Rochester's drive-in movie screen, the First Freewill Baptist Church on nearby New Durham Ridge, and to the north any number of mountains.

The Belknap Mountains, near to the northwest, present unusual outlines. They hide Lake Winnipesaukee, from whose shores and waters the angular silhouettes and rounded ridges are more often seen. The Belknaps also hide several summits on the western edge of the White Mountains, but if you look closely between Mount Major and Mount Belknap, you'll see Mount Moosilauke's barren dome on the horizon.

14

Fox State Forest

Distance: 4¼ miles
Walking time: 3 hours
Vertical rise: 600 feet
Map: USGS 15' Hillsboro

In 1922 Mrs. Charles A. Fox of Boston gave the state her 348-acre farm with its fine house and barn. Since then the state has expanded this holding north of Hillsborough to 1,432 acres, most of them abandoned farmland where woods have taken over the fields. The interior of the house has been remodeled into offices. To fulfill the conditions of the original trust, the state combines forestry practices and related experiments with education and nature trails. The environmental center, built in 1972 for ecology classes and conservation meetings, contains a forestry museum. More than twenty miles of well-marked trails wind through the forest.

The simple day hike I'll describe (over the loop path named the Ridge Trail) conducts you through the eastern part of the forest. It includes a detour to a glacial "kettle" with the inevitable name of Mud Pond and a return down Hemlock Ravine. The western part of the forest and a lookout tower are attractions for another day. (See *Walks and Rambles in the Upper Connecticut Valley* by Mary L. Kibling, Backcountry Publications, 1989.)

Turn north at the blinker in Hillsborough toward Hillsborough Center. The road cuts through the forest. After 2 miles turn in, to the right, at the sign "Fox State Forest." Park in the shade of the spreading sugar maples. The white house with its spacious porch suggests leisurely summer days and rocking chairs. Beside it a glassed bulletin board opens for free literature. A pamphlet, *Fox State Forest Trail Guide,* displays a map and lists points of interest. Additional information is available at the offices in the house.

The Ridge Trail begins at a sign on a tree north of the maples and to the right of a larger parking area. It passes the house, curves downhill along a woods road, and then branches left. The way is blazed with vertical red stripes. Keep past the Mushroom Trail, which forks left. You walk down into a growth of hemlocks and pines.

At the bottom of the hill the trail turns sharply left before low ground and tall grass. In 100 yards you cross Gerry Brook to a junction with the Hemlock Ravine Trail coming down, on the left, from Gerry Cemetery on Concord End Road. Hemlock Ravine Trail will be your return route.

Swing right along the Ridge Trail.

Pines and hemlocks grow on the higher ground to your left as the trail parallels a sunny swamp and beaver pond on the right. Tangled alders, grass, and ferns partially hide Gerry Brook. Warblers are at home in this green jungle. During June, myriads of mosquitos command attention. The trail rises up a slope beside a stone wall on your left, and then enters an impressive grove of virgin hemlocks.

Here the Ridge Trail veers left. The right fork is your detour to Mud Pond. In a few minutes this trail crosses a woods road. All intersections are clearly marked and the way is shown by white dot blazes. The trail continues a short distance to the pond. You'll return to the woods road after exploring part of the bog.

A walkway across slabs leads off the trail to the left and provides dry access to the sphagnum moss and shrubs that float out from the west shore. Further investigation means wet feet and a moment of trepidation when you first see and feel the bog's mat undulating beneath your weight. You realize the origin of the term "quaking bog." Caution is advisable, especially near the water's edge. Keep a wary eye for holes in the bog.

The rootless sphagnum moss has the capacity to spread out and grow across water. It forms a mat that becomes a seedbed for other plants. Eventually the bog will fill the pond with peat. Present-day sphagnum bogs are relicts, having survived from the glacial era. Because the chemistry of sphagnum moss makes its environment acid, other plants must be able to thrive in such a condition. Various members of the heath family can do this. In Mud Pond's bog you see blueberry bushes, bog rosemary, sheep

Heading out of Fox Forest

laurel, cranberry vines, and leatherleaf. There are two insectivorous plants: sundew and pitcher plant. Two pink orchids, pogonia and calopogon, bloom in late June. (I'm sure you know they're not to be picked!) The bog supports stunted tamarack and black spruce.

To pick up the Ridge Trail again, retrace your steps as far as the woods road and turn right. In dry pine woods the Ridge Trail soon joins the road from the left and follows it a short way before branching right. Here it winds through a young hardwood forest. Less than a half hour from the pond you come to the east edge of the forest at the Bog Road Four Corners. Three of the roads are asphalt. Follow the fourth, a woods road, as it heads west past the cellar of the Davis farmhouse on your right.

A few yards beyond the cellar, the Ridge Trail leaves the woods road northward under lofty trees. These leafy trees give way to hemlocks as you climb a moderate slope and find yourself picking your way among scattered boulders, which force the trail into a twisting pattern. You come to a rounded rock. Water seeps from under it and away to the right. It's the spring shown on the map in your Trail Guide. Don't count on it in a dry season.

Climbing steadily now you walk through a gap in a stone wall beside basswood trees. You are ascending Jones Hill. Beyond a narrow opening extending left and called Oak Lot Road, beeches replace the oaks, maples, and birches. A blue post near a stone wall marks the forest's boundary corner.

Look left toward daylight in a brushy, higher clearing. A giant oak rises up to a broad mass of foliage. Its circumference is eleven feet.

Over the hill you go, as the trail curves left and levels. Watch for the faint trace of Jones Hill Road, which the

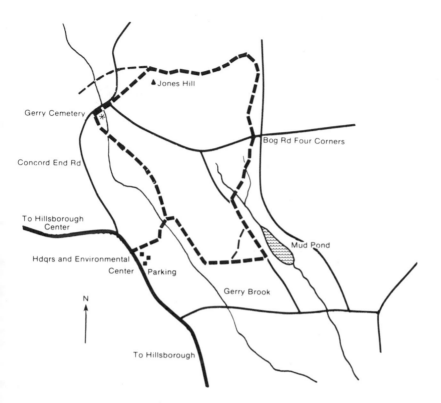

Ridge Trail crosses. When you spot it, turn left. A shortcut to Concord End Road, it slants downhill to the junction. Now follow the graded dirt of Concord End Road to the left. In a few yards you reach a bend where the road branches left to Bog Road Four Corners. Beyond a big tamarack on the right a grassy path takes you through the bushes to the cellar of the Gerry-Kimball farmhouse.

Return to Concord End Road. Under it Gerry Brook flows through a stone culvert. Farther along on the left you come to the family cemetery. Headstones show different early spellings of the later "Gerry".

At the cemetery turn left off Concord End Road, onto a woods road downhill. This is the Hemlock Ravine Trail. You first enter leafy woods. In the small trees' shade, through royal ferns, you cross Gerry Brook and arrive at the hemlock woods. They grow so close along the brook that the name, Hemlock Ravine is appropriate indeed.

You descend to the junction with the Ridge Trail near its crossing of Gerry Brook. Step across the brook to your right and retrace your earlier route to the woods road. Turn right and climb to the parking area.

A visit to the museum will give more meaning to the hike. The western part of the forest remains as an inducement to return another day.

Lovewell Mountain

Distance: 4½ miles
Walking time: 3¼ hours
Vertical rise: 925 feet
Map: USGS 15' Lovewell Mountain

Lovewell Mountain makes me think of a blunt galleon boring south into a forested green sea. The prow points toward Mount Monadnock. The foredeck is the open ridge below the upper deck of the summit's spruce woods. The sails are clouds.

At other times I try to imagine how Lovewell must have looked as a treeless mountain pasture during the 1800s, when surrounding farms in the town of Washington turned out sheep and cattle for the summer grazing on its broad slopes. Now all but the south ridge is forested. The stone walls exist as relics without a purpose. The old road at the mountain's south base was once a thoroughfare between the village of Washington and the farm community at East Washington. It still is suitable for horse-drawn wagons but that's about all. Don't be misled by the USGS Lovewell Mountain Quadrangle map, which classifies the road as "light duty" as far as, and somewhat beyond, the trail head.

As in earlier days, the present village of Washington with its store, new post office, brick library, old white church, town hall, and fine houses, remains spic and span, unspoiled in its high isolation

on NH 31 northwest of Hillsborough.

The gazetteer notes that Lovewell Mountain "received its name from Captain Lovewell, who was accustomed to ascending it to discover the wigwams of Indians, and who, on one occasion, killed seven Indians near its summit."

To approach the scene of Captain Lovewell's legendary exploit take a road that forks southeast from NH 31 opposite the store and post office in the center of Washington. You immediately pass the church and town hall on your left. After .5 mile a left turn around a big house takes you to Halfmoon Pond. Shorefront cottages appear on your left. Continue past Halfmoon Pond for a total of 2 miles from NH 31. The East Washington road branches off to the right. A little way in, a smooth broad ledge offers parking at the right.

Rectangular white blazes on the trees indicate that you're on a section of the Monadnock-Sunapee Trail or Greenway. Along this old road between stone walls, evergreens and leafy trees blend around a few larger hemlocks, oaks, and one monster spruce beside a little cliff. The gradual ascent consists of ups and downs leading to a level height-of-land at 1,620 feet. Alerted by the double

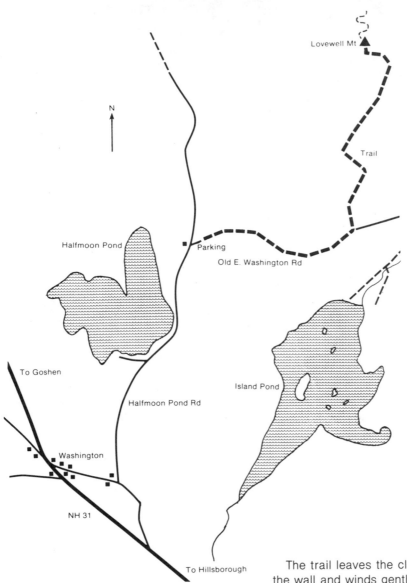

N

Lovewell Mt

Trail

Halfmoon Pond

Parking

Old E. Washington Rd

To Goshen

Island Pond

Halfmoon Pond Rd

Washington

NH 31

To Hillsborough

blaze that indicates a turn on the Greenway, you find the trail leaving the road north and left.

A glaciated ledge emerges from the dirt road and slants up under a remarkable stone wall. The granite slabs could have been stacked by a giant. Through a gap in the wall the trail enters a clearing with junipers. You are about 1 mile from your car.

The trail leaves the clearing beyond the wall and winds gently up into spruces whose branches have been cut to open a tunnel toward the next clearing. The trees alternate with open spaces. Cairns are older than the white blazes. You walk through waist-high meadowsweet and between head-high blueberry bushes. More junipers will in time die as shade spreads over them

Cairn on the south shoulder

from growing trees; junipers must have sunshine.

About twenty minutes from the old road and height-of-land, you come to a stone wall on your right. The trail swings left and angles across the dampness accumulating from a dubious spring on your left. It may have provided water for the house that has vanished from the crude foundation in the grassy clearing on your right.

The reentry into the woods is somewhat obscure to the left. Watch for the white blazes. Rising more steeply and slabbing into a patch of lovely green New York ferns, the trail climbs left onto the south shoulder. Northward looms the summit.

Once more cairns mark the way, which now leads northwest through scattered small spruces and low blueberry bushes. A much larger cairn, six feet high, stops the trail's northwest bearing and turns you to the right into a broad patch of meadowsweet, bracken, and spruces. Thereafter the trail curves northeast, again in the open, past another large cairn built of flat rocks.

Frequent small cairns guide you to the trail's final entry into the upper spruce woods and more white blazes. You climb steeply to a spur trail on your right. Take this a few yards for a lookoff above an intervale farm and East Washington. Back at the main trail a short climb brings you to a rock from which you can see the islands of Island Pond (behind you to the south). Beyond, Highland Pond is a long channel.

After this view the trail rises to a low rock face. Keep left at its base. You climb a short distance to the summit ledges surrounded by spruces. For a northern outlook keep to the right past the summit cairn. Across the upper valley of Woodward Brook there's a long ridge on the horizon. Below this, and as though struck into the woods with blue pencil, Ayers Pond appears as an irregular line. Directly north Mount Sunapee rises beyond its southern ridges.

For the return go back to the summit cairn, bear left across the ledge into the spruce woods, and pick up the trail you ascended.

The Monadnock-Sunapee Trail continues from the summit, to the right of the cairn as you face south, and descends along the north ridge before dropping into a valley and crossing the extension of the road past Halfmoon Pond. On your Lovewell Mountain Quad this rough logging road is shown as the route of the Monadnock-Sunapee Trail. It was — before the 1938 hurricane. The present Monadnock-Sunapee Trail, fifty-one miles of it, has been relocated and reopened under the auspices of the Society for the Protection of New Hampshire Forests with the aid of the Appalachian Mountain Club. Thus for the adventurous and sturdy hiker atop Lovewell Mountain a loop is possible down to the logging road; then go left on it to the south and back to the fork where your car is parked. (Maps and directions for the Monadnock-Sunapee Trail are available at the society's office, 54 Portsmouth Street, Concord, N.H. 03301 and at its summer centers in Monadnock State Park and Lost River Reservation.)

Mount Kearsarge

Distance: 2 miles
Walking time: 1½ hours
Vertical rise: 1,105 feet
Map: USGS 15' Mt. Kearsarge

Atop this mountain — not to be confused with Mount Kearsarge North between Conway and Jackson — the bare rocks and stunted spruces represent a harsh and primitive world in contrast to the man-made tower, warden's cabin, airplane beacon, and relay cones. When the wind is right, hang gliders launch themselves from the cliff like gaudy birds and land at Winslow State Park picnic area, (except when they land in trees). The trail for this hike starts at the picnic area.

To reach the mountain and park take the Warner Road, which runs south from NH 11 between Elkins and Wilmot Flat. (Or from the south pick up the Warner Road via 1-89, Exit 10, and Sutton.) The intersection with NH 11 is marked by signs. After 1.5 miles on the Warner Road, you are directed left onto the park access road by another sign. From here it's 2.5 miles to the parking spot. Signs will keep you from taking any side roads. Mount Kearsarge looms ahead as this asphalt road winds up through farmland and woods.

There's a gate near the ranger's cottage and a booth for collecting the nominal fee before you drive to the picnic area and the site of the Old Winslow

House. Grassy banks now surround the cellar hole. Birches shade some of the picnic tables and fireplaces. Wide views stretch away, but the 2,937-foot mountain dominates the scenery.

The Northside Trail to the summit starts at the southeast corner of the picnic area. Through spruces it is wide and at first presents springy duff to walk on. Then it becomes eroded and steeper, making rough climbing. You swing into a more gradual eastward ¼ mile. White birches mix with the spruces for a time. At a higher elevation the woods change almost entirely to spruce and fir. These evergreens rise above thick, perfectly formed, new undergrowth. A difficult bypass forks left.

Next smooth ledges test the grip of your boot soles. Kids run up the rocks like young goats. A lookoff rock, to the left, is worth a visit for views and a breather. Trees get smaller through here.

The trail takes you into the open. Barren rocks, marked with red paint arrows, lead you in a southerly curve through islands of scrub spruce. A final knoll of rock supports the tower. Another crest beyond a little hollow is a foundation for the beacon. The

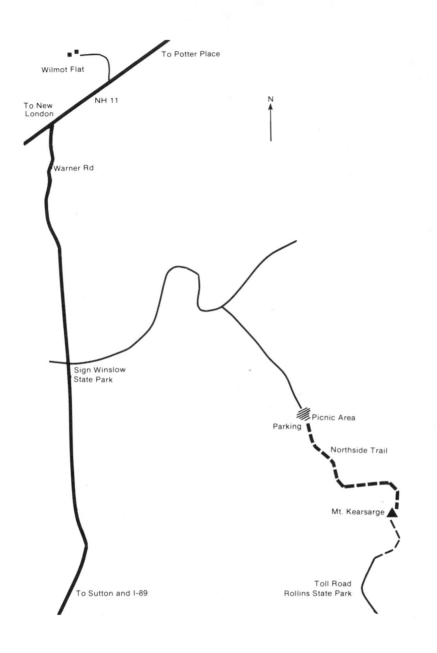

To Potter Place

Wilmot Flat

To New London

NH 11

N

Warner Rd

Sign Winslow State Park

Picnic Area

Parking

Northside Trail

Mt. Kearsarge

Toll Road
Rollins State Park

To Sutton and I-89

warden's cabin, north of the tower and lower than the summit, avoids the prevailing west winds. The ledges, through the years, have been profusely chiseled with names, initials, dates.

People wander about, climb the tower, study the views, or watch the hang-glider daredevils launch into space. Some of the pilots carry rope around their waists to lower themselves from accidental landings in tall trees.

You may also wonder about apparent tourists in nonhikers' clothing. They *are* tourists, having driven out of Warner to park half a mile below the summit. This auto road through Rollins State Park is also the access route for the hang-glider people. The tourists seem to regard the trail from the road's end as a city walk. It's not. Mount Kearsarge can be suddenly cold and blustery or very wet.

The view is wide to all points of the compass. Pleasant Lake on the west reflects sunlight, and farther away parts of Lake Sunapee gleam near Georges Mills. Identified by their ski trails, King Ridge and Mount Sunapee are easy to locate. To the northwest you see the mountains along the Connecticut River above Hanover: Smarts and Cube, particularly. Nearer, Cardigan's rock dome topped by a tower drops off to the shoulder called Firescrew, because the holocaust that burned the forest to bedrock in 1855 twisted smoke and flame into an awesome spiral. In the distance, Moosilauke, the westernmost peak of the White Mountains, shows itself.

Swinging your gaze more to the northeast, you see the long Sandwich Range's varied peaks. Mount Washington stands out on the horizon. The Ossipee Range billows from ridge to ridge in a form of great solidity and breadth beyond the few visible patches of blue water in the Lakes Region. The Belknap Mountains are nearer, south of Lake Winnipesaukee.

Much closer, the valley only four miles northeast shelters the village of Andover, where white houses, brick school buildings, and a church steeple look like toys set among artificial green trees and fields. The town, like all the countryside, is watched over by the New Hampshire state warden ever alert for smoke. You may hear him — or her — talking to other wardens, exchanging compass bearings on strange smoke, and speculating whether it's caused by a dump burning, an out-of-control grass fire, blueberry bushes being burned over, or a lightning strike in the forest.

Your descent to the picnic area will be quick. You'll need only a half hour to return along the paint marks and down the wooded trail.

View south from the summit

17

Red Hill

Distance: 3½ miles
Walking time: 2 hours
Vertical rise: 1,370 feet
Maps: USGS 15′ Winnipesaukee;
 USGS 15′ Mt. Chocorua

I lived only twenty miles from Red Hill for thirty-eight years before I climbed it. Now I wish I had long ago known enough to take my two daughters up it before having them tackle Mount Washington, Moosilauke, and Lafayette. It would have been good experience and conditioning. What a view we'd have had: lakes all around and peaks arrayed to the north along the Sandwich Range — a fine reward for so easy a hike.

None of this implies that Red Hill is ignored by others. Many hikers enjoy it. You'll have lots of company. Its 2,029-foot dome, topped by another New Hampshire state fire tower (now closed), rises in flat country 1,500 feet above Lake Winnipesaukee to the south and Squam Lake to the west. Heavily traveled NH 25 between Center Harbor and Moultonborough curves under Red Hill's eastern shoulder.

Driving northeast from Center Harbor 1.7 miles you'll notice a motel, stores, and a service station where the Moultonborough Neck Road branches to the right. Stay on NH 25, slowly. About .2 miles beyond this intersection bear left onto a side road. This was once the main highway. It brings you in .1 mile to

your left turn onto Red Hill Road. Drive 2 miles straight along Red Hill Road, past the end of asphalt and the beginning of gravel. Watch for a farm on the left where a road forks west to the Bean Road out of Center Harbor. Keep past the farm and uphill straight ahead another .2 mile to parking at areas cleared from the woods.

The Red Hill Trail starts eastward up the jeep road with which it coincides all the way to the summit. There's a locked gate barring vehicles. A turnstile accommodates hikers. This jeep road across private land is strictly a service road for the firewarden's use. It follows the general route of an old farm wagon track, making a right turn up to a bridge over a brook, which starts as a spring halfway up the mountain. Red oaks grow over most of Red Hill. The forest floor seems to suit fringed polygalas with their evergreen leaves and flowers that flare like pink wings in May and June. In spring, oaks are late in putting out leaves. Maples and beeches begin to close in the aisles of gray trunks long before the end of May, and hemlocks sprout new tips on darker green branches.

A turn of the road to the left circles a

barn foundation and cellar hole surrounded by shrinking fields and sumac bushes. You enter a long, gradual rise. Hikers ambitious for steeper climbing avoid the easy route by turning right up a path under the telephone poles, but the road is more relaxing. Beyond the straight section it leads upward in winding S-turns. A cut has eroded to glaciated ledge marked by the tire tracks of the warden's four-wheel drive vehicle. The road passes bracken ferns, blueberry bushes, and swamp cranberries, these last at the highest altitude I can recall. These are not mountain cranberry's creeping vines, but upstanding little plants that grow in bogs with leatherleaf and sphagnum moss. I ate some one fall and proved them to be cranberries, and properly puckery, to my own satisfaction.

The road levels for a few yards until, on the left, you see spring water gushing from a pipe. Some folks once called such a treat "Adam's Ale," especially if the pipe were absent and the water bubbled into a sidehill pool.

Winding on up past oaks and some pines, the road lifts you higher. You see the last curve to the tower on the topmost ledges. Walking past the garage, the generator shed, and the shingled cabin, you climb the gray and white rock to steel girders. In the surrounding glade amid oaks, blueberry bushes and grasses compete for the earth unoccupied by protruding ledges.

Leafy vistas of lakes and mountains open to a 360-degree panorama as you climb to the second landing of the closed fire tower and look over the treetops.

There's no way to describe the view briefly. I must list it to get it all in. So here's the panorama starting southeast and turning full-circle to south, west,

South across Lake Winnipesaukee

north, east, and southeast again: Mount Major across Lake Winnipesaukee, Mount Belknap also across the lake, Mount Kearsarge (the southern one), Mount Cardigan across Squam Lake, Smarts Mountain also. There's Cube, Stinson, Carr, Kineo, Moosilauke, Kinsman, Cannon, Welch (nearer in front of Cannon), Black, at the Sandwich Range's west end, then Sandwich hiding the Franconia Range. Next, and nearer, rises Israel. Away back is Carrigain to the left of Tripyramid. Sleepers,

Whiteface, Passaconaway, Paugus, Wonalancet are nearer. Again far back, come the Moats left of Chocorua's rock spire, and then Cranmore, Pleasant in Maine, the Ossipee Range (best view of it anywhere), more Winnipesaukee, and Copplecrown in Wolfeboro.

I've forgotten to mention the white and yellow and red sails of boats on Lake Winnipesaukee and Squam Lake. They look like kites in an upside-down blue sky.

Old Croydon Turnpike

Distance: 12 miles
Walking time: 6½ hours
Vertical rise: 975 feet
Maps: USGS 15' Sunapee;
　　　USGS 15' Mascoma

This long woods walk follows old roads. It also offers freedom of choice, because you need not hike the entire twelve miles. I'm inclined to think, however, that you will go the route when you find how easy and pleasant the miles are. You'll walk on the old turnpike to Chase Pond, detour to Lily Pond, and follow along a great fence that encloses a game preserve once known as Corbin Park. You'll see miles of stone walls. You'll pass the foundations of dwellings and a mill. A hundred years ago here in west-central New Hampshire north of Newport and Claremont, fields and pastured cattle and sheep would have comprised the scenery. All is woods now.

To reach this turnpike built for horses, you'll probably drive your steel box on a modern turnpike: I-89 between Concord and Lebanon. Take Exit 13 for Grantham and NH 10. Drive north on NH 10 for 2.5 miles toward North Grantham. Watch for the access road on the left. It's marked by small signs reading "Miller Pond Road" and "Sherwood Forest Camping." Turn onto it, to the left and west, from NH 10. Soon you pass under I-89. Up a steep grade along Skinner Brook (on your right) continue

straight past a right turn to "Sherwood Forest." The road becomes gravel past Mill Pond, also on the right.

This small lake, half hidden by trees, links with larger Miller Pond, to which a housing development's road branches right. Your road continues on the left but has obviously been abandoned to log skidders and erosion. Park your car out of the way of both roads and walk up the left fork.

You soon cross a forest brook and climb uphill steeply to the Old Croydon Turnpike at a four corners. On your right a small cabin bears the sign "Blue Mt. Snowmobilers Club Grantham." At the corner, signs directing the way to towns beyond the scope of this walk can be checked on USGS topographical maps (see head of hike description). You are about fifteen minutes, or ½ mile, from your car. The turnpike runs roughly southeast-northwest. Straight ahead and higher lies Lily Pond, but Chase Pond to the west should be your first destination. Turn right onto the Old Croydon Turnpike.

At once you come to a cellar hole on your right. It's the first of several you'll pass during the hike. A family once lived here when this was farm country.

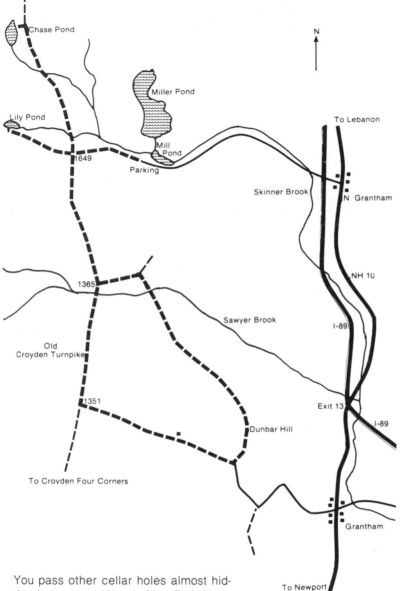

You pass other cellar holes almost hidden in trees and brush. You find them near apple trees and lilac bushes. At a small brook, the outlet from Lily Pond, freshets and the years have demolished the stone culvert. Now the turnpike takes you up into rougher land. You cross the outlet from Chase Pond. On the left a stone foundation identifies the site of a vanished sawmill or gristmill.

The road levels toward Chase Pond along the Grantham-Cornish town line. Chase Pond, 1 mile from your first corner on the turnpike, is in Cornish. (The township of Croydon begins south of this hike.) The pond's east shore benefits from the shade of tall, unusual Norway spruces, which someone planted. The pond is an elongated oval. At the south end skeletal trees mark the shoreline as it existed before beavers moved in and built a dam across the outlet.

Now you turn about and walk back to the first intersection, where you began the walk on the turnpike. Take the road, now on your right, to Lily Pond. You climb uphill beside a fence on the left — and what a fence! Paralleling the woods road, the heavy wire mesh eight- and one-half-feet high stretches between posts as stout as small telephone poles. The wire closes gullies and stream beds. Locked gates and signs appear occasionally.

In the late 1880s Austin Corbin, a New York banker and railroad man, bought 26,000 acres north of his birth-place, Newport. He enclosed the property with thirty-six miles of this fence. The cost of the park and the wild animals he stocked it with came to over a million dollars. He bought elk, buffalo, moose, and wild boar. Today the park, without exotic animals, is a private club owned by the Blue Mountain Forest Association.

Lily Pond appears through the evergreens on the right. About the same size as Chase Pond and at the same elevation, 1,800 feet, the still water has a completely different setting. Pointed firs and spruce match reflections in the pond. Water lilies thrive. Beavers are more active. There's a northern atmosphere, helped along by the scent of balsam fir. Lily Pond could be farther north in the White Mountains.

The ecological contrast between the two ponds may hold you here for lunch. Then you return to the first, main intersection and continue exploration of the Old Croydon Turnpike by turning right, to the south.

A stone wall borders the turnpike on a wooded slope to your left. To your right the great fence leads on through the woods. For a time the walking is almost level.

After about 1 mile from that now-familiar first intersection, you come to a left-branching woods road leading to Grantham. It's at the foot of a hill with fine oaks. Just ahead is a plank bridge over Sawyer Brook. (You'll return to this corner via a loop to the east.)

Keep straight on the turnpike. Before you leave the bridge you may want to pause and admire the minnows darting about the brook. For another 1 mile of level walking in shady woods you stay on the turnpike. Then you come to a second left-branching road. Follow it. (The Old Croydon Turnpike keeps south to Croydon Four Corners.) This road might show more jeep tracks than the turnpike because it traverses damp ground as it leads up and down over two little rises. A seasonal brook is not quite dry. Watch for cellar holes on the left. One is notable for long stone sills displaying peculiar split marks made during quarrying. They are shaped like miniature spades instead of the usual halves of round holes. I can't visualize how these holes were drilled, nor have I seen any like them elsewhere.

Beyond the cellar and through spruce woods you pass above low ground, where the road's grade was built across a swamp. On your left are piled rocks cleared from an upper field and dumped into the swamp, probably from a "stone boat" or drag pulled by oxen. The gradual slope upward along the field takes you to a fork. Bear left a few yards and step out on a gravel road near Dunbar Hill. This junction is marked by a sign reading "Old Post Road." Turn left. (To the right the gravel road leads 1¼ miles to Grantham and NH 10.)

Old cellar hole in the woods

Open fields on your left give a clear view of Grantham Mountain and its gray ledges. In June 1953, a stubborn forest fire devastated the mountainside. Along this road you can expect a car or two. It slants downhill past a farmhouse on the right. Next you walk along level ground through more woods and across a swampy little brook. About a mile from where you took to this road it turns sharply to the right before reaching a house that you can see ahead on the right. Bear left here on the continuation of the old road, which at once returns to its abandoned condition and setting. In the close-growing trees it resembles the woods road you've been walking along earlier in the day. It bears northwest past a branch road on your right. About twenty minutes past the last junction you cross a bridge over Sawyer Brook. The bridge is in disrepair, although its girders still support planks.

Climb the far bank and walk along a short level section. You come to a junc-tion with a road running west (left) to the Old Croydon Turnpike. (To the east — right — it joins a road to Grantham.) Turn left. Shortly you rejoin the Old Croydon Turnpike, just west of the first bridge over Sawyer Brook. At this junc-tion turn right.

Now the way is familiar, although you are climbing the oak-grown hill instead of descending it. Then you reach the easy walking between stone walls that stretch as far as your first intersection. There turn right, downhill, to your car.

Note: This hike is a good route for learning elementary use of USGS topographical maps. You'll need two maps: the Mascoma quadrangle and the Sunapee quadrangle. Most of the hike is on the Mascoma sheet. The ponds and the various roads show plainly, and the contour lines may be used to form a picture of the elevations and valleys hid-den in the forest. You can identify the road intersections by the elevation figures printed at them. The first in-tersection is marked 1649; the next to the south, 1365; the third, 1351.

Lake Solitude/Mount Sunapee

Distance: 7¼ miles
Walking time: 5 hours
Vertical rise: 1,550 feet
Map: USGS 15' Sunapee

Most people travel partway to Lake Solitude in gondolas — not the Venetian kind but the metal capsules traveling on cables to the top of Mount Sunapee. From the gondola terminal and summit lodge they walk the mile and a half to the lake. For hikers there is a better way: Andrew Brook Trail.

Mount Sunapee State Park features a ski area on the north slopes of the 2,743-foot mountain, with the standard assortment of park headquarters, summer picnic grounds, and lifts. There's also the state park beach on Lake Sunapee. An extensive forest insulates Lake Solitude from these attractions. Approached from the south by the Andrew Brook Trail the little pond at 2,500 feet seems far removed from the activity on the northern side of the mountain.

The road to the Andrew Brook Trail leaves NH 103 about 1 mile south of Newbury and the southern end of Lake Sunapee. On the USGS map it has the engaging name of "Between the Mountains Road." It's commonly called just the Mountain Road. A small sign so designates it on the east side of NH 103, although the Mountain Road diverges west. The asphalt ribbon winds up the valley westward 1.2 miles to

start of the Andrew Brook Trail on the right. There's usually a sign, but you can identify the trail by an opening in the woods just before a bridge over the brook. A wide road shoulder accommodates several cars on the same side as the trail.

Initially, the Andrew Brook Trail follows an old logging road. It keeps east of the brook and then crosses to the west bank. Soon a curve in the brook confronts you with a crossing back to the east bank. The grade becomes steeper to the next crossing, which puts you again on the west bank. The logging road bears off left among beech trees. The trail, now a woods path marked with orange paint blazes, continues straight. Stay on the path.

Rather overgrown with bushes here and there, the Andrew Brook Trail continues to live up to its name with another return to the water — your fourth stepping stone lesson. Thereafter you find climbing easier. You pass several extremely large, isolated yellow birches among the lesser leafy trees.

Approaching the lake, the trail leads through a boggy area of evergreens (mostly red spruce) levels for a short distance and surmounts a geologic for-

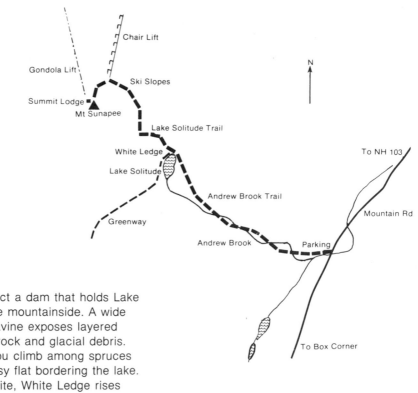

mation, in effect a dam that holds Lake Solitude on the mountainside. A wide and shallow ravine exposes layered metamorphic rock and glacial debris. Beyond this you climb among spruces to a little grassy flat bordering the lake. Directly opposite, White Ledge rises from the shore for two hundred to three hundred feet.

After this first outlook the trail turns right and skirts the eastern shore. Water laps at the trail, thanks to the beavers whose dam across the outlet insures a high water level. At the north end of the lake and a little east of the cliffs, Andrew Brook Trail ends at a junction. You take the Lake Solitude Trail uphill on the right. Because it is now part of the fifty-one-mile Monadnock-Sunapee Trail, or Greenway, it's marked with rectangular white blazes similar to those on the Appalachian Trail. Signs direct you up northward, as the trail soon angles left steeply above the cliffs, but still in the woods.

As you climb above the cliffs to the top of White Ledge, you step out on a great lookoff — and it is white! Far below, Lake Solitude reflects blue sky. Looking out and away your eyes cannot take in the panorama all at once. It begins to the south at the Uncanoonucs near Manchester and sweeps east and north to the Franconia Range.

From White Ledge, which extends into the woods fifty yards north from the cliff, the trail descends to a wooded col. Along with the white blazes are older orange paint marks. The sinuous course of this path should be explored at a leisurely pace for it traverses a varied mountain environment. The forest becomes mixed evergreen and deciduous. In June warblers flit in the trees that shade white star flowers, pink lady's slippers, and hobblebushes that display their large white blossoms. The trail rises over a slight knoll and levels again. The woods open up. Sunlight ahead turns out to be shining on the grass of a cleared slope east of the summit.

The trail swings across the ski slope and under the chair lift to another ski trail called the Skyway, which it crosses toward the Gondola lift's access path. Here you turn left and climb the last yards to the summit lodge.

Crossing green lawns you walk up steps to open sundecks around the lodge. You are level with leafy treetops and spires of evergreens and level, too, with blackpoll warblers, cedar waxwings, and perhaps a male redstart fluttering its black and flame-colored plumage. The sundeck also shows off the far northern mountains and nearby Lake Sunapee.

Inside the lodge you can refresh yourself at the snack bar and rest at the benches and tables. A huge fireplace and windows with wide views lend a general air of spaciousness.

The return is by the same route. Descending across the ski slopes, don't become too absorbed with the scenery open before you. Watch for the blazes at the entrance into the woods. Later at the junction near Lake Solitude, keep left onto the Andrew Brook Trail. Take a last look at the blue water below White Ledge. Then you're ready for the descent through the woods.

Mounts Morgan and Percival

Distance: 5¾ miles
Walking time: 4 hours
Vertical rise: 1,475 feet
Map: USGS 15' Plymouth

This hike up two of the Squam Mountains starts from NH 113 north of Squam Lake. On a warm June day after a rain the air here is heavy with the aroma that stirs my memory. The scent is from Balm-of-Gilead trees growing near an old cellar hole. I think of summer days when I was a boy. These poplars or aspens give off a cloying but delightful odor. My past has nothing to do with Squam Lake, but homes in my boyhood were often shaded by Balm-of-Gilead trees.

Here at the beginning of the Mount Morgan Trail the large granite foundation and tree-grown pit are all that remain of such a house. From among the scented trees it must have overlooked wide lawns and commanded a view across fields and pastures to Mount Morgan.

At Holderness just west of the bridge on NH 3, turn northward onto NH 113. Drive along the winding asphalt, which follows many of the irregularities of Squam Lake's shoreline. After 5 miles you pass a road to the right marked for Rockywold and Deephaven camps as NH 113 bears uphill north of Rattlesnake Mountain. About .5 mile beyond the camp road along NH 113

you'll see a sign on the right for the Old Bridle Path up Rattlesnake. Opposite it on the north side of NH 113 through an opening in a stone wall, the Mount Morgan Trail begins. There's parking — and if you're lucky, the aroma of Balm-of-Gilead trees.

The Mount Morgan Trail leaves northwest from the clearing and left of the cellar hole. Also keep to the left of a rough logging road. The trail continues in a northwest direction following an old road that shows on the current USGS map, which was surveyed in 1928. It heads more westerly, away from Mount Morgan, but don't worry, you're on the right trail. The good path is wide and worn but not overused. It's maintained by the Squam Lake Association, whose yellow paint blazes mark it between neat signs at the junctions. After a twenty-minute warm-up with easy walking, you discover that the trail assumes its true character as a mountain path. You turn north, to the right, from the old road and begin the real climb.

The mountainside seems to have been cut over several times, and thus there's more reason for wonder at the survival of a huge, recently fallen, hemlock you pass at about the 1-mile mark. It's the biggest hemlock I ever saw. Nearby a large pine and several monster oaks have also managed to escape the axe and saw.

Beyond the big trees and up more steeply for ¼ mile or so, you come to a spring on the right. It's a good place to pause for a drink — if there's water. The Squam Mountains are mostly dry on the higher ridges. You continue to climb and soon approach a hairpin turn where the trail forks. Both branches lead to the Crawford-Ridgepole Trail west of Mount Morgan. (The Crawford-Ridgepole Trail extends the entire length of the Squam Mountains from the Sandwich Notch Road to Cotton Mountain near Holderness.)

I like to take the left fork and approach Mount Morgan along the ridge. This left fork is less used, climbs up into thick woods of beech, maple, yellow birch, and is overhung with ferns and hobblebushes. You reach the Crawford-Ridgepole Trail in a growth of spruces at a small swamp atop the ridge.

Here in 1974 the trail sign provided a snack for a black bear, judging by the claw marks, dental punctures, and scattered pieces of wood lying about. The bear had eaten several miles of the distances posted by the Squam Lake Association.

At this junction turn right onto the Crawford-Ridgepole Trail. You walk for ¼ mile along high ground closed in by spruce and fir woods. The other fork of the Mount Morgan Trail joins from the right. You begin to get glimpses ahead as the trees open toward the rocky summit and a cliff appears on the left.

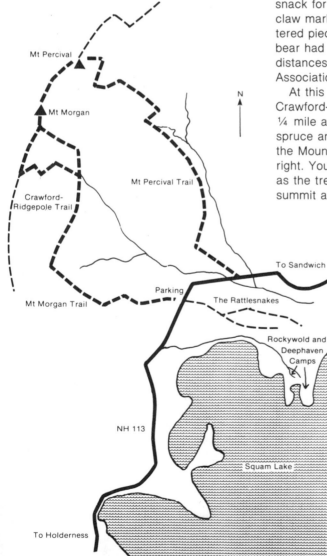

Under the cliff a path leads left to the base. Once scaled by wooden ladders, the rock faces are now for rock climbers only. Straight ahead is safe. The trail curves below fallen rocks and the eastern precipice. Then it climbs left through thick spruces. You pass a junction where the Crawford-Ridgepole Trail bears right on its way to Mount Percival, ¾ mile away. You'll return here after climbing to Mount Morgan's lookoff and summit. Keep left up through the spruces.

After a few yards you see daylight to the left. A spur trail leads to a rounded ledge wide open to the south. In that direction the lookoff affords better views than the summit. Squam Lake extends east and west beyond Rattlesnake Mountain. Larger and farther away is Lake Winnipesaukee. The blue waters are intricately patterned with peninsulas and islands. Small ponds and lakes lie cupped in the forest. Ossipee Mountain, really a range of summits, looms in the east.

Returning to the summit trail, turn left and climb a few steps to a north view from the 2,243-foot elevation. A rock cluster for a lookoff gives you wooded Sandwich Mountain and its west shoulder, craggy Black Mountain, above Sandwich Notch.

Now go back to the Crawford-Ridgepole Trail and turn left. Avoid an old trail branching right to a minor viewpoint. It may attract your feet despite the rope or poles barring the way. Before the barrier, the main trail's yellow paint blazes and arrow lead up a ledge to the left.

The trail is then plain enough as it curves toward Mount Percival over rocks and past oaks, with vistas on either side. You can see Mount Percival from some of the knolls. You climb finally over a rough section between small evergreens and then step out on

Summit ledges

the open rock. Eastward you face a dropoff. The true summit is to your left, a rounded knob at 2,235 feet.

Southward as on Morgan the lakes absorb your attention. I wouldn't be surprised if Percival shows you more fresh water than can be seen anywhere in New Hampshire. The Belknap Mountains rise beyond Lake Winnipesaukee. Lake Kanasatka lies between Squam and Winnipesaukee. You see the northern tip of narrow Lake Winnisquam almost due south.

For mountains, turn east and north. Mount Chocorua's pinnacle identifies the eastern end of the Sandwich Range. Then nearer, Mount Paugus announces itself by its slides. Mount Passaconaway is a rounded triangle beyond Mount Whiteface. You recognize the long hump of Sandwich Mountain. With binoculars on a clear day you can see the tower on Mount Carrigain. It's to the left of Sandwich's west shoulder. You can also see Osceola and two ski trails on Tecumseh.

For the descent turn southeast and walk down the ledges to the woods where a sign marks the Mount Percival Trail. (The Crawford-Ridgepole Trail continues east along rocks with yellow blazes and cairns.) I'm never sure whether this first rough section of the Mount Percival Trail would be easier

climbing down or up. A steep jumble of loose rocks and jagged chunks provide the most rugged terrain of the hike.

The trail curves to the right then gradually levels out in oak woods as it swings left to avoid a logging road and a slash straight ahead. Watch for blazes. The trail takes you on a long descent toward the southeast. You may find water along here on the right, but there'll be more water farther on at upper Smith Brook.

Out of place in the woods, a stone wall appears, and the trail leads through it where there originally must have been a gate or barway. The land was once a hill farm. You pass a cellar hole on your left. Two great white birches grow on the chimney base. Stone walls continue under the trees. The trail follows the old farm road, which soon shows the gouging tracks of a modern log skidder.

These lead to a clearing or log yard. The Mount Percival Trail follows a truck road down to NH 113. At the asphalt you turn right, to the west, for the ½ mile to your car. You pass the site of a former beaver pond on your right, which Smith Brook flows through. The narrow winding road and lack of traffic are in keeping with the Balm-of-Gilead trees: they seem part of another era.

The White Mountains

Crawford Notch from Mount Willard

Mount Willard

Distance: 2¾ miles
Walking time: 1¾ hours
Vertical rise: 925 feet
Map: USGS 15' Crawford Notch

The little railroad station at the north entrance to Crawford Notch is an information center operated by the Appalachian Mountain Club, which has acquired the site of the vanished Crawford House. There at the station you might ask about visibility before you climb Mount Willard; only a day of "ceiling and visibility unlimited" does justice to the breathtaking views from the summit cliff.

For the Mount Willard Trail, hikers park their cars near the station or on the wide shoulders of US 302. Across the road, and despite the whizzing cars, Saco Lake manages to preserve its charm and typifies the romantic term "mountain tarn."

From the station — usually called the Crawford Depot — you step over the Maine Central tracks and take up the trail, which coincides with the Avalon Trail as you enter the woods and come to a junction. Turn left and follow the Mount Willard Trail through woods at the base of the slope. (The Mount Avalon Trail continues ahead to Mount Avalon and Mount Field.)

Soon you come to a right turn onto the old carriage road. It once served guests from the famous Crawford

House, which burned in 1977. The property is now the site of an AMC hostel. The carriage road at once leads upward. You are scarcely breathing a bit faster before you find that the trail swings to the right away from the road to avoid a totally eroded section. It climbs through the woods above a brook and shortly returns to the road.

A right turn keeps you on the grade that was engineered for horses pulling heavy surreys and passengers to the top. You can probably cover the same route with a half hour of walking. It brings you out on top of the cliff.

There before you spreads a vast and open sky. Mount Chocorua is the rocky peak. Nearer on the right looms Mount Willey, solid, bulky, and so steep its spruce forest is scarred by slides. Fortunately they have been less devastating than the slide that buried the Willey family in 1826. Nearer you toward the right Mount Field rises to 4,326 feet. That's twenty-four feet more than Mount Willey. You are standing at 2,804 feet.

Opposite across the notch and forming its eastern bastion, cliffs brace Mount Webster. Beyond Mount Webster, the southernmost of the Presidential

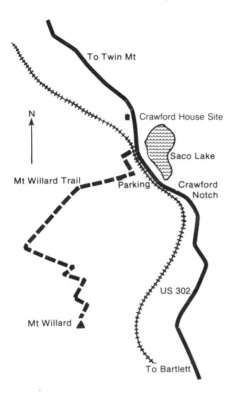

To Twin Mt

N

Crawford House Site

Saco Lake

Mt Willard Trail

Parking

Crawford Notch

US 302

Mt Willard

To Bartlett

Range's peaks, Mount Jackson, carries a tangle of spruce and fir to its topmost crags. Beyond those rocks, Mount Washington is a splendid sight against the sky. You may see above the western ridge a puff of smoke from the cog railway's engine.

So far your eyes have been distracted out and aloft. If vertigo is no problem you can gaze down into the impressive depth of the notch below the cliff. It's 1,300 feet — and no protection — down to the highway and railroad tracks. The combination of Mount Willard and children tends to make parents nervous. A length of clothesline and a sturdy tree might be the best solution. Cliffs attract kids to the very edge.

People come and go. This is a popular hike. The universal reaction at the instant of stepping out on the rock is awe blended with delight (usually indicated by an involuntary gasp). The impact lingers in your memory. It's not the scenery alone; it's the power underlying our green and stone-ribbed world.

Descend by the same route. The only turn to watch for is left into the woods off the carriage road at the top of the badly eroded section.

The Sugarloaves

Distance: 2 ¾ miles
Walking time: 2 hours
Vertical rise: 1,150 feet
Map: USGS 15' Whitefield

The two Sugarloaf summits, burned to the rock by a forest fire in the spring of 1903, handily satisfy the mountain climbing urges of campers at Zealand and Sugarloaf campgrounds. Boys and girls in groups of fifteen or twenty, families, couples, and loners run, walk, and saunter to the open ledges. The trail is easy and short. The summits are spectacular.

Except for some bushes and scrub spruces on Middle Sugarloaf, the views are totally exposed. North Sugarloaf lacks northern vistas because of screening spruces. Another peak in the series, South Sugarloaf, has no trail. It's not, therefore, part of this hike although it's the highest of the trio at 3,023 feet. Middle Sugarloaf is 2,526; North Sugarloaf 2,317. The series forms a ridge that runs north and south, separating the Zealand River on the east from the Little River on the west.

The two Sugarloaves in this hike, rising only ten miles west of Mount Washington, present one of the finest views of the peak as your reward for a climb that is only a slightly strenuous jaunt. Surely another reason why the Sugarloaves attract hikers is their challenging appearance, peculiar in

their rounded, bare rocks. They resemble not today's sugar cubes, of course, but oldtime conical loaves that housewives had to take a hammer to before pulverizing the pieces with mortar and pestle. The barren summits catch your eye while you drive past on US 302.

To reach the Sugarloaf Trail turn south off US 302 onto the Forest Service's Zealand Road, 2.5 miles east of Twin Mountain village. The paved road is the entrance to Zealand Campground.

Here tents and campers have replaced sawmills, lumberjacks, teamsters, and railroad men. Zealand was a busy lumber settlement north of the present US 302 until 1897 when the sawmills and houses went up in smoke. This put an end to J.E. Henry's Zealand operations, but he went on with his other lands and became the lumber baron of Lincoln and the Pemigewasset River's East Branch country. The upper Zealand River valley, and incidentally Henry's logging railroad camps, suffered their most devastating fire in 1886. From Middle Sugarloaf you can look south and see how miraculously the forests have returned.

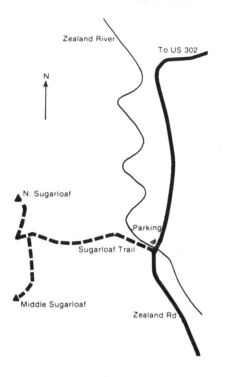

Follow the Zealand Road over the Ammonoosuc River and uphill, where the pavement gives way to dirt. High on the flat above the river you pass to the east of the Sugarloaf Campground. You are approaching the tributary, Zealand River, and at a little less than 1 mile from US 302 you come to a bridge over it. There's plenty of parking to the right before the bridge. (The Zealand Road continues another 2.7 miles to a dead end and the start of the Zealand Trail up the river to Zealand Pond and AMC's Zealand Falls Hut.)

The Sugarloaf Trail begins on the far side of the bridge. Initially it coincides with the Trestle Trail beside the river. The path is level along the west bank. The stream flows transparently, showing each stone on the bottom. After ¼ mile the Sugarloaf Trail leaves the river at a sharp left turn. (The Trestle Trail continues ahead to complete its loop over the river on a bridge and back to the road.) Turn left. Soon you pass two monstrous rocks

pried loose by the glacier and dropped here, along with smaller ones farther on. Both peaks show the rocky southeast faces typical of mountains filed down by the great ice sheet's rock teeth.

Soon the trail leads up more steeply to switchbacks and steps of sawed logs. As you approach the col between Middle Sugarloaf, on the left, and North Sugarloaf, on the right, the trail forks. Bear left at the fork and cross a flat with spruce woods and high bracken ferns. At an abrupt rise the trail bears right and then gradually left as it circles to its final approach in the upper spruces. The last steep angle on crumbly rock and gravel takes you to the bare granite summit.

Beyond a scattered line of bushes and two boulders, to the southwest, you see North Twin Mountain rearing its sharp, wooded peak above a precipitous buttress. North Twin seems to join the ridge that extends left toward South Twin. (It doesn't.) Walking west toward the edge, you look down on Twin Mountain Airport and the long line of motels, stores, restaurants, and amusement enterprises. By moving south past a large bush and over the low vines of three-toothed cinquefoil (white flowers in late June), you come to the cliff of rocky outcroppings I've previously mentioned as having been filed away by the glacier. Before you, Mount Hale appears two miles away as a truncated pyramid slightly notched on top.

But these views are pale in comparison to the great panorama — the Presidentials — eastward. Beyond the Rosebrook Range on the horizon, sometimes in haze or clouds, sometimes as sharp as its broadcasting towers, Mount Washington displays its treeless summit. Mount Monroe flanks it on the south. Clay, Jefferson, and Adams do the same on the north. Directly north and nearer stands

Boots on North Sugarloaf

isolated and shapely Cherry Mountain.

Middle Sugarloaf is more popular than North Sugarloaf. You are more likely to find privacy for sunning and lunch by heading back to the col between the peaks and keeping straight toward North Sugarloaf. A path leads across the forked main Sugarloaf Trail to a junction and sign. Turn left and walk about 200 feet to the beginning of the downward slope. The trail to North Sugarloaf branches right. There is no sign.

Under the partially wooded cliff two routes are possible: east or west around the rock face and its short chimney. Either way involves hoisting yourself over crevices and discovering passages between slabs before you reach the summit.

Your more northern viewpoint here reveals another Presidential peak beyond the Rosebrook Range. It's Mount Eisenhower. "Peak" is a misnomer for this bald dome.

Descent from North Sugarloaf presents a problem only for those who are troubled by looking down on treetops. The east route is the less trying. At the base of the rocks, and facing south toward Middle Sugarloaf, you pick up the spur trail leading to the fork from the main Sugarloaf Trail. Turn left, to the east, and you soon come to the trail worn by hikers who have settled for Middle Sugarloaf and have missed the adventure of North Sugarloaf. Now you have a relaxing half-hour walk back to the Zealand Road.

Mud Pond

Distance: 5 miles
Walking time: 2½ hours
Vertical rise: 890 feet
Maps: USGS 7½' Mt. Moosilauke;
    USGS 7½' East Haverhill

Approaching the western slope of
Mount Moosilauke, the Tunnel Brook
Trail rises gradually from the south to a
little-known notch so acutely angular
that slides have skidded down into it.
There in a mountainous setting lies the
destination of this hike — repulsively
named Mud Pond.

Of the many Mud Ponds in New
Hampshire, I have yet to find one that
wasn't interesting, and this pond at the
source of Tunnel Brook is one of the
more fascinating. It now could be called
Bog Pond because beavers have
engineered an environment more varied
than that of a simple body of water. It's
a teeming place. Bog plants flourish,
birds pursue insects, and shy animals
leave tracks in the mud.

To reach the south end of Tunnel
Brook Trail, follow NH 25 to Glencliff
between Warren and Haverhill. Turn
north onto the Old Sanatorium Road
(still known by the name although the
state tuberculosis institution is now a
home for the elderly). After 1 mile
watch for the North and South Road
branching left, downhill, at two forest
service signs, one urging environmental
care and another stating that the road
is not maintained in winter.

A third sign directs hikers on the Appalachian Trail, which at this corner
leads north over Mount Moosilauke via
the Glencliff Trail, and south via the
Town Line Trail to NH 25 and beyond
for the climb past Wachipauka Pond.

Turn onto this gravel road, which
became a way through the forest to
Benton when the Civilian Conservation
Corps built it during the 1930s. Drive
past the Town Line Trail on the left.

The Tunnel Brook Trail begins .2 mile
down the North and South Road. You'll
see the sign, on the right, at an access
road to a cottage. Park off the North
and South Road.

Beyond this small cottage and a
tributary to Slide Brook, the trail takes
up the route of the old Tunnel Road.
(Tunnel Brook itself flows north from
Mud Pond in the notch.) The ancient,
graded woods road, which keeps to the
valley, has been used for logging in
modern times. Before that it linked the
settlements of Warren and Benton.

The maples and beeches above the
old road have shed leaves on it for
years, so you walk on a cushion of
forest duff. Shade deepens under occasional hemlocks. The two crossings of
Slide Brook are on rounded stones.

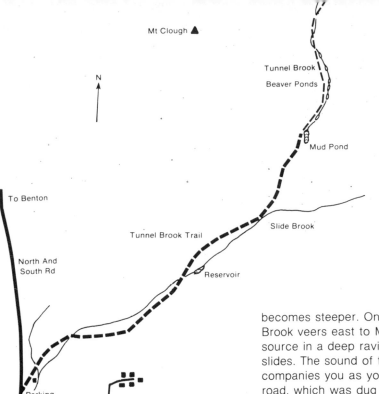

Mt Clough ▲

N

Tunnel Brook

Beaver Ponds

Mud Pond

To Benton

Tunnel Brook Trail

Slide Brook

North And
South Rd

Reservoir

Parking

Old Sanatorium Rd

To Glencliff

becomes steeper. On the right Slide Brook veers east to Moosilauke and its source in a deep ravine scarred by slides. The sound of falling water accompanies you as you climb the old road, which was dug out of the slope. Spruces and firs take over near the height-of-land. The change to northern drainage is evident only as the beginning of a slight downgrade, which soon takes you to the open slot between Mount Clough on the west and Moosilauke on the east. Partially screened by evergreens, spectacle-shaped Mud Pond lies to the right beyond a slide off Mount Clough. (The Tunnel Brook Trail keeps on 2 miles to Tunnel Brook Road in Benton.

The pond floods back from a long beaver dam of poles and mud and takes up most of the notch's level area. Beyond it the eastern wall rises to Moosilauke's broad flanks and massive ridge. Mixed hardwoods, often blown into dipping swirls by gusty winds, give way to scrub spruce and rocks below the 4,560-foot South Peak. The main summit, elevation 4,810 feet, is hidden by the long northern ridge extending from South Peak. Opposite it Mount Clough rises beyond a shoulder. The

The brook is clear and sparkling. You'll appreciate the water's transparency if you stop at the little reservoir on the right 1 mile from the North and South Road. Held back by an earthen dike with bushes and by a concrete dam, this pool supplies water to the home for the aged. It is so clear that you look down and see distinct grains of sand.

Beyond the reservoir the trail

Mud Pond **101**

3,560-foot summit forms the west wall of the notch.

From Mud Pond northward beaver ponds and slides border Tunnel Brook Trail. By following the trail for ½ mile you'll see six more examples of beaver hydraulics, logging, and lodge building. The slides from Mount Clough's gashed steepness continue through the notch. At one beaver dam a Clough slide fans out to meet another from Moosilauke. A sight-seeing excursion beyond Mud Pond and back is a nice finishing touch for a hike into this western-most notch in the White Mountains. It adds only about 1 mile to the 5 miles I've listed.

Arethusa Falls/Frankenstein Cliff

Distance: 4½ miles
Walking time: 3½ hours
Vertical rise: 1,200 feet
Map: USGS 15' Crawford Notch

Arethusa Falls and Frankenstein Cliff: such baroque names for a waterfall on Bemis Brook and a series of exposed rock strata above US 302 in Crawford Notch State Park — but they are special.

Plunging more than two hundred feet, Arethusa Falls are the highest in New Hampshire. The orchid arethusa, with its magenta crimson flowers, is said to have once bloomed at the falls. This orchid usually displays its three-pronged, tongued flowers in bogs. There is no bog at the falls. I wonder whether some poetic young lady of the horsedrawn carriage and hotel era named the falls while reading Shelley. The nymph Arethusa appears in his poetry.

The magnificent geologic formation that drops Bemis Brook at the falls appears again northward as Frankenstein Cliff. Named not from Mary Shelley's novel, but for an artist, Godfrey N. Frankenstein, who loved to paint the mountains, the cliff provides a lookoff to sweeping views of the Notch.

A loop hike takes you to both of these natural wonders. The opportunity to study a man-made wonder — the steel railroad trestle — is a bonus. I suggest a visit to the falls in early sum-mer or after a rainy spell, when the flow of water is more spectacular than during dry weather.

Three miles south of the Willey House Site on US 302, or about 8.5 miles north of Bartlett, a large sign on the west side of the highway identifies the approach to Arethusa Falls. A blacktop access road leads uphill to a parking area. Beyond the Maine Central Railroad tracks there's a white cottage with an apple tree on the lawn. It is known as Willey House Post Office from days gone by.

You'll find the path and the sign for the Arethusa Falls Trail on the far side of the railroad tracks to the left of the house. Frankenstein Cliff dominates the northern view along the tracks.

The 1½-mile trail to the falls is easy and popular. I've met tourists in city clothes and street shoes. More comfortable clothes and sturdy shoes are necessary for a full hike around the cliffs.

The path leads up a slope with fine white birches. Soon Bemis Brook Trail forks left at a sign. (It leads to pools and minor falls before returning to the main trail.) Now you begin to climb. You pass the upper junction of Bemis Brook

N

To Crawford Notch

Maine Central RR

Frankenstein Cliff

Saco River

Willey House P.O.
Parking

Bemis Brook

Arethusa Falls

US 302

To Bartlett

Trail and find yourself high above the brook, which is mostly hidden by trees on the precipitous bank. The trail, more level, clings to the valley wall.

Trail wear here has exposed spruce roots in an intricate pattern. They do a good job of stopping erosion. You can see how their intertwined tentacles hold the earth on mountainsides.

Gradually the trail slants down to the brook, which you cross on boulders. The trail remains close to the brook. It becomes rough. Then you see the falls through the branches of big spruces.

The water forms a long, narrow veil over the cliff. During times of freshets the cascade becomes a clear drop. For the best view, and for the distance necessary to get the falls in a camera viewfinder, cross the brook as the trail sign indicates and observe the falls near the trail's entrance into the woods.

Continuing through the spruces, you are now on the Arethusa-Ripley Falls Trail. Don't assume this graded path will continue for the remainder of your loop hike. Just enjoy it for about a half mile. There is still rugged hiking ahead.

Arethusa Falls

The Arethusa-Ripley Falls Trail leads you toward Frankenstein Cliff. You swing left over a ridge and up between trees that line a small stream on your right. The trail turns north again as you cross the brook at an abrupt right angle. You leave behind the graded section.

Climbing more steeply to a fork 1 mile from the falls, you leave the Arethusa-Ripley Falls Trail and keep right onto the Frankenstein Cliff Trail. It descends easterly and you soon come out on a glacier-smoothed stone dome. The trail skirts the north side of this rounded ledge and enters a notable spruce forest where tree trunks are tall, straight, and without branches for twenty feet or more. The spruce needles are springy underfoot. The trail is ten or fifteen yards from the cliffs, so you pass various lookoffs.

After walking about ½ hour from the Arethusa-Ripley Falls Trail junction you come to the best view. Over the treetops and across the valley a broad, green slope rises toward the summit of Mount Bemis. The white line at the head of the valley is Arethusa Falls. Bemis Brook drains into the Saco River, which flows between wide sandbars on its way to meadows in Bartlett and Conway. Miniature cars speed along US 302. The highway is straighter than the Maine Central tracks curving along the grade above it. The more you look down, the higher you seem, although elevation is only about 2,000 feet above sea level. The total drop to the parking area and your car is 800 feet.

Looking out, Chocorua displays its distinctive spire in the far distance southeast, with the long ridge of Moat Mountain to the left. Mount Paugus is a hump to the right of Chocorua over-shadowed by Mount Passaconaway. Eastward across the highway and up the ridges beyond the Saco River you see Mount Crawford's squared crown at its northside cliff.

When you've enjoyed the scenery, follow the trail again on a gradual descent through the spruces that continue growing to the cliff's edge. Here you must watch for the woods to change from spruce and fir to leafy trees, because the trail is obscure as it drops abruptly to the right down a break in the cliffs. You could be misled by the easier walking straight ahead in the leafy trees; I was.

Keep to the right climbing down among ledges and small maples and beeches. A big fallen oak confuses the trail as the slope moderates. Several switchbacks in the hardwood forest are poorly marked with old axe blazes and faded yellow paint, but your general direction is north under more cliffs. Steep descents alternate with slabbing. Soon you turn south (right), and you have to scramble over fallen rocks in the cool shade where water drips off a cliff. From here you enter beech woods once more.

Rotten stone grades the trail with gravel. It results from the natural weathering of certain granites. Rain and carbon dioxide form carbonic acid; this washes out the orthoclase, or potash feldspar, so the rock almost literally comes unglued. The effect is common in many areas of the White Mountains. On steep slopes the gravel can be treacherous underfoot.

During the final descent you'll be walking through the open woods. Looking ahead you'll see black lines gleaming through the oaks and beeches. You are approaching the great steel curve of the Frankenstein Trestle's girders, while in the distance on US 302 you hear the sounds of the machines that have put the railroad out of business.

The trail takes you under the massive, curving steel frame whose giant legs rest on foundations of squared rock, not on concrete. If you look up and study the girders you'll see, under layers of black paint, the name "Carnegie."

Beyond the trestle the trail forks at a sign where Frankenstein Cut-Off, your route, bears right. (The Frankenstein Cliff Trail leads ¼ mile down to US 302.) The cut-off keeps to the contours below the railroad grade. To your left you look into the tops of beeches and yellow birches. A moderate slope up at the end of a ½-mile cut-off brings you back to the parking area.

By the way, don't walk on the tracks. That's trespassing, which, like investigating the trestle, is strictly forbidden.

Welch and Dickey Mountains

Distance: 4½ miles
Walking time: 4 hours
Vertical rise: 1,860 feet
Map: USGS 15' Plymouth

The sparsely wooded, rocky hump of Welch Mountain looms up from the north bank of Mad River at the entrance to Waterville Valley. Tourists on I-93 speculate about the strange and barren formation. Hikers at once want to climb it.

Welch, elevation 2,591 feet, is a small yet varied peak. Exciting ledge scrambles lead to spectacular views and a rare evergreen: the little jack pine of the far north.

Dickey, 2,720 feet, a short distance north of Welch and similarly composed of rounded rock faces and flat ledges, provides an unusual look at Franconia Notch and the mountains bordering that famous pass.

Welch and Dickey are fine for a spring hike, because snow melts early on the open, southerly rocks. In autumn, these two give you a really special foliage hike. The treetops in the depths west of the summits are dazzling in sunlight. I have stared into the gigantic montage and thought I must be seeing every conceivable blend of red and yellow.

From Campton, off I-93's Exit 28, NH 49, the route into Waterville Valley, leads east along the Mad River. At Goose Hollow, 2.7 miles from the traffic lights in Campton, it crosses the river. Stay on NH 49 another 1.7 miles, then turn left onto the Upper Mad River Road. At once you cross Six Mile Bridge, which despite its name is only 4.5 miles from Campton.

Beyond the bridge drive up a steep hill. Keep going past "Gateway" on the right, and several other roads for the homes and condominiums nearby. At .7 mile from Six Mile Bridge, turn right onto a road marked with a small sign, "Welch Mountain Trail," and drive another .7 mile. Just beyond a sign reading "Woodwinds" and a driveway on the left, you come to a sign marked "Parking," followed by a turnaround.

This hike loops up and over both Welch and Dickey Mountains, descending down Dickey's west shoulder to your car here at the parking area. The trails meet at a junction in the woods to the left, opposite the entrance to the parking area.

I must warn you against undertaking this climb in wet or icy weather, as it involves many steep, bare rock faces. But in good weather it's a joy.

At the junction mentioned above, take the fork to the right, the Welch Moun-

Tripyramid in distance

tain Trail. It follows an old logging road, soon crosses a brook, and maintains a moderate grade up the east bank through fine hardwoods. On at least one of the beeches you may notice the claw marks left by a bear climbing after beechnuts. The view to the left, in seasons when the trees are leafless, reveals the cliffs of Dickey Mountain. You will descend along the tops of them.

As the Welch Mountain Trail becomes steeper it also turns right. Well-marked with yellow paint blazes and signs, it begins a series of switchbacks up into spruces. Near the top of the ridge you step out onto sloping, bare bedrock, typical of the trails over these mountains. Not far above, and about ¾ hour from your car, you reach the barren

ridge below Welch. The trail joins a former route up from the south. Turn left (north) toward the crags leading to Welch's summit.

Here you walk along cliffs overlooking boulder-strewn Mad River, the ribbon of asphalt called NH 49, and the eastern valley. Across the river and highway the great ridge is Sandwich Mountain. The gap to the south is Sandwich Notch.

Beyond this lookoff, the cairns and white or yellow paint blazes lead you up among the ledges and sparse, wind-blown trees. The summit crown rises directly ahead. Trees grow below and above a huge stone sphere that seems to protrude from the mountain. The grade is easy but impressive because you're climbing the spherical face.

You walk through an entrance into

the spruces; the trail curves high to the left and then to the right into jumbled rocks. Here you encounter a briefly demanding climb and passages through narrow clefts.

Angling up open ledges, you find yourself among jack pines. They occur in three other New Hampshire areas — near Mount Chocorua, Mount Webster, and at Lake Umbagog. Short, twin needles surround tight cones that cling for years to the wiry branches. Limbs protrude in twisted toughness along the length of the trunks. Some of the jack pines grow as high as twenty feet.

Beneath the sheltering boughs snowshoe hares have scattered numerous pellets as they nibbled at undergrowth during the snowy season, to which they adapt by turning from summer brown to white. A more obvious scat than the pellets decorated a ledge when I was last there. It was a product of a bobcat, who is, as was demonstrated by the compacted white hair, higher on nature's food chain than the hare.

Climb on to the summit. The crags offer an almost entire round of distant mountains closed only to the north, where Dickey's stone knob and scrubby trees hide Franconia Notch.

To the east the slide on the southernmost of three peaks identifies Mount Tripyramid. In the opposite direction, to the west, Mount Moosilauke stands above adjacent mountains. The pool of water in the forest southwest of the rock ridge that braces Dickey is Cone Pond.

To complete the panorama continue

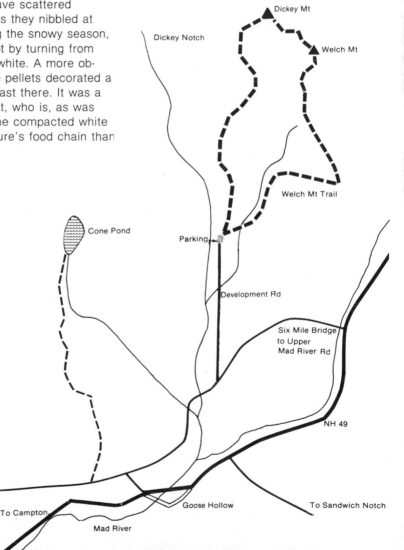

the hike for a look north from Dickey, only another ½ mile on. Descent north from Welch begins along white blazes on the summit rocks and continues down ledges that form natural, wide steps. Cross the open col and enter spruce woods. You climb to the broad, spherical rock face, similar to Welch. The trail, however, here bypasses the rock with a left turn along the base in the woods. Then you turn right and climb into the open, where you can walk up the rest of the ledge.

A sign on a tree to your left points back to Mount Welch. Another on your right points to "North Outlook." Follow the yellow paint blazes on the ledges straight ahead for Dickey's summit, where bushes and evergreens surround areas of rock. Notice a sign reading "Highway" on a tree. It points the direction along the trail for the second half of this loop hike. A nearby sign again points back to "Mt. Welch."

Look to the east and you'll see an extensive bare rock surface beyond scrub spruces. For tremendous views up into Franconia Notch you must go to that rock surface. This is the "North Outlook" mentioned on the sign. You may return to the sign and follow a trail through the spruces, or you may descend the summit ledges and take a more direct route marked by random cairns and footpaths in sphagnum moss and scrub.

As you walk up the easy slope of the rock, you see glacial erratics scattered all about, and several little cairns piled here and there, apparently by energetic children or larking adults. On the long dome, if you can look down from the panorama, you'll see a distinctive vein of white quartzite in the bedrock as straight as a chalk line.

Far up the valley of the Pemigewasset River, silhouettes sharply outline the northern horizon. Mounts Lafayette, Lincoln, and Flume rise as triangular peaks east of deep Franconia Notch. For a contrast in mountain shapes, Cannon Mountain west of the notch appears as an inverted bowl. Looking south and west you see Moosilauke, Kineo, Stinson, and distant Cardigan.

For your descent, return to the summit of Dickey. Follow the direction of the arrow-shaped "Highway" sign north into evergreens and thicker woods by a well-defined trail. There is another outlook toward Franconia Notch before the trail turns left and you start down. It soon emerges from the woods and crosses areas of rough but rounded rock, mostly slanting south toward the valley that separates you from Welch. You briefly enter woods again, only to cross more bedrock exposed to the sky. Watch for a blaze on a tree at the far side of each open rock slope. It shows you the entrance into the next patch of woods.

About fifteen minutes from Dickey's summit the trail turns left up a rock knob, then descends along a rounded rock ridge bordered by trees on your right. You begin an interesting walk along the dropoff over the cliffs. Because of the rounded surface, there is no actual "edge" in the usual sense of the term. Keep close to the woods on the right.

Below the rock ridge you enter the woods and pass to the right of a vertical ledge eight or ten feet high and over a hundred feet long. The trees change from evergreens to deciduous, with many large red oaks. The trail keeps to the top of a narrow ridge that slopes gradually down to an ancient logging road. Keep to the right, then after five minutes turn left at a junction with another woods road. You soon step out of a little ravine into the parking area.

Mount Doublehead

Distance: 4 miles
Walking time: 3¼ hours
Vertical rise: 1,776 feet
Maps: USGS 15' North Conway

There's a Mount Doublehead near Jackson and another in the Squam Range. I'm talking here about the Doublehead northeast of Jackson. The rounded, wooded summits have elevations as nearly identical as their contours: North Doublehead, 3,056 feet; South Doublehead, 2,938 feet.

I recommend this loop hike for the views and for the log cabin atop North Doublehead. The outlooks from the ledges are fine and sweeping. The Presidentials, the Carter-Wildcat Range, and the Saco Valley are all seen from unusual angles. The cabin is so perfect it belongs in a museum. A U.S. Forest Service project built long ago, and an adjunct to the old ski trail, the cabin is as delicate as the mountain environment. I hope the steep, 1¾ mile climb protects it from overuse and vandalism.

The access road toward Doublehead leaves Jackson north of the stores. It's the east section of NH 16B. (Don't take NH 16B west of the stone bridge.) Drive up the hill, bearing right on NH 16B at a fork. From the hilltop you can look to your right across fields and woods to Doublehead. Drive down to the corner at Whitney's Inn and turn past onto the Dundee Road. (NH 16B forks left.) Keep past the Black Mountain Ski Area and the Black Mountain Road on your left. Less than .5 mile from the Black Mountain Road you come to the start of this hike's climb: Doublehead Ski Trail, also on your left, 2.5 miles from Jackson.

But don't get out of your car yet. Drive on another .5 mile and park off the road opposite the New Path, which will be your return route. Shoulder your rucksack and walk back down the road to Doublehead Ski Trail. This warm-up for the hike leaves your car ready and waiting when you descend by the New Path.

If confronted with Doublehead Ski Trail, the modern skier probably wouldn't believe that this twelve-foot corridor winding up through hardwoods was a ski trail at all (or if he did he'd chuckle over the quaintness of it.) I shudder to think that we skied such corkscrews in the 1930s, not to mention first climbing them. The forest service, anticipating disaster, housed a rescue toboggan and other emergency equipment in a small shed partway up the trail. On posts to raise it above snows and lined with tin against squirrels and mice, the shed's age shows on its mossy shingles.

After about a half hour you pass a branch trail, the Old Path, forking right from the ski trail. (The Old Path leads to the col between North and South Doublehead.) Midway up the mountain you come to a spring, the only water. There's none at the cabin. The overflow runs across the trail. As you climb on, following the curves from contour to contour, you may wonder where all the mountain came from; it didn't look so big as you drove toward it. The trail goes at the steep upper section without much regard for the angle. Evergreen woods are deep in forest duff, which supports thriving colonies of clintonia and bunchberry.

The cabin appears through the spruces just north of the trail junction with the col trail to South Doublehead, on the right. Evergreens nearly surround the cabin. An outlook has been cut to show Mount Washington, Lion Head above Tuckerman Ravine, and Huntington Ravine. In the opposite direction from the cabin an opening in the woods reveals the eastern view to Mountain Pond and the Saco River's East Branch valley.

Sunlight and shadows pattern the cabin's peeled spruce logs. They have a special sheen that seems remarkably light despite two generations of weathering. The walls are joined at the corners by rounded notches on the lower side of each log so no rain can accumulate to rot the wood — and they fit snugly. Asphalt shingles on the roof

are more recent protection. Inside the green door with its strong hinges and latch, the center room has only essential furnishings: two heavy tables and four benches. The chunk stove has been removed. Off this communal room four bunkrooms, two on each side, contain two bunks apiece. Windows have twelve panes.

Everywhere is evidence of skillful work by men using simple tools such as axe, crosscut saw, and adze. The rafters fit true to the plate logs so the roof is absolutely true. Walls inside dividing off the bunkrooms are made of smaller poles carefully trimmed and fitted. Door frames set nicely into the logs. A cabinetmaker might well approve of all the joints in the cabin — allowing for the tools and material used.

This is the cabin all of us dream about at one time or another when the real world becomes too much for us. It should be preserved and cared for not only by the forest service but by those who use it without permit or fee for daytime shelter or overnight lodging.

The trail to South Doublehead begins at the junction south of the cabin. It descends through the evergreens to the col and rises again as lookoff ledges appear on the right. Beyond this, spruce and fir blend with deciduous trees, which become sparse at the junction with the New Path down to the Dundee Road. (For your descent you will return to this junction after going to the top of South Doublehead.) Ascending farther south, the trail leads to the east-west summit ridge with various open outlooks.

Explorations among these reward you with views to Kearsarge North and Jackson Village. Vistas east reveal Chatham, Baldface Mountain, Evans Notch, and Kezar Lake in Maine.

The west lookoff from South Doublehead shows you Mount Washington and a section of the auto road at the Horn. The Wildcat summits, Carter Notch, and Carter Dome appear from the unusual angles I mentioned. You can see the Dome's southeast shoulder and eastward as far as the rocky eminence at the headwaters and beaver ponds (out of sight) on Red Brook, which drains into Wild River.

Northwest with binoculars you can pick out the summit cairn on Mount Eisenhower in the line of southern Presidential peaks. To the south Moat Mountain's craggy summits show clear-ly, and farther away, to the west, Mount Carrigain can be identified with binoculars by locating the lookout tower. I would not guarantee any of these views for long. The evergreens are growing fast.

When you return to the New Path for your descent, remember that the junction is between the two ledges. Watch for two small cairns under the spruces. The way is steep and easy to follow. Soon you drop to a growth completely mixed with mountain trees: spruce, fir, mountain maple, moosewood, birch, and poplar. The trail, continuing steep but very little eroded, becomes well defined as it takes you into larger spruces. Here in mid-June, white lady's slippers grow in open shade. The forest becomes leafy with beech and yellow birch. Cairns occasionally mark the way. Two logging roads joining emphasize the route. The trail twists and turns. Blowdowns may also interfere.

Following another old logging road, the trail completes its descent to the Dundee Road. You pass stone walls built when all this was pasture and cropland. Your car is nearby.

Profile of Doublehead

Black Mountain

Distance: 4½ miles
Walking time: 3 hours
Vertical rise: 1,800 feet
Map: USGS 7½' East Haverhill

Two or three New Hampshire elevations named Black Mountain come to mind. I have often wondered if the adjective originated when early settlers looked up at the dark spruce forests in the days before logging and fires laid bare the summits. This one in Benton, with its 2,836-foot elevation, exposes to the sun a long ledge that sparkles with quartzite. An open shoulder gives you a half-hour climb among spruces and bare outlooks before you reach the summit. The ledge offers wide views. This western outpost of the White Mountains overlooks forested valleys to the east toward imposing Mount Moosilauke. To the west it shows you the Connecticut River valley and green farmland extending to the Vermont hills.

If you climb Black Mountain during the last week of May or early in June, you'll find splendid rose purple masses of flowers among the upper rocks. The shrub rhodora blooms before its leaves unfold, so there is almost no green. On a sunny day when you climb over a creamy quartzite ledge and look down on a pocket of solid magenta, the color literally hits your eyes.

Although the mountain rises in Benton, your route to the Chippewa Trail lies through Haverhill, or more specifically through East Haverhill. The village is on NH 25 between Pike and Glencliff. In the center of town, take the Lime Kiln Road north off NH 25. After 1.5 miles bear left at a fork. Drive 1.3 miles more on this dirt road to the Chippewa Trail on your right. There's a small clearing where you leave your car.

The fence at the edge of the clearing accommodates hikers with an opening formed by two posts; a third post set between them bars the way to farm animals. You may have to remove your rucksack to slide through. The trail at once descends to a small seasonal brook in low ground, then curves left along the edge of the woods, from which you see a house and field. You cross a larger, mucky brook. To the right it looks as if it once flowed into a beaver pond, now a brushy swamp.

Ten minutes from your car you step up a few yards to a woods road. Turn right and walk about 50 yards to a fork. Keep left as indicated by an arrow on a tree. The road leads uphill into spruces.

Blueberry Mountain from Black Mountain

From the right another woods road joins. You climb to an open field beyond a stone wall. In the cellar of a vanished house white birches grow. You've been walking an old farm road. Follow the cairns spotted with blue paint left. Ahead you look up at Black Mountain rising steeply. To the right is a similar, quartzite-crowned mountain, Sugarloaf.

At the edge of the field the trail goes directly upward among dense pines and then leads through more open growth among junipers and young leafy trees. The trail is dirt, like a cow path, but this one is not from cow's hoofs. It goes up too straight. Cows, no longer in evidence here, always graze along contours.

Ahead to the left a big yellow arrow on a rock points skyward. The direction is not entirely in error, as you learn when you cross an old high pasture on short, poor grass that still holds out against the returning forest. At the left corner you enter spruce woods and begin the skyward climb. It's quite serious for about twenty minutes. Then a turn to the right gives you a respite with more level going. But a left turn takes you up steeply again, this time into a fine stand of spruces thriving on the mountainside as far up as you can see. Branchless for twenty feet or more, straight as plumb lines, they're just right for a log cabin.

Large white blazes on the trees, many of them now red pines, lead you up until the trail begins to wind between looming stone outcrops. Smooth and rounded by the glacier, the ledges show striations etched by sharp rocks imbedded in the ice sheet. Here rhodora and blueberry bushes grow in the openings, and you can look west to North Haverhill and to green meadows bordering the Connecticut River.

About an hour and twenty minutes from the car you climb out onto the

open shoulder. About 100 feet to the right a lookoff ledge shows you a vista south down the valley. The trail bears left, marked by yellow arrows on the rock. You climb toward the blue sky and are now and then briefly in spruces. You feel like a mountaineer as you scramble with both toeholds and handholds. You are exposed to white rock, cool shade, sun, and wind. Then you are entirely clear of trees on a bright quartzite knob, and suddenly ahead, beyond a short col, a cliff rises to the topmost ledge.

At the base of the cliff the Chippewa Trail turns sharp left. Keep left around the cliff's base. There's a short grade through spruce woods; turn to the right. (Ahead the Black Mountain Trail descends 2½ miles to a town road in Benton.) You leave the evergreens behind and step up on bare rock.

From the summit you face a sweep of forest all the way to Moosilauke, massively occupying the horizon beyond Mount Clough. To the left of Mount Clough, almost hidden in trees, Long Pond's shoreline extends to a glimpse of blue water at the north end. Nearer on the right, Sugarloaf presents its rocks, now lower than you are by 230 feet. From it a ridge called The Hogback extends to Blueberry Mountain. Away to the left, to the northeast, bulky Mount Kinsman hides some of the Franconia Range.

For views to the south, walk along the ledge. I like to look south because I can see the hills of Orford, my boyhood summer home, and Mount Cube, my first mountain. Its shining quartzite stands out between wooded Piermont Mountain to the north and Smarts Mountain to the south.

One of the main attractions on Black Mountain is the bird watching from the summit. Swallows always skim by; sometimes there are hawks and ravens; warblers and white-throated sparrows are often in the spruces.

Two more attractions await you northward. Keep to the crest of the ledges. You may find faded yellow arrows in places. Pick your way down to a narrow line of evergreens and into open space again. Tipping Rock is plainly visible to your right. Maybe once this glacial erratic, seven or eight feet through and equally high, actually tipped. Now it rests solidly above the cliff on rocks jammed under it. For the second attraction, a cup of icy water, continue northward. You must watch closely on your left for a path diverging from the open rock and thin topsoil. It's nearly hidden by waist-high brush, but once your boots are on it you can follow it to an opening in spruces and an easy trail down to a spring. A buried can and cover, once painted green, protects water so cold it makes your teeth ache.

Back at the summit and ready to descend, you'll be facing west toward the green valley. North Haverhill appears as a double row of toy houses along the main street. Beyond the Connecticut River in Vermont you can see Newbury's church spire above the treetops. The serene fields, farms, and villages contrast with the wild forest and mountains behind you.

The descent is the Chippewa Trail in reverse. Below the summit turn left, to the south. Below the cliff turn right. Down past the lower field where the woods road forks, keep right. Later for the entry to the trail through the wooded low ground, turn left at an arrow on a tree. One more corner to watch for comes after the brooks and just before the brief climb to your car. There turn right and uphill past a blue arrow on a tree to your left.

If you've had the forethought to park your car in morning sunlight, it's probably shaded and cool now in the afternoon.

Mount Tecumseh

Distance: 4¼ miles
Walking time: 4 hours
Vertical rise: 2,000 feet
Map: USGS 15' Plymouth

A springtime mountain, Tecumseh overlooks sunny Waterville Valley from the west, and its slopes receive the warmth necessary for a new hiking season. Of course, you'll have to expect snow under the shading spruces as you approach the summit, as well as back across the ridge to the ski-lift terminal. But during your descent, the ski slopes will be bare turf and gloriously open to the mountains and the greening valley.

I've climbed Mount Tecumseh as early as May 3. I carried no snowshoes and relied on packed snow in the trail left by winter climbers. Snowshoes, however, if you plan to hike early in the season, would be good insurance.

From Campton NH 49 follows the Mad River to Waterville Valley's ski resort. Ten miles from Campton a left turn puts you onto the Tripoli Road and across the river. Drive 1.2 miles to the access road for the Tecumseh Ski Area on the left. Drive past the parking lanes and the lodge. The Tecumseh Trail begins on the left 100 yards north of the lodge. (The ski area is closed during the summer.) The scarred mountain to the east is Tripyramid with its North Slide.

In early May you'll notice the trees are still bare as you climb an easy grade along the south bank of Tecumseh Brook, which has a seasonal flow and should not be expected to provide drinking water in the summer. At a small cascade flowing over a plank dam, a red arrow on a tree directs you left up the bank a few yards to a grassy ski slope. This is ½ mile from the parking area. Keep to the north edge about 200 yards to another red arrow marking a woods path. This leads up about 300 yards to another ski slope. Midway up the first really steep pitch, and 1 mile from the parking area, another red arrow on a tree, to the right, points into the woods for the beginning of the trail that continues to the summit. (Note: the U.S. Forest Service may soon relocate all the trails in the woods north of the ski slopes.)

The great advantage of spring climbing is the leafless forest. Yellow birches have green-tipped twigs, buds on beeches are lengthening, but the sudden bursting of foliage is a week or two away. No leaves hide the view north to Mount Osceola and its separate East Peak. Ahead you see a spruce-clad, flattened dome, which is your destination on this hike.

Below these wide views, tree trunks stand in scattered rows along aisles extending in all directions. The forest is spacious and lively with migrating birds. A myrtle warbler, yellow, white, and black among a shadbush's white lace flowers, can make you a lifelong bird watcher.

The seasons reverse themselves as you climb. Early spring surrounded you at the start along Tecumseh Brook. There all kinds of plants were rushing to airy life after a winter protected by fallen leaves. Now at 3,000 feet late winter encloses you. Snow crunches beneath your boots, and the air is cold. If you step off the packed track, you plunge at once to your knees. The woods have changed to wintry evergreens.

The trail swings northerly up toward the summit. The Sosman Trail, on the left, joins and will be part of your descent route. After about 200 yards, it branches left up through the spruces; the Tecumseh Trail keeps on straight. Either will take you to the summit, but for spring walking on a packed snow track, Sosman probably offers more solid footing.

So turn left onto the Sosman Trail. It circles west of the summit, opens to a good view toward Mount Moosilauke, then climbs steeply in an S-turn past wooded ledges to the partially open summit rocks. You are four feet above the 4,000-foot contour. (The Mount Tecumseh Trail, arriving at the summit from the east, descends north to the Tripoli Road 3¼ miles away.)

The northern horizon is the commanding sight from Mount Tecumseh. In May it centers on snowy Mount Washington, seen between Mount Osceola and East Peak. It is left of Mount Carrigain.

After lunch return by the Sosman Trail. Beyond the section where it coincides with the Tecumseh Trail, it branches right and descends before climbing to a 3,740-foot nameless knoll with excellent views. You look northwest to Mount Liberty, Mount Lafayette, and Cannon Mountain's spectacular precipice south of the famous Profile ledges and above the Franconia Notch.

Beyond this lookoff and lofty knoll the trail's general direction is southsoutheast through open spruce woods. About ½ mile from the Tecumseh Trail,

View to Waterville Valley

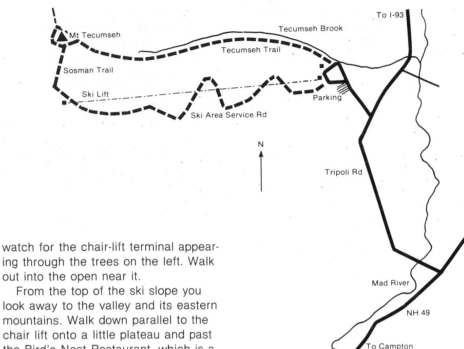

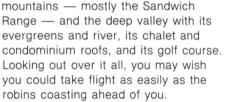

watch for the chair-lift terminal appearing through the trees on the left. Walk out into the open near it.

From the top of the ski slope you look away to the valley and its eastern mountains. Walk down parallel to the chair lift onto a little plateau and past the Bird's Nest Restaurant, which is a refreshment building for skiers. Beyond this to the right and past another control booth for the next chair lift, a work road crosses the slope to the right, heading down. The gravel road zigzags across the precipitous mountainside providing good walking all the way to the base. You can relax and walk with minimum attention to your footing and maximum enjoyment of the surrounding mountains — mostly the Sandwich Range — and the deep valley with its evergreens and river, its chalet and condominium roofs, and its golf course. Looking out over it all, you may wish you could take flight as easily as the robins coasting ahead of you.

Mount Israel

Distance: 8½ miles
Walking time: 5½ hours
Vertical rise: 1,770 feet
Maps: USGS 15' Mt. Chocorua;
 USGS 15' Plymouth

This 2,620-foot mountain north of Sandwich could be climbed in an afternoon. You'd get the striking views of Lake Winnipesauke, Squam Lake, and the Sandwich Range, but you'd lose out on a memorable loop hike that includes part of the ancient Sandwich Notch Road.

From Center Sandwich take the road northwest opposite the store. Watch for signs to Mead Explorer Base Camp and Sandwich Notch. Beyond the village and at the foot of a hill keep to the left fork up a long grade. After the view at the top you enter the woods and head downhill. Pass a road on your left and another on your right. At 2.5 miles from the village the Sandwich Notch road forks left. (It will be your return route afoot.) Keep right and drive across the intervale past a Devon cattle farm on your left. The road ends .2 mile beyond the farm at Mead Explorer Base Camp, an old white house. Park in the field below the house.

The Wentworth Trail begins at the north edge of the clearing, passing to the left of the house. Rising steeply into the forest, it crosses a small stream and slabs to the right through a gap in a stone wall. A growth of maples on the

nearly vertical slope suggests that this might have been a sugar orchard, although gathering the sap would be a feat in mountaineering.

The wide path narrows and zigzags to get you up the mountainside. Soon you enter spruce woods as the trail leads northeast across a shoulder. Then it swings northwest. You pass a lookoff that opens left to Squam Lake and Winnipesaukee.

Now a curve to the north takes you to another view from a wide ledge. The massive ridge is Sandwich Mountain. It's so bulky that the elevation appears less than the 3,993 feet. Sometimes called Sandwich Dome, it forms the south wall of Waterville Valley. Its west end, called Black Mountain, terminates the Sandwich Range above Sandwich Notch.

Between Mount Israel and Sandwich Mountain lies the valley where Beebe River begins as a brook draining Black Mountain Pond and Guinea Pond. Swamps down there attract moose after they've spent a winter "yarded" on Black Mountain. A former logging railroad grade traverses the valley.

From this viewpoint the Wentworth Trail dips down to the left into spruces and then curves right to the main, eastern summit. It passes the Mead Trail, on the left, a few yards below the rocky crest. (The Mead Trail will be your route of descent.) The summit is a rectangular rock extending above the spruces and firs. The opening again reveals Sandwich Mountain and also the whole range to the east: Mount Whiteface, Tripyramid, Passaconaway, Paugus, and Chocorua's rock-faced pinnacle framed by spruces. In the opposite direction toward Moosilauke, cutover areas mark the U.S. Forest Service's Hubbard Brook Experimental Forest.

For the descent and the next section of the loop, return the few yards west to the Mead Trail and turn right for a rapid downgrade through the spruce woods to a leafed forest. A spring on the left becomes first a trickle and then a little brook beneath hobblebushes and towering yellow birches. The trail follows an old logging road. There is a crossing of the brook to the west bank and another

at a tributary. Bright sunshine ahead becomes, as you walk into it, the long opening under a power line. The trail crosses below the cables through bushes and tall grass. You are down from the mountain.

The Mead Trail ends at the Guinea Pond Trail running east and west through the valley. It mostly follows the old railroad grade you saw from above. (Opposite the Mead Trail at this junction, the Black Mountain Pond Trail leads to the pond and shelter and then up Black Mountain to the Algonquin Trail for Sandwich Mountain.)

Turn left, to the west, onto the Guinea Pond Trail. (To the east it links with the Flat Mountain Pond Trail and Bennett Street Trail from the area of Whiteface Intervale on NH 113A.) The Guinea Pond Trail gives you flat walking for a change as it crosses the swamps. Although generally above the water by only a few feet, the trail is sometimes on the same level as the beaver ponds, or bears left to higher ground. These large flats of water make the country

open and sunny. Bordering the road, tall grass grows with Joe-Pye-weed In mid-summer the weed's pinkish purple blossoms, high as your head, stand out against the drowned skeletons of trees in the bogs.

The road and trail slant down beside Beebe River on your right. You walk under the power line and join the Sandwich Notch Road within sight of the bridge over the river. This is the terminus of the Guinea Pond Trail.

Here you turn left, to the south. The dirt road ascends a long hill. Chopped from the forested notch about 1800, the road became a thoroughfare for the people of remote northern settlements. Those pioneers needed markets and products available only in towns settled earlier to the south and even as far as the coast and Portsmouth. By 1850 well-established families had occupied the notch, along the road's eight miles. They logged and operated farms, sawmills, a tavern, a whiskey still, and school houses. Now all that remains are a cemetery and cellar holes beside the road.

At the top of the hill you've been climbing there's a sandy excavation on your right. Walk across it to the cemetery. This primitive burying ground and its headstones are hidden in the trees and surrounded by a wall. The hill is called Mount Delight.

Back at the road you pass a cellar hole on the right in which poplars and raspberry bushes have made themselves at home. You enter the woods again. Branches interlace overhead. You may not realize you are walking across the height-of-land. It's about 1,480 feet in elevation, and almost imperceptible. You know you've passed the area when you come to an open ledge slanting to the right from the edge of the road. The shape of depressions on it resulted in an appropriate name: Devil's Footprints.

A little farther, but on the left, an early advertisement for a general store still announces its message to the traveler. Letters chiseled on an overhanging rock read: P WENTWORTH 6 MLS 1838.

Two more points of interest are worth investigation. First, the Pulpit, a pinnacle of rock on the left beyond the second of three bridges across the brook that grows into the Bearcamp River. The rock provided a stone rostrum from which a Quaker preacher, Joseph Meader, spoke on fair-weather Sundays to the assembled people of the notch.

The second, Beede Falls and Cow Cave in the Sandwich town park and picnic area, may be reached from a parking area, on the left, about halfway down the road's last slope. A path leads to the Bearcamp River — here still a brook—and Beede Falls. A wide, misty curtain of water slides down a rounded ledge into a pool surrounded by dark hemlocks. Cow Cave is downstream and farther east in the woods. Legend has it that a wandering cow was marooned there one winter. It's a long rock formation gouged out by the ice sheet's melting water ten or fifteen thousand years ago.

Back on the Notch Road it is only ¾ mile to the junction with the road to Mead Base. Turn left and walk past the field of the Devon cattle farm.

Cherry Mountain

Distance round trip: 5¾ miles
Walking time: 4½ hours
Vertical rise: 2,450 feet
Maps: USGS 15' Whitefield;
      USGS 15' Mt. Washington

Perhaps next October when the leaves are yellow and red I'll see from the ledges called Owl's Head those colors in sunlight carpeting the ten miles to Mount Washington. I've never chosen the right autumn day. Once I was on the summit in an October snowstorm. One year I climbed too late, for the leaves had already fallen.

This hike includes Cherry Mountain's main peak (Mt. Martha on the USGS map) and a pinnacle named Owl's Head. The spruces around the summit's clearing have been trimmed away in two places for views of Mount Washington and the Presidential Range, or Mount Lafayette and the Franconia Range. Owl's Head, ¾ mile northeast of the main peak, offers open ledges and a more impressive panorama. This to me is the real destination, but if you want to shorten the hike you need not continue to Owl's Head.

The Cherry Mountain Trail leaves the east side of NH 115 at a forest service sign 1.7 miles from US 3 north of Twin Mountain. If the sign is missing, watch for a blacktop road opposite the trail and a small house on the northwest corner.

The trail begins as an old farm road

recently used for logging. You'll notice a few yards into the road a glistening tank on the right and a hose suspended from trees. Their purpose is the storage of maple sap from a grove up on the mountainside. These woods were once cultivated fields and pastures as you'll realize when you see a stone wall and a strand of barbed wire. Keep straight ahead at a right fork. The trail leads more uphill. Waterbars drain melting snow and rain into the woods, so the old road is not eroded. Climbing more steeply, you enter spruce woods and then emerge into an open forest of beech, maple, and birch. The woods road becomes a mountain trail along the angular slope. A stream on the right flows through a ravine below another ridge.

One of the sources of this Carter Brook trickles across the trail about halfway up the steep climb. A few yards higher a 50-foot spur trail on the left ends at a spring. Moosewood and mountain maple grow in thickets under large yellow birches and other hardwoods, which blend into the upper evergreen forest.

Above the spring the Cherry Mountain Trail continues straight despite the steepening angle. This is the style of old trails before switchbacks came into common use.

The trail becomes rocky, then levels somewhat toward the junction with a service road for the former tower. Turn left toward the summit. (The Cherry Mountain Trail follows the service road to the right and descends about 3 miles to the Forest Service's Cherry Mountain Road between NH 115 and Fabyan.)

For ¼ mile you're on easy grades and switchbacks. You enter the grassy clearing at the site of the tower, which was removed in 1982. Like other forest service lookout towers, its usefulness in fire protection was over. Plane patrols now spot fires in the White Mountain National Forest.

After you enter the flat clearing on this 3,554-foot summit, turn left for the cutaway outlook to Mount Washington and the Presidential Range. The second opening through the spruce and fir that surround the summit is beyond the pile

of debris remaining from the old tower and treetops that blocked views after the tower was razed. Mount Lafayette dominates the Franconia Range to the southwest. Here you see nearer and to the east at a definitive angle Mount Garfield, North Twin, and South Twin.

Now for the great view from Owl's Head. You will find the trail, Martha's Mile, at the northeast edge of the clearing. You pass an outlook ledge among spruces on the right. Don't linger;

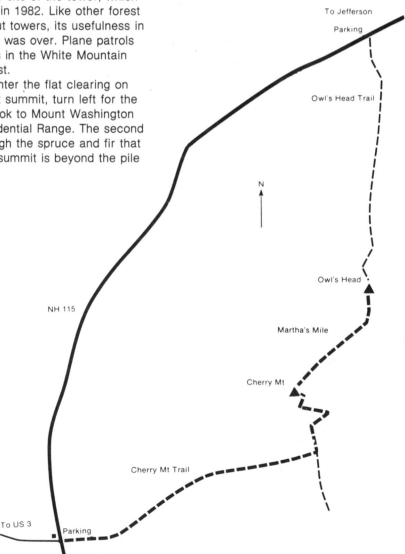

there's a far better vista in store for you. The trail descends along the ridge in an evergreen forest deep in moss, fallen trees, and shade. Maintaining elevation along the 3,140-foot col, the trail approaches big rocks that loom ahead and provide a short climb to the left. A log ladder assists at one ledge.

The trail swings to the right. All at once the spruces part around barren stone, and you're looking back west across the green slope toward the site of the tower and over to the Lancaster-Whitefield area, the Connecticut River valley, and Vermont. Then ahead a few yards there are the Presidentials: Mount Monroe south of Mount Washington, its unspoiled rocks contrasting with the buildings and broadcasting towers on Washington. Looking north and east, you see three more peaks: Jefferson, Adams, and Madison.

Between the Presidentials and the mass of Mount Willey on the west, a gap — Crawford Notch — opens all the way to Mount Chocorua. The nearer ridge between you and Mount Washington includes Mount Dartmouth and Mount Deception. In the valley, squares of lighter green have been logged by clear-cutting. Away to the distant east and north, seen past spruce branches, stretches the Mahoosuc Range with Mount Success, Goose Eye, and Old Speck. Your hike plan should include an hour here for lunch or for just looking. It's one of the great sights in the mountains.

To make sure you can say you've surmounted Owl's Head climb the knoll above the rock lookoff. Through the branches of spruces you catch glimpses northwest to Whitefield Airport and Cherry Pond in Pondicherry Refuge, a preserve of the Audubon Society of New Hampshire. From this knoll the Owl's Head Trail to NH 115, formerly discontinued because of logging, has been reopened by the Randolph Mountain Club. It descends precipitously at first along the upper section of a disastrous slide, now grown to evergreens except for the bedrock in the trail. After a cloudburst in July 1885, tons of boulders, trees, and mud destroyed a farm on the lower slopes. The trail turns sharp left into the cutting and follows skidder routes, crosses an access road into woods and grown-over farmland. It meets NH 115 at 4.1 miles from the start of the Cherry Mountain Trail. There a New Hampshire historical marker commemorates the slide. Hiking parties with two cars may choose this descent.

Most hikers return from Owl's Head by way of Martha's Mile and the summit. Watch for the right turn off the service road onto the Cherry Mountain Trail. You can easily keep swinging down past it.

View from Owl's Head of the Presidential Range

Carter Notch

Distance; 9½ miles
Walking time: 6 hours
Vertical rise: 1,650 feet
Maps: USGS 7½' Carter Dome;
   USGS 15' North Conway

The remote and craggy gap between Mount Wildcat and Carter Dome has two approaches through long, forested corridors. I think of them as the front door trail and the back door trail. The popular front door opens from NH 16 north of Pinkham Notch as the Nineteen Mile Brook Trail. This is the usual way to the notch, the two ponds, the ice caves, the AMC hut, and bunkhouses. I prefer the less traveled way from the south. This back door trail is more private and more in keeping with the primitive character of the notch and its wild mountain scenery. Take the Wildcat River Trail out of Jackson.

The trail head is 5 miles north of the village. Drive just west of the stone bridge over the Wildcat River and turn straight north onto NH 16B. You pass a hotel on the left and then reach the valley by a steep hill beside the river. After about 2 miles NH 16B branches right across a bridge. Keep straight ahead on the Carter Notch Road. It follows the river to the valley's steep upper end. Asphalt has improved the road as far up as the last house, after which there is gravel to a log cabin on the left. The road beyond narrows, but is well graded and graveled.

Drive carefully for .7 mile to a fork. The right fork, although an unmaintained woods road, can usually be driven for another ¼ mile past a cottage, left, to a turnaround. Parking at the fork is easier on the nerves if your car is as low as mine. There is space for three cars off the road or at turnouts before the fork.

Whether you drive or walk up the right fork, you'll find signs at the turn-around — a Forest Service sign for your entry onto Bog Brook Trail, and an AMC sign for Wildcat River Trail where the trail enters the woods. Bog Brook Trail and Wildcat River Trail coincide for ¾ mile. The blue #5 tags you see on trees mark ski trails for the Jackson Ski Touring Club.

From the right, or southeast, arc of the turnaround, the trail descends slightly, and you soon cross a tributary of the Wildcat River. The trail then levels along the contour.

You cross another tributary in a little ravine and swing left, again following the slope's contour. Wildcat River appears as a sparkling clear stream in a bed of smooth stones, ¾ mile from the trail head. At low water you step across in the plentiful rocks. I've also waded it.

Up the east bank, the trail takes you a few yards to a former logging road and a sharp left turn. This ancient grade will be your footpath north for most of the next 3 miles until the final climb to the notch. Almost at once it takes you to the sign for Bog Brook Trail branching right, also marked by blue #5 ski trail tags. (Bog Brook Trail links to the Wild River Trail 2 miles east.) Another sign directs you straight ahead on the Wildcat River Trail. The ski trail tags here are yellow #43. Paint blazes on trees are blue.

After a ten minute walk you come to a Forest Service gravel road just to the right (east) of a bridge over the Wildcat River. Keep straight across, climb the bank, and take up the old logging road once more.

There's fine walking with a few steep pitches at times, on the east bank of the river, which becomes smaller as it divides toward its sources. About 1¼ miles upstream from the crossing to the east bank you come to a major tributary, Bog Brook. The trail angles left at the junction of the two streams and then turns right along a narrow little embankment between them for 10 or 15 yards in alders and returns to open woods again. This seems to me the only possible puzzle along the way.

The junction with the Wild River Trail 1 mile beyond Bog Brook marks the approach to real climbing. (The Wild River Trail forks right to Perkins Notch and eventually reaches the Wild River Campground 9 miles east.) The Wildcat River Trail bears left at the junction and soon makes the final crossing of Wildcat River. It has dwindled so here the term *river* would be applied only by an elf running the rapids on a beech leaf.

The trail follows the uphill grade of another wide old sled road. It curves around a shoulder and leaves the brook.

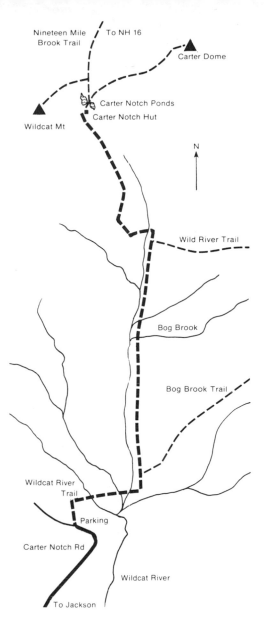

You walk up this loggers "dugway" excavated from the ridge. It's an easy climb, but you're about to leave it for the heights. There's 1,000 feet of vertical gain in the next mile.

At a sidehill spring trickling across the trail to your right, extemporized campsites down in the spruce and fir woods show that backpackers often lack either cash or reservations for the AMC bunkhouses at the notch. Carter Notch is a Restricted Use Area in the White Mountain National Forest, which means no camping.

The trail winds upward, rough and rugged over boulders and spruce roots or around ledges. Vistas to Carter Dome's south ridge begin to open through the evergreens. Boreal chickadees may flit nearby as you look past treetops. Great rocks and other debris from cliffs block the entrance to the notch itself. You make your way to the top of this 3,450-foot elevation. You can look to your right and see the massive jumble of rocks known as the Rampart. The geologic term for the rocks is *talus*. Your imagination must conjure up the great ice sheet thousands of feet thick. It wrested the rocks from Carter Dome and Wildcat while it scoured out the notch.

Keep past a spur trail to the Rampart. You pass the first of two bunkhouses in the evergreen woods. They are long, low frame barracks enclosing a porch under each roof. The trail descends a short distance to the old stone hut built in 1914 and now converted to a dining room, kitchen, and crew's quarters. Carter Dome's crags dominate the scene. Evergreens hide the ponds.

Continue down from the earthen platform in front of the hut. You come to the elongated pool into which the larger pond drains. Beavers, eager to build a dam across any running water, once plugged the pool's outlet and raised the water level. Scarcity of food trees (beavers require leafy species), and perhaps sore paws from the rocks, caused them to abandon the dubious project. The neglected dam opened up and lowered the water to its former level, but exposed accumulated silt.

The larger pond, a circular acre of perfect blue water, fills the notch and reflects the pointed spruces and cliffs. At the south shore a huge boulder offers a scramble for a wider view and a look down into the sunny shallows where little trout lie motionless. The pond is never over fifteen feet deep and always ice cold. It was stocked years ago by Fish and Game Department conservation officer Paul Doherty and others.

Mount Wildcat just west of the pond rises almost straight for a thousand feet. Carter Dome's summit on the east side is as rounded as the name implies; yet the mountainside is so steep that slides have gashed down it.

Save time for the Rampart. Beyond the last bunkhouse turn left onto the spur trail. Leaving the spruces behind, you walk or crawl among the giant boulders. You feel the refrigerator chill of the air in the ice caves — it lingers long into the summer. Higher climbs to boulder crests open wide views south to the valley floor, Jackson, and away to the Saco River. The scene is pastoral in contrast to the jagged cliffs and overpowering dome behind you.

I always leave Carter Notch with reluctance and consequently sometimes reach the road at twilight. The fast downhill walk along the logging road, after you descend the upper rough section of the trail, can take you out in 2½ hours.

Nancy and Norcross Ponds

Distance: 8 miles
Walking time: 5½ hours
Vertical rise: 2,100 feet
Map: USGS 15' Crawford Notch

Four related attractions combine to make this hike worthy of an annual excursion. As with Shakespeare's Cleopatra, "time cannot wither" the enticements, because the surrounding 460 acres have been set aside by the U.S. Forest Service as a scenic area preserved within the White Mountain National Forest. The four major rewards of the hike are, in order of their appearance: Nancy Cascades, virgin spruce woods, remote ponds, and an outlook into the federally-created (1984) Pemigewasset Wilderness.

Two landmarks help locate the Nancy Pond Trail on the west side of US 302 between Bartlett and Crawford Notch. A mile north of the trail and east of the highway is a large asphalt parking area for the Davis Path to Mount Washington, about 15 miles away. Just beyond this but west stands the Notchland Inn, whose granite walls rest solidly above a grade crossing for a side road that once was US 302. The Maine Central no longer runs trains through the notch.

Approaching the Nancy Pond Trail from the south, it is 1.2 miles from the Sawyer River Road, which branches west from US 302 just north of the Sawyer River Bridge.

By driving US 302 slowly toward the Nancy Pond Trail from either north or south, you'll see the trail sign to the west of the highway. Park off the shoulder.

The trail first follows an easy woods road, so, for the moment, you may trust your hiker's subconscious to select places for your boots while you think about Nancy. In the fall of 1788 after an absence from her work for Colonel Whipple's family in Jefferson, she returned to find that she apparently had been deserted by the man she was to marry. He had left the settlement that day without explanation but *with* her two years' wages, which she had given him for safekeeping. Believing he had started for Portsmouth by Crawford Notch, she followed him. A fierce snowstorm and darkness overtook her. She froze to death on the south bank of Nancy Brook. Colonel Whipple's men found her body the next day. She had walked thirty miles through the forest following blazes on trees, fording streams, and making her way among the rocks of the wild notch.

The Nancy Pond Trail turns left off the woods road after ¼ mile and winds among trees to a crossing of Halfway Brook. About a hundred yards beyond the brook, you come to a logging road.

Turn left, uphill. There are houses visible ahead through the trees. Stop and look back at the trail junction. This old woodsman's trick will give you a picture to watch for coming back. There is no sign.

You walk up the south bank of Nancy Brook for about ½ mile through a forest of large beeches and yellow birches. Then the logging road heads for the brook. A cairn, logs, and brush partially block the road. You should be alert for this and for the trail's sharp left turn up the bank. *Don't* go straight ahead to the brook.

Climbing, you enter spruce woods. Some of the trees are tremendous specimens that bulk and tower over the trail where it slabs above the stream. Along here you cross the boundary into the Nancy Pond Scenic Area.

The trail descends to the brook. This time *do* cross it. On the far bank, washed-out stones obscure the beginning of another steep uphill logging grade on the left. Now you climb among leafy trees. Beyond a narrow section of trail above the brook, you traverse the base of a slide, climb over rocky rubble, and step down from a massive spruce trunk half buried in gravel.

At the brook once more the crossing is plain enough, but on the south bank the way is a bit confusing (at least on returning). An unmarked branch trail, on the left, leads to a small clearing. The inclination is to press on to the falls, which appear as a shining whiteness through the spruce branches. But pause and look back so you'll fix this section in your mind for the return trip. Heedless hikers, having lingered overly long at the falls, have been known to hurry inadvertently into the little clearing and then take a false trail leading only to the bosky wilderness.

The falls are as lovely as any in the mountains. A circular pool to the right of the trail catches white water pouring down sixty feet or more over a ledge closed in by spruces. Your eyes follow the cascades upward. The glinting water, three hundred feet up, contrasts with the dark evergreens.

The trail turns left and surmounts the valley's headwall. Switchbacks take you up to lookoffs across the Saco River valley to Mount Crawford and Giant Stairs. As the trail angles to the cascades, you can look down over the falling water. The third switchback takes you to more level ground beside the stream sliding quietly to the dropoff.

You find yourself walking through a virgin forest of red spruce and balsam fir. The trees were too remote and the terrain too difficult for profitable logging. They grow on gradually ascending slopes that extend across the 3,000-foot contour to Nancy Pond. Because it's a climax forest, as seen by the first explorers of the mountains, you can observe complete cycles from seedlings through mature trees to fallen and decaying logs. Notice the dead stubs from which the bark has fallen. Sometimes weathering exposes the fibers in spiral array. Ever wonder at the strength of trees? You're looking at it — the power of continuous arches.

Split log walkways here keep you above the boggy sections. The last water for canteens trickles from several springs in the upper ground to your left. Ahead you'll have only undrinkable pond water. Shade-loving plants abound: clintonia, goldthread, and wood sorrel.

You step across the main branch of Nancy Brook draining from the pond. The trail swings over a knoll with silent footing on a cushion of spruce needles. Now you begin to see through the trees to the four-acre pond. The trail follows

Nancy Brook

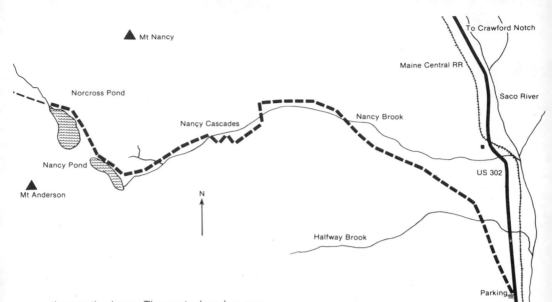

the north shore. The water's edge supports varieties of wet-root species known generally as "water brush." In this bog environment grow leatherleaf, sheep laurel, blueberries, and viburnums. White spruce, rare in the mountains, grows beside the common red spruce. You can easily compare the distinguishing characteristics. Tamaracks thrive in the wetland.

Beyond Nancy Pond an almost imperceptible ascent takes you over a height-of-land into the Pemigewasset-Merrimack rivers watershed. Norcross Pond drains that way.

Its seven acres are studded with rocks, and skeletal spruces bear stark witness to the beaver dam at the outlet that raised the water and drowned the trees.

For the final reward of the hike circle the north shore. The trail turns left at the west end and crosses the outlet. Here, to your left and above you, a bedrock plug holds Norcross Pond against the base of Nancy Mountain. Climb to the top of the plug and face about. Before you stretches the vast Pemigewasset Wilderness. The smooth rock on which you stand is your destination. (The Nancy Pond Trail continues to the Carrigain Notch Trail 3 miles farther on.)

Facing northwest, you are looking to Mount Bond, the dominant mountain of the East Branch valley. To the north, on the right, the rounded, connected summit is Mount Guyot. Between them seven miles away, Guyot Shelter's backpackers awaken in the morning to see the rising sun gleaming on the water behind you. All the country before you was logged and much of it burned. Protection by the National Forest allowed natural regrowth to heal the land.

Upon starting the return trip by the same trail, be sure to keep right along Norcross Pond's north shore. An old logging road on the left toward Mount Nancy could mislead you. Below the falls keep left past the little clearing I mentioned. And on the lower logging road near the houses, watch for the turn to the right among the beech trees as the trail heads for the crossing of Halfway Brook.

Webster Cliff/Mount Webster

Distance: 5½ miles
Walking time: 5½ hours
Vertical rise: 2,633 feet
Map: USGS 15' Crawford Notch

Webster Cliff is an awesome series of precipices opposite the Willey House site in Crawford Notch State Park. The Webster Cliff Trail begins 1 mile south, where the Appalachian Trail crosses US 302 to follow this spectacular route. After parking off the highway you cross the Saco River on a footbridge and discover that the trail heads northeast through the woods. It's taking you around the cliffs that would demand expert rock climbing technique if approached head-on.

After ½ mile the Webster Cliff Trail curves northward to your left. You climb the steep slope on carefully built steps of logs and stones. Because it approaches the perpendicular and negotiates the mountainside by switchbacks, the trail leads you toward the sky. You can be confident that you'll reach a lookoff — and you do, about 1½ hours from your car.

Thereafter the trail continues above the Saco River valley to many viewpoints atop the cliffs. You are treated to bird's-eye views of rugged Crawford Notch. You look down on the ribbon highway and its miniature cars. The other line curving parallel to US 302 has steel tracks — the Maine Central

Railroad. Everything down there appears as if seen through the wrong end of a telescope. Toy roofs protect the buildings at Crawford Notch State Park. There Samuel Willey, Jr., and his family died in the terrible landslide of August 28, 1826.

Mount Willey, from its preeminent position across the notch, presents you with a gauge for your progress, although you'll not quite equal its 4,302-foot elevation on Mount Webster. Slides scar the solid pyramid, which rises all at once from the highway and railroad.

On the night of violent storms and cloudbursts during which the Willey family perished, the Saco River rose twenty-four feet. Samuel Willey, his wife, five children, and two hired men fled from the house. They were all crushed or drowned in the avalanche of debris and water that poured down into the flooding river. The landslide, ironically spared the house.

In 1832, when Nathaniel Hawthorne visited the mountains, he heard the story of the Willey family from Ethan Allen Crawford. Hawthorne wrote a tale based on his conversation. He called it "The Ambitious Stranger."

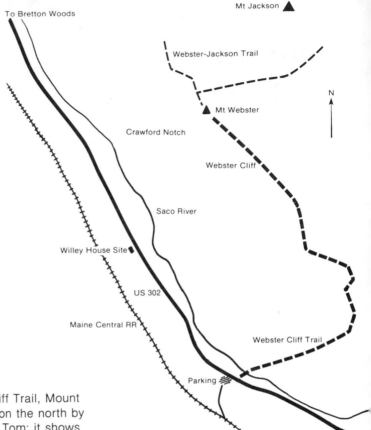

To Bretton Woods

Mt Jackson ▲

Webster-Jackson Trail

N

▲ Mt Webster

Crawford Notch

Webster Cliff

Saco River

Willey House Site

US 302

Maine Central RR

Webster Cliff Trail

Parking

To Bartlett

From the Webster Cliff Trail, Mount Willey appears backed on the north by Mount Field and Mount Tom; it shows its foundation at the head of the notch in the cliffs of Mount Willard. As you climb from lookoff to outlook, you gaze down on Mount Willard's summit (2,804 feet). The clearing there was for generations a viewing point for guests at the Crawford House, which burned in 1977. Hikers now arrive at the same spot by way of the carriage road; earlier, Crawford House guests rode up in style behind teams of horses.

But the notch is the great recurring interest. You draw nearer to, and high above, the rocky cleft where it narrows to the few yards that admit only the highway and the railroad between the ledges. Originally a footpath, the first road (1803) occupied all the space in the cleft. Blasting opened the way for the railroad.

The railroad trestle over Willey Brook, which drops out of the valley between Mount Field and Mount Willey, lacks the impressiveness of an engineering feat when seen from atop Webster Cliff; yet below in the notch and seen from the highway it's imposing enough. The nearby, one-time boarding house for trainmen and track crews has burned, leaving only the foundation for you to pick out.

When you reach the pinnacle near the north end of the cliffs you see ahead a spruce-grown knob beyond the final vertical rocks. It's Mount Webster's wooded summit. Then you descend a few yards and climb again to the uppermost viewpoint, where you look down 2,400 feet to the highway.

After this your rugged climb to the true summit at 3,910 feet takes you into the shade of spruce and fir, which is welcome indeed on a hot, bright day. (The Webster Cliff Trail keeps on for 4 miles to Mount Jackson, AMC's Mizpah Spring Hut, Mount Clinton, and the Crawford Path.)

For a lunch spot, descend a few steps beyond the summit rocks and turn right. Spruce woods are level to a vista, left, which opens away and away. You see north to Mount Washington, east across the Presidential - Dry River Wilderness Area to Montalban Ridge, and all the way to the southern Presidentials. Mount Jackson is the nearer craggy summit, and beyond it are Mizpah Spring Hut and Mount Clinton. For this view alone you should save Mount Webster for a clear day.

Return is by the same route you climbed. The afternoon light will change the scenery and reveal unnoticed valleys and peaks.

Storms in the mountains overtake you quickly. I'll describe an escape hatch in the woods beyond Mount Webster in the event that you need to protect yourself from lightning and a sudden downpour. Instead of venturing onto the exposed trail you climbed, follow the Webster Cliff Trail 200 yards beyond the summit to a left fork. This is the west branch of the Webster-Jackson Trail. It leads down through the woods 2½ miles to the highway between the notch's northern end and Saco Lake not far from the Crawford House site. You'll have to hitch a ride south about 4 miles on US 302 through the notch to your car. But that's better than dodging thunderbolts on Webster Cliff.

Webster Cliffs from Mount Willard

Imp Profile/Middle Carter Mountain

Imp Trail only:
Distance: 6 miles
Walking time: 4¾ hours
Vertical rise: 2,275 feet
For climb to Middle Carter add: 3½ miles
3¼ hours, 1,164 feet
Map: USGS 7½' Carter Dome

The Imp Trail reveals not only a vast panorama across Pinkham Notch to Mount Washington, the Great Gulf, and the northern Presidentials, but also connects with the North Carter Trail, which leads you, via the Carter-Moriah Trail, to the summit of Middle Carter Mountain. Yet you need not climb the extra distance to Middle Carter: the Imp Trail alone makes a fine day hike, especially at the beginning of a season before your legs and lungs are in the best condition.

The Imp Trail loops from NH 16 up the western slopes of North Carter and returns to within ¼ mile of its start. I like to begin at the northern end. The trail leads to the top of the cliff whose lower ledges form Imp Profile at 3,175 feet. Then it swings across the rim of Imp Brook's ravine, passes the North Carter Trail, and makes a leisurely descent by old logging roads to the highway.

The addition of Middle Carter (4,610 feet) provides the hike with a peak that's included in the AMC Four Thousand Footer Club's list. Mount Washington and its neighboring summits appear in a new perspective. There are vistas across the Wild River Valley to the mountains along Evans Notch as you pass just below the summit of Mount Lethe.

On the east side of NH 16 about 2.2 miles north of the Mount Washington Automobile Road and the Glen House site, a U.S. Forest Service sign marks Imp Trail's south end. The other end, which I think of as the beginning, is .2 mile north. I leave the car off the highway at the south end and walk the gravel shoulder to start at the north end.

My northern beginning is almost opposite the Dolly Copp Picnic Area, from which you can look up at Imp Profile. The best view is from Dolly Copp Campground, whose access road is about 1 mile farther north. There, a monument marks the site of the homestead that Hayes Dodifer Copp cleared from the forest. His wife Dolly named the profile, which she could see from the dooryard of their house.

Between 1832 and 1884 the Copps

The author on Imp's "forehead"

lived on their farm. Each year Hayes chopped out more open land until he cultivated or pastured seventy acres. The Copps sold produce and put up travelers. Dolly charged seventy-five cents for a night's lodging — bed, board, and care of horse. Her blue wool homespun cloth and her maple sugar became prized by vacationers who began coming to the mountains in the 1850s and 1860s. On the golden jubilee celebration of her marriage to Hayes, Dolly made the comment still quoted in the mountains: "Hayes is well enough, but fifty years is long enough for a woman to live with any man." They sold the farm to their son, Nathaniel E. Copp, and Dolly went to live with a daughter in Auburn, Maine.

But to return to Imp trail, the 2¼ miles to the cliff atop Imp Profile takes you through big woods of mixed spruce, beech, and birch. Occasional towering hemlocks spread over the trail, which stays on the south bank of Imp Brook for the first ½ mile. Then it crosses to the north bank. There are two crossings, really, as the brook forks. This is the last reliable water till the head of the ravine beyond the Imp lookoff.

Leaving the brook valley you climb a ridge to the north. The trail levels in beech woods. On some of the trees the smooth gray bark shows initials and dates carved in the 1940s. Now you begin a moderate grade during a swing east over another ridge. Then the trail becomes steep and approaches a ravine. It turns abruptly right, to the south, avoiding the ravine, and you climb a rough section of mountainside. Spruce and fir begin to take over the forest cover.

All at once you step out onto open rock. You are standing on the Imp's "forehead". It's like a balcony six hundred feet high. Mount Washington and its ravines, on a clear day, look to be just across NH 16, yet the cars on the auto road, around the great bend known as The Horn, are bugs. Their windshields and tiny mirrors sparkle in the sun. Off to the right of the auto road the Great Gulf's glacier-hollowed bowl drops away and rises again to Mounts Jefferson, Adams, and Madison.

From your eagle's aerie look left toward Pinkham Notch's east rim. Beginning at the south you can see Wildcat Ridge and Wildcat Ski Area, Carter Dome, South Carter, Middle Carter, Lethe, and the spruce-grown skyline leading toward North Carter, which is hidden by a nearby knoll.

Imp Trail leaves the clifftop for the spruces on that nearby knoll. You climb briefly in the trees before turning down, to the right, to a minor lookoff into Imp Brook's ravine, where the sound of falling water rises from cascades far below.

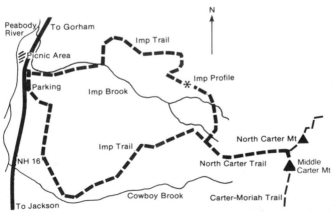

The trail continues southeast and then gradually swings south around the head of the ravine. It's rough in places but pleasant under the spruces that shade the green wood sorrel and ferns. Beyond the trickling sources of Imp Brook the trail begins to turn west. It descends a short distance to the junction with the North Carter Trail on your left. You are almost 1 mile from Imp Profile's forehead.

Here you may choose the 3½ mile round trip to Middle Carter, to the left, or you may bear right on Imp Trail and walk down 3 miles to NH 16.

If favorable skies and your own fitness tell you that this is the day for Middle Carter, turn left onto the North Carter Trail.

A moderate climb becomes steeper, but you should be able to keep at it steadily. After about an hour from the Imp Trail, and 1¼ miles, you reach the junction with the Carter-Moriah Trail. Turn right, south. (The Carter-Moriah Trail along here is part of the Appalachian Trail.) Keep going ½ mile over wooden walkways across boggy ground, then over rocky knolls to the bare summit of Middle Carter.

From this angle, higher than from the Imp lookoff, Mount Washington and the northern Presidentials appear more remote. To the east you look into the broad valley through which flow Wild River and its many tributaries. The range of summits between you and Evans Notch includes North and South Baldface, Eagle Crag, Mount Meader, West Royce, and East Royce.

You return to the Imp Trail the way you came. Make sure you turn left off the Carter-Moriah Trail and onto the North Carter Trail.

At the junction with Imp Trail go straight down the south half of the loop. Soon you are walking on an old logging road above Imp Brook ravine.

The good path changes to washouts among rocks like a dry brookbed. Then you leave erosion behind and follow a steady downward slant on the old logging road. The trail makes a sharp right turn away from Cowboy Brook past open slash and brushland on your left. The remaining mile of trail parallels the highway as you walk north. Car noises penetrate the forest. The everyday world is off there through the trees. Make the most of the forest.

Mount Hale

Distance: 8½ miles
Walking time: 6 hours
Vertical rise: 2,320 feet
Maps: USGS 7½' South Twin Mountain;
      USGS 15' Crawford Notch

On Mount Hale's 4,077-foot summit you use your compass for fun. Holding it in hand beside the big cairn, which marks the site of a former tower, you can watch the needle swing toward the rocks. Move around the cairn and the compass continues to point at the magnetic rocks instead of at magnetic north. Compasses can lie. Ask any deer hunter who once forgot that the steel of a rifle will attract the needle.

To reach Mount Hale drive along US 302 between Twin Mountain and Fabyan. East of Twin Mountain village 2.5 miles, turn south at Zealand Campground. Follow the U.S. Forest Service's Zealand Road 2.5 miles along the Zealand River to the sign on the right for Hale Brook Trail. (The Zealand Road ends 1 mile farther south.) The Hale Brook Trail is the first section of this loop hike, which, from Mount Hale, descends the Lend-a-Hand Trail to the AMC Zealand Falls Hut. From there your return follows the Zealand Trail and the Zealand Road.

The lower forest along the Hale Brook Trail consists of the familiar leafy trees common to 1,700-foot elevations in the White Mountains. The pleasant path, mostly graded along its 2⅜ miles,

rises into evergreens.

Early in the hiking season the leafy forest is open, but the leaves spread out and close the aisles by June. When the last snow melts into rivulets and mud, reviving plants appear as green points emerging from fallen leaves. Heavy snow has so flattened and packed these brown leaves that the new points, spearing upward, often lift them inches off the ground. Clintonia does this before the tuliplike leaves unfold. (The pale yellow flowers mature into clusters of blue berries giving the plant its alternate name, blue bead lily). The green sprouts also turn into lady's slippers, purple trilliums, and painted trilliums. Up among the barren trees, shadbushes bloom earliest and decorate the woods with white lace.

Snow lingers in the upper spruces as late as the last week in May. Its melting turns Hale Brook into a lovely torrent. Approaching the first crossing ½ mile from the car, you see the brook ahead in cascades like white surf. Above this gushing the brook runs quieter, and you cross on big rocks.

The trail goes up more steeply into

*View of Zealand Notch (near) and
Carrigain Notch (far)*

spruces bordering a gully. It enters a white birch forest along a gradual traverse of the valley's steep north bank. The brook is far below. At the head of the valley the trail turns sharply left. You step across the diminished stream and climb to another branch, which is the final drinking water. Your way is eased by switchbacks into evergreens. As you proceed, the trees become smaller and form dense thickets.

The summit opens wide across green turf and stony earth that once surrounded a fire tower. You're facing South Twin Mountain and its connecting ridge to North Twin. You look south to Mount Carrigain, from here a solid pyramid. Turn around northeast and there's Mount Washington.

The panorama between Carrigain and Washington, starting at the narrow pass east of Carrigain (which is Carrigain Notch) includes Mounts Lowell, Anderson, Nancy, and Bemis. Blue distance follows and then Mounts Willey, Field, and Tom. Over beyond those summits are Mount Jackson and the top of Webster Cliff forming the east wall of Crawford Notch.

Toward Mount Carrigain you look across Zealand Notch to Whitewall Mountain. It was burned to bedrock by a forest fire in July 1886, along with 12,000 acres and much of J.E. Henry's logging railroad, camps, logs, and equipment. In 1903 flames extended the devastation by sweeping over 10,000 acres in the Zealand River valley. The new forest is, quite simply, a natural miracle.

As for your compass pointing to the rocks in the cairn, the explanation, as you've probably guessed, has to do with iron. The rocks are of volcanic origin and contain iron.

This loop hike's next section, the 2½-mile Lend-a-Hand Trail, begins in

thick spruce and fir growth south of the summit. On the southwest North Twin Mountain, seen across the deep valley of Little River, vanishes behind evergreen branches. But the trail becomes scenic after you dip down among and over the big rocks on Mount Hale's shoulder. You enter open woods, and the sun beats down. White birches, often stunted and twisted, rise only ten or fifteen feet above bracken ferns. The spruces and firs, shapely in their pointed outlines, might be growing in a neglected park. Ruby-crowned kinglets flit among the trees and white-throated sparrows call from the branch tips.

Dropping down the lower half of the Lend-a-Hand Trail, you come to spruce and fir woods again and small bogs. The trail spans the muck on split-log walkways.

The Lend-a-Hand joins the Twinway within sound of Zealand Falls. Turn left onto Twinway. (Twinway extends 7 rugged miles over South Twin Mountain and other peaks to the AMC Galehead Hut.) You'll also hear voices from Zealand Falls Hut and shrieks from girls in bikinis and guys in trunks splashing out of the icy pools along the cascades.

From the hut's porch and its gunsight aim through Zealand Notch to Mount Carrigain and Lowell, the Zealand Trail descends a steep 200 yards to the level of Zealand Pond. Soon you cross the pond's southern outlet. Turn left (north) for the return section of your loop hike, 2¾ miles of the Zealand Trail and 1 mile along the Zealand Road. At this corner the Ethan Pond Trail branches right (south) in brushy flatland, where you may see a vireo or a veery. The former usually prefer tree branches; the latter stay near the ground.

The Zealand Trail keeps mainly to the grade of a former logging railroad. Almost a hundred years old, its gravel fill overlooks the east shore of Zealand Pond to your left. A bridge takes you over the northern outlet. You pass the A-Z Trail branching right from the wide path.

The stream, hardly yet worthy of the name Zealand River, flows into low ground on the right. Beavers have diverted the water into broad pools. These bogs are noted for the magenta flowers of rhodora that bloom here in June. The trail crosses low ground of poplars, willows, viburnums, and alders. Along the water's edge the insectivorous sundew plants show their little clusters of sticky-haired leaves all ready to trap bugs. You must look closely to locate them.

The Zealand River becomes a mountain brook flowing faster over smooth rocks in evergreen woods. Briefly leaving the railroad grade to wind among spruces, the trail regains the level before a small brook crossing and the Zealand Road. Suddenly you find yourself among parked cars, and you are greeting other hikers.

The Zealand Road is the last mile back to your car at Hale Brook Trail.

Mount Tremont

Distance: 7 miles
Walking time: 5 hours
Vertical rise: 2,600 feet
Map: USGS 15' Crawford Notch

Tremont's deficiencies are also its charms. It's removed from any popular trails between important peaks; it's only 3,384 feet above sea level; and it's wooded to the crest.

The spruce forest is part of the charm. On the steep northeast slope the big trees have never been cut off. This is one of the few places in the mountains where you're not seeing second- or third-growth timber.

On the summit ledges, smaller evergreens are taking over after fire or hurricane, but the views are wide and impressive. The Swift River flows through the Passaconaway Valley. One or two sections of the Kancamagus Highway could be the curves of a black river. The northern ridges of the Sandwich Range's many summits appear spread out east and west. Beyond the irregular oval of Sawyer Pond in its green setting, a smaller blue gem, Little Sawyer Pond, suggests a chip of lapis lazuli. Mount Carrigain, five miles to the west, is the eyecatcher until you turn southeast and see Mount Chocorua eight miles away, viewed bright and clear through a frame of green boughs.

Stepping out on the ledges, you may not at first notice Mount Washington

behind you. It seems distant in the composition of spruces and blue sky, and it *is* distant: fifteen miles.

This is another hike off US 302 near Crawford Notch. The Mount Tremont Trail ascends the most southerly and highest of the three summits that form a ridge west of Bartlett and south of the highway. There are no trails on the other two.

Three miles west of Bartlett the Saco River and US 302 begin their curves north. The Mount Tremont trail leads into the woods here. Parking is on the highway's wide north shoulder a few yards from the trail sign on the south side.

Following an old logging road up a gradual slope in beech and birch woods, you soon come to Stony Brook on the left. The stream forms dark pools below cascades that sparkle in the morning sun. Hemlocks are several shades of green, from the deepest, almost blue, to the delicate tones of new growth. In the valley of Stony Brook light and shade are the theme.

After about an hour and a quarter there's a short, steep climb, and the trail swings up in an S-turn. The brook is now far below. You walk into a

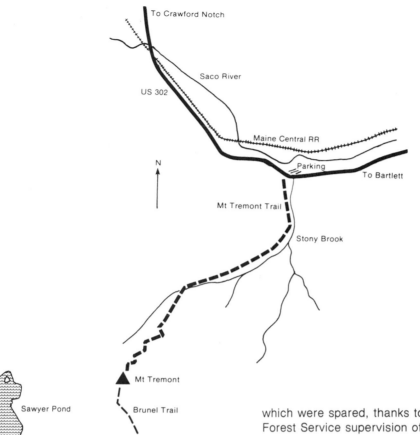

grassy clearing (recently bulldozed during logging) fifty feet across, with a green gully down left to the brook. Ahead, to the west, a wide and unused road disappears into a clear-cut area growing sprouts twenty feet high from sawed stumps.

You should take note of a peninsula of woods on the left. Into this arm of spruces and hemlocks the trail enters by a relocated route that is rather obscure for 100 yards as it winds among windfalls and through a wet area before rejoining the old trail. The way becomes clear once more. It takes you along the high bank above the brook. The logged slash, to the right, appears as an opening beyond the trail's woods,

which were spared, thanks to U.S. Forest Service supervision of the cutting.

You enter a growth of white birches; shortly after, the trail slants down to a brook crossing. This west branch of Stony Brook is the last water. The trail heads upstream but climbs steeply above the brook and eventually leaves it behind by a series of switchbacks through woods almost entirely of white birch.

Spruce and fir gradually take over, first as low growth seeding in from higher on the mountain and then as young trees six feet or more tall.

Now several dead spruce stubs of unusual diameter appear, suggesting fire (as did the white birches that often reforest burned land). A little farther on living trees seem to tower into the clouds as you look up. They are red spruces. I suspect there may be two possible explanations of why this virgin forest was saved: (1) it was too remote and steep to be profitably logged; (2) a fortunate change of wind or a sudden rainfall stopped the forest fire before the trees went up in smoke.

This is virgin forest complete in itself from the seeds in its cones to the decay that replenishes the earth. Trunks having coarse, ancient bark seem ageless and the upper branches forever vernal. But they live out their time; eventually the thriving undergrowth engulfs the fallen trees.

Through this forest the trail — narrow, rocky, leading over roots and logs as your shoulders brush the big trees — winds upward between thickets of hobblebush and colonies of trillium, goldthread, and wood sorrel.

Here on the mountainside you can occasionally look off to Crawford Notch and to Mount Washington beyond its long southern ridges and valley. The trail zigzags up at a knee-bending angle toward light above. The evergreens become smaller and younger. You've left the virgin forest. (My guess is that the summit burned over once.)

An opening between trees leads to a lookoff ledge on the right atop a cliff that falls away to green treetops. Sawyer Pond shines blue 1,447 feet below and a mile away. Mount Carrigain rears up between Carrigain Notch on the northeast and its southwest neighbor Mount Hancock.

About 100 feet farther, the Mount Tremont Trail ends at the summit. (The Brunel Trail descends south 3 miles to a forest service road at Rob Brook, 2½ miles from the Bear Notch Road.) A little brushy gap in the ledges surrounded by evergreens may be called the top, although the line of rock to the southwest is a few steps higher. The thirty-foot, slanting rock face offers a precarious seat and footholds for studying the mountains and valleys. To the southwest, 2,903-foot Green's Cliff rises beyond Sawyer Pond (100 feet deep and 47 acres). South of Sawyer Pond another small lake is Church Pond. The entire Passaconaway Valley — also called Albany Intervale — extends clear to a bend in the Kancamagus Highway over toward Mount Osceola.

You can see all the way to the mountains around Waterville Valley. Besides Osceola (minus its fire tower), there's Tecumseh and its ski slopes and Tripyramid, whose slides are hidden from this vantage. Swinging east from Tripyramid the next peaks you see are Whiteface, Passaconaway, Paugus, and Chocorua.

A cooling breeze blows across the rock face from the western mountains. There's plenty of time to enjoy the view. The descent back down the Mount Tremont Trail is much faster than the climb up, or so it seems on the steep places. Two hours, however, should allow for another leisurely traverse of that majestic spruce forest.

Mount Paugus

Distance: 9 miles
Walking time: 6½ hours
Vertical rise: 2,370 feet
Map: USGS 15' Mt. Chocorua

Paugus is a remote little mountain with a low profile in the Sandwich Range. However, this loop will force you to revise any prehike expectations you may have had about it being mediocre or easy to climb. Sharing a characteristic with humans of this type, Mount Paugus conceals more surprises than at first seem probable.

The 3,200-foot summit is tucked away between dramatic Mount Chocorua and bulky Mount Passaconaway. To reach the access road take NH 113A from the four corners in Tamworth and drive toward Wonalancet. Three miles from Tamworth, NH 113A crosses a bridge over the Swift River.

A road forks right. It is known as the Fowler's Mill Road, and it extends between NH 113A and NH 16 at Chocorua Lake. Follow it about 1¼ miles to a Forest Service sign and a side road on the left beyond a bridge over Paugus Brook. This is the Paugus Mill Road. Turn onto it and drive ¾ mile to a parking area and a Forest Service gate. The Liberty Trail leaves on the right for Mount Chocorua. Your route north lies ahead along Brook Trail, here a gravel logging road.

Walk the Brook Trail for five minutes until it also forks right to Mount Chocorua

along the gravel road. Your way, the Bolles Trail, bears left to a stony crossing of Paugus Brook. Beyond here, the Bolles Trail turns northwest away from the stream. In ½ mile you come to the next link in this loop hike: the Old Paugus Trail begins on the left for the mountains's ascent. (The Bolles Trail leads due north 5 miles to the Kancamagus Highway. See Hike 43.)

Turn left onto the Old Paugus Trail. Almost at once you are crossing Whitin Brook on rocks. The Old Paugus Trail follows an ancient logging road. Just beyond Whitin Brook you pass the Bickford Trail. (The Bickford Trail surmounts the west ridge 2 miles to Wonalancet.) You are entering the Sandwich Range Wilderness.

Along the wide curve of the logging road you circle the wooded flat that once was flooded by water behind a dam. The pond stored logs before they were hauled into Paugus Mill, whose by-product, sawdust, still forms a heap among the trees east of the stream.

The Old Paugus Trail here provides grand walking as it swings gradually up the valley beside Whitin Brook through a fine leafy forest. You cross to the north bank of Whitin Brook. The graded sled road of lumbering days and the trail coincide so pleasantly for 1 mile that you must watch for the junction where the Whitin Brook Trail takes over the road. Close to Whitin Brook on the left, the Old Paugus Trail turns north at a right angle up the ridge. The Whitin Brook Trail starts straight ahead. (The Whitin Brook Trail will be a section of your return loop.)

Now begins the real climb as the Old Paugus Trail ascends a steep slope to a relatively level breathing place past left-branching Big Rock Cave Trail. (The Big Rock Cave Trail aims southwest over Mount Mexico to Wonalancet.) Beyond graceful white birches you scramble up a gully to the first cliffs. The trail skirts the base between the smooth rock face and spruces towering on the right. Then you climb steadily around the cliff's east end.

On springy brown spruce needles the trail leads along the mountainside and plunges into a green tunnel. You clamber over roots and old logs where trail crews sawed clear the spruces flattened by the 1954 hurricane. In open woods again, the Bee Line Trail joins from the right. (The Bee Line Trail links the Old Paugus Trail and Mount Chocorua.) Beyond it you ascend — hands helping boots and legs — a jumble of rocks to a ledge, on the right, overlooking the forest toward the Ossipee Mountains. Ossipee Lake shimmers in sunlight.

A white arrow guides you from the ledge into spruce and fir woods that shade you above several smooth slopes of New Hampshire bedrock. The trail levels and then descends to a junction from which a spur trail used to lead to Old Shag Camp and a spring ¼ mile beyond it.

Sagging Old Shag Camp, gone but not forgotten! One evening my companion Doc Sharps whistled up a flock of migrating white-throated sparrows to entertain us with *their* clear, descending notes—and blackflies and mosquitoes devoured us till we built a smudge. The log walls dated

A midday break

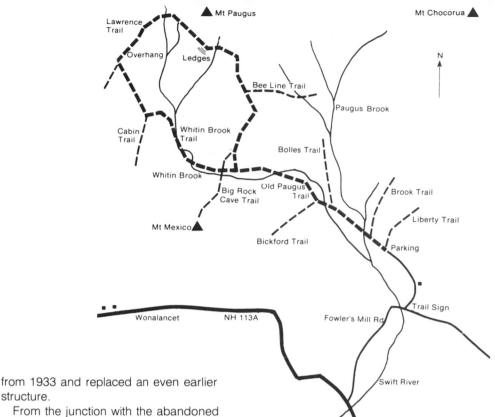

from 1933 and replaced an even earlier structure.

From the junction with the abandoned path the Old Paugus Trail turns south a few yards and then bears sharply right across a trickle of water dark from the swamp that was once a beaver pond. At almost 3,000 feet it was perhaps the highest of such ponds in the mountains.

The last short climb up rocks and over tree roots surprises you when you look back. Mount Chocorua's bare peak rises only 2¾ miles away. Another summit, to the west about the same distance, greets you beyond sparse evergreens as you step out on open ledges. It is the triangular silhouette of Mount Passaconaway.

Here the Old Paugus Trail ends. Beyond open rock, to the west, a sign on a tree marks the Lawrence Trail, which is the first section of your return loop.

But there's time for lunch and enjoyment of the sunny, glacier-smoothed ledges, which fall away into fragments rimming the valley of Whitin Brook. Although the true summit is about 100 feet higher and ⅓ mile north in woods without a trail, this lookoff at 3,100 feet is summit enough, as the view manifests the more you study it. Attached to Mount Passaconaway by a long ridge, Mount Whiteface drops to the wide lake country. Away to the south the ski trails you see are on Mount Gunstock in the Belknap Mountains.

The Lawrence Trail, identified by blue blazes, winds briefly among spruces before it precipitates you down into two ravines and the sources of Whitin Brook. Beyond them you are facing the climb to the Overhang.

This unsung delight consists of a fascinating array of fallen rock, precipices, tangled spruce and mountain maple over which the trail keeps to a seemingly impossible route. The steepest part is the descent down a gully under the overhang and into a forest of beech and maple.

Spruce begin once more at the junction with the Cabin Trail. Turn left onto the Cabin Trail, a short link (less than ½ mile long), to the Whitin Brook Trail. Turn left onto the Whitin Brook Trail. (The Cabin Trail continues 2½ miles south to Wonalancet.)

The Whitin Brook Trail here is a narrow corridor down through a thick stand of spruce and fir. It is studded left and right with the sawed butts of old "blowdowns." The trail was closed for a time after the 1954 hurricane.

The spruce forest ends abruptly in the valley's beeches and yellow birches. Make a sharp right turn. Watch out for rotten bridges. After crossings of tributaries forming Whitin Brook, however, you can stride down the good footing of the old logging grade beside the main brook, on the right. Pass through a junction with Big Rock Cave Trail. A few steps farther you meet the Old Paugus Trail descending from the left to take over the road. This is the end of the Whitin Brook Trail.

The route is familiar now, but in reverse. Make the final crossing of Whitin Brook, turn right onto the Bolles Trail, and walk to Paugus Brook and cross it. Then the gravel road is open, bringing in the Brook Trail on the left, and leading you back to your car.

Probably the time is late afternoon and that delicious weariness of complete relaxation cradles you better than two martinis. Mount Paugus is just right.

Mount Osceola: East Peak

Distance: 8½ miles
Walking time: 6½ hours
Vertical rise: 2,605
Maps: USGS 7½' Mt. Osceola;
 USGS 15' Plymouth

Thrusting above the precipices west of Greeley Pond, East Peak's 4,156-foot wooded spike presents a climb of 1,876 feet in somewhat over a mile—steep enough for most of us. Greeley Pond is a perennial joy, so I like to climb East Peak by the trail north of the pond, rather than from the main summit of Mount Osceola, as peak baggers do (thus collecting two four-thousand-footers in one hike). But that's not me.

Ten miles east into Waterville Valley from Campton, the Tripoli Road branches left off NH 49 across the Mad River before you reach the golf course and buildings of this mountain resort. Drive on the Tripoli Road past the Tecumseh Ski Area road on your left and continue along the Tripoli Road for 1¾ miles from NH 49. Turn right onto a road and bridge over the Mad River's West Branch. (The Tripoli Road climbs north and west through Thornton Gap between Mount Tecumseh and Mount Osceola, descending to I-93 near Woodstock.) Just beyond the bridge you keep left at a fork. It takes you in ¼ mile to parking on the left at a gate. Walking with your pack beyond the gate, you come in a few minutes to a clearing known from early logging days as Depot

Camp. More recently it was again used for yarding logs.

The hike begins at the clearing. Walk around a second U.S. Forest Service gate and across a small bridge. Take a former logging road to the left. It's the Greeley Ponds Trail. (Straight ahead the old Livermore Road giving access to the valley's upper ridge leads 3 miles past Mount Tripyramid to the Livermore Trail, which crosses Livermore Pass to the Kancamagus Highway 6 miles from Depot Camp.)

The Greeley Ponds Trail stays on the logging road for 1 mile up the west bank of the Mad River. You leave the road at a fork and keep right across a footbridge. The trail stays near the stream for 1¼ miles. Newly located sections and bridges have eliminated several shallow crossings. The old forest mostly survived the gale of December 3, 1980, which devastated Waterville Valley; its striking specimens of spruce and fir rise between spreading hardwoods. Lower Greeley Pond is the elongated, boggy stretch of water on your right. Soon the trail passes a cold spring on the left and approaches Upper Greeley Pond. The lovely, deep, dark mountain lake appears through the spruces under towering west cliffs and is cupped on the east by massive Mount Kancamagus.

Greeley Ponds are preserved as a National Forest Scenic Area. No camping, just enjoyment of the green, craggy setting is allowed within the 810 acres. Perhaps with this protection, and with nationwide reduction of deadly pesticides — particularly DDT, the cliffs will again become a nest site of peregrine falcons.

After you have enjoyed the views of the stupendous cliffs from the little beach at the east shore beyond the outlet, return to the Greeley Ponds Trail. Walk on northward into the spruce-fir woods above the west shore. The trail crosses the inlet and climbs ¼ mile to Mad River Notch and the Mount Osceola Trail on the left. You are 1¼ miles from East Peak. In the dense hardwood forest the notch appears more like a height-of-land, but you'll discover notch steepness. (The Greeley Ponds Trail continues down 1¼ miles to the Kancamagus Highway.)

Turn left onto the Mount Osceola Trail. It rises sharply at once and bears off southwest at a vigor-testing slant. You are heading back toward the almost vertical wall above the pond. On the far side of the notch rises trailless Mount Kancamagus. Among evergreens the trail's pitch eases. You climb under a 200-foot cliff, which drops off a shoulder of East Peak on your right. Soon the trail joins the old route and bears right at a serious grade. You achieve a sharp ridge upward at a steep angle in smaller spruces. The ridge leads to a false summit from which you glimpse the true summit. It's nearer than you think, and the trail takes you abruptly up to the top of East Peak's wooded cone. (From here the trail dips downward into the col between East Peak and Mount Osceola and beyond down to the Tripoli Road 4¼ miles away.)

Despite spreading branches, East Peak intrigues the hiker with views glimpsed through windblown branches. They give a sense of overlooking unex-

Osceola (left) and East Peak (right)

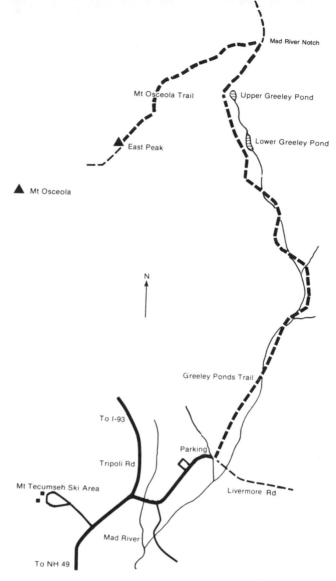

plored terrain such as an eighteenth-century trapper might have seen. That impression is sharpest looking north into the Pemigewasset Wilderness.

Of course, you must disregard the Kancamagus Highway and forget that the "Pemi Wilderness" is alive with backpackers. The trapper would have been intrigued not by the views but by the beaver pond down on Cheney Brook. Beavers have returned since they were trapped out and loggers cut the first forests and wasted the streams.

The descent from East Peak should be leisurely. Concern for sure footing and for those downhill leg muscles dictates a cautious pace. There'll be occasional views you didn't notice climbing up. At the junction with the Greeley Ponds Trail turn right for the easy walk past the ponds and along the brook to Depot Camp and your car.

North Moat Mountain

Distance: 9½ miles
Walking time: 6½ hours
Vertical rise: 2,740 feet
Map: USGS 15' North Conway

Moat Mountain, an elongated, craggy ridge, establishes the horizon west of Conway. It is clearly seen along the much used highway, NH 16. There are three summits: North, Middle, and South. North Moat, rising to 3,201 feet beyond Cathedral ledge and White Horse ledge, is the highest. The colloquial name for the mountain is "The Moats". The term goes back to the time when settlers applied it to beaver ponds along streams flowing from the mountain. On this loop hike over North Moat, you'll follow a branch of Moat Brook for part of the descent.

The unnatural treeline at 2,700 feet resulted from a fire in September 1854, when flames consumed the trees on this once-forested landmark above the Saco River. The Moats stand alone between major mountain ranges, and you can see in all directions. I know a man who was hooked on mountaineering for life by the exhilaration that comes from a hike on the Moats.

The trail up North Moat begins west of North Conway at the road leading to potholes called Diana's Baths on Lucy Brook. From the north section of North Conway's long main street turn west onto the road that links to the West Side

Road. (This turn is just north of the Eastern Slopes Inn.) You drive under the old railroad trestle and across the Saco River. Keep straight past the left turn onto the West Side Road. You head northwest for a clear .5 mile in fields and pass the left-branching road to Cathedral Ledge. Your road curves above the Saco River's sandbars on your right. Drive through a series of curves and cross Lucy Brook on a narrow bridge. About .2 mile beyond the bridge flat farmland surrounds a house and a large barn on your left. There's a dirt road on your left also. This is the access road to Diana's Baths. It's easy to miss, so slow down as you pass the barn. Drive to the edge of the woods and park on a shoulder. A gate closes the road from here on. There is a sign for the Moat Mountain Trail.

Walk the road for ¼ mile among the tall red pines. Lucy Brook flows by on your left, and you pass an old mill foundation. Diana's Baths in the rocks above and to your left are basin-like potholes, much wider and shallower than usually found. Lucy Brook drops over ledges squared into steps of a few feet.

The Moat Mountain Trail passes the

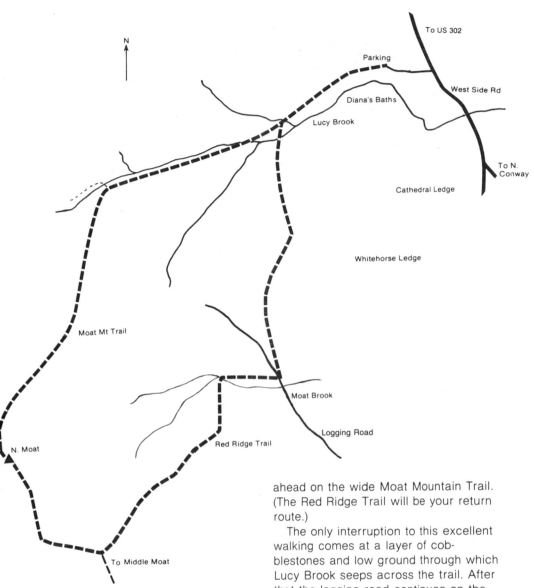

N

To US 302

Parking

West Side Rd

Diana's Baths

Lucy Brook

To N.
Conway

Cathedral Ledge

Whitehorse Ledge

Moat Mt Trail

Moat Brook

Logging Road

N. Moat

Red Ridge Trail

To Middle Moat

base of the rocks where an old logging road enters the woods. A curve left soon has you climbing the slope among hemlocks and pines. The road levels along Lucy Brook. About ½ mile from Diana's Baths the Red Ridge Trail forks left across the brook. Keep straight ahead on the wide Moat Mountain Trail. (The Red Ridge Trail will be your return route.)

The only interruption to this excellent walking comes at a layer of cobblestones and low ground through which Lucy Brook seeps across the trail. After that the logging road continues on the south bank of the brook to the base of North Moat, 1¾ miles from Diana's Baths. Last water until Moat Brook.

Here at a trail junction turn left up the mountainside. (Straight up the brook the Attitash Trail leads to West Moat and Bear Notch Road 6 miles away.) The ascent at once becomes steep as you climb this northwest shoulder of

Diana's Baths

North Moat. The grade moderates somewhat at 2,000 feet and then you go up again steeply into smaller spruces and over occasional ledges. Moat Mountain is of volcanic origin. Like Mount Hale and a few others it's a recent formation — geologically speaking. Can you imagine magma and molten lava flowing where evergreens now grow?

From the treeline spruce and fir you follow the yellow blazes up the final ledges. Then you're facing off the peak toward the length of the Moats. The ridge is above treeline for most of its three miles. To the left you look east across the Saco River valley at North Conway's ski area on Mount Cranmore. You are also looking at nearby ridges whose eastern, hidden cliffs are Cathedral Ledge and White Horse Ledge. The conical peak with the tower is Kearsarge North, or Mount Pequawket, another volcanic mountain formation.

To the west the Kancamagus Highway traverses the valley of the Swift River. You can see Bear Mountain, Mount Carrigain, Mount Willey, and Crawford Notch.

But the grand view is to the north. Perhaps Mount Washington hides under a white cloud penetrated by broadcasting towers. Washington often makes its own vapors. They are a trademark and distinctive notice that this is *the* peak in the White Mountains. But you see all of the Southern Peaks — Monroe, Franklin, Eisenhower, Clinton, Jackson — clear to Crawford Notch. East of Washington, Carter Notch is a slot between Wildcat and Carter Dome. Still more easterly there's a bare summit, which I take to be one of the two Baldfaces in Chatham.

After lingering and lunching, follow the yellow blazes of Moat Mountain Trail south beyond the summits crags. You descend into spruces and cross an open shoulder with views to the west. The trail swings left and down steeply over ledges. You go down 640 feet. From this col you climb briefly. Emerging from the woods you come to the junction with the Red Ridge Trail on your left. Two smooth rocks slope up on your right. The Moat Mountain Trail turns ninety degrees to the right and west of them. (The Moat Mountain Trail stays on the ridge and then descends from South Moat to the Dugway Road 4 miles away.)

Now you begin the spectacular Red Ridge Trail. Leaving the junction through spruce woods, the trail soon takes you out on a series of open shoulders. These are Red Ridge. You walk down ledges split into steps seemingly for your use. The trail is well marked with cairns and yellow blazes. I should warn you about the lichens on the rocks. Although innocent looking, they are slippery when wet, especially the map lichens.

Among these ledges you pass colonies of sheep laurel and blueberries. Smaller plants protect themselves from exposure by growing close to the ground: three-toothed cinquefoil, mountain cranberry, and crowberry. The small trees are red spruce, red pine, and white birch.

Entering taller woods, the trail swings left toward a branch of Moat Brook out of sight in a deep ravine. Care is required as you cross smooth ledges where scattered gravel along the top edge of the ravine slides down to the brook. Then you descend steeply among evergreens.

At the brook you cross on stones to a short bank and climb several yards into spruce/fir woods. The trail turns to your right. Watch for blazes and small arrow signs as you descend a slight grade through the woods and away from the brook. At a gravel logging road you'll need to pause and make sure of signs and blazes on the far side. Cross to the opening in the woods where the trail angles to your right away from the gravel road.

Proceed north through a logged area, staying alert for any confusion of the trail. At two forks, arrow-signs on trees point your way left. A slight rise in the forest floor lifts you to a junction with the Red Ridge Link Trail on your right. Keep to the left. (The Red Ridge Link Trail leads to White Horse Trail from Echo Lake State Park.)

You are only about 1¼ miles from Diana's Baths. The trail passes through notable growths of ground hemlock. Also called American yew, this low evergreen is often scraggly and sparse. Here it grows luxuriantly under hemlocks, pines, oaks, and other leafy trees.

Lucy Brook appears to your left, and you make the shallow crossing on stones. Turn right at the junction with the Moat Mountain Trail. You're walking the last ½ mile back to Diana's Baths. On a hot summer's day those "baths" can cool your feet — or more of you.

King Ravine

Distance: 7 miles
Walking time: 6 hours
Vertical rise: 3,400 feet
Map: USGS 15' Mt. Washington

Exploration of this mighty glacial cirque includes scrambling through the jumble of stupendous rocks, touching perpetual ice in caves, and sensing the doomsday weight of boulders above you. Then after a climb up the east wall, with rockbound Mount Adams looming beyond your perch on barren Durand Ridge, you gaze back into the depths and see the rocks reduced by distance to what looks like crushed stone for a road. This hike does not include Mount Adams' summit. King Ravine deserves a whole day.

From US 2 in Randolph, trails to the northern peaks of the Presidential Range lead south from a parking area known as Appalachia, which was its flagstop name on the Boston and Maine Railroad. It's 5.5 miles west of Gorham.

Your trail at the beginning and end of this loop hike is Air Line. Facing the mountains, take the path from the right hand corner of the parking area. Cross the railroad tracks. The path forks, Valley Way bearing left, Air Line right. Keep to the right under the powerline. At the edge on a tree is a sign for Air Line, which leads ahead into maple woods.

You pass several of the many trails that crisscross these northern slopes.

First, the Link and the Amphibrach diverge to the right; then you cross Sylvan Way and, after a few minutes, Beechwood Way. Now you are approaching Short Line ¾ mile from Appalachia. Turn right onto Short Line. (You will return here in the afternoon, descending Air Line.)

This fine trail provides easy, fast walking southwesterly up through the forest. At a gradual angle in big woods Short Line joins the Randolph Path and they coincide for almost ½ mile. (The Randolph Path continues 4 miles to Edmands Col between Mount Adams and Mount Jefferson.)

Short Line branches left, and you climb steeply to sparkling Cold Brook on your right. The stream is well named. Its source is the perpetual ice under the ravine's headwall and the destination of this hike. The environment itself becomes cooler as you approach 3,000 feet of elevation; the woods change to spruce and fir interspersed with white birch and mountain ash. The terrain becomes rough and rocky but levels somewhat along the brook.

In 1857 Thomas Starr King, author of *The White Hills,* and his companions climbed this way into the ravine that now bears his name. Those early mountaineers followed Cold Brook from the valley and camped beside it.

Short Line ends at its junction with the King Ravine Trail, which comes from the right. Turn left along the King Ravine Trail. Almost at once you face exquisite little Mossy Fall. Here Cold Brook pours from a ledge between two huge boulders covered with emerald green moss. Beyond and far above the ravine's precipitous sides rise before you.

Here you should make sure that the rocks are *dry,* and will continue so. They and their lichens give you only treacherous footing when wet.

The trail beyond Mossy Fall disappears among the first gigantic rocks. They engulf you for a short distance until the trail swings left. You climb for a steep ¼ mile among spruce, fir, and twisted birch, which somehow cling to the rocks and survive the fierce north winds. A final S-turn upward takes you into the open on the floor of the ravine. You're at 3,500 feet and have climbed into a vast amphitheater — the typical bowl shape of a glacial cirque.

Immobile rivers of rocks extend ahead to the base of the headwall and also to your left and right. The boulders were torn from bedrock during the glacial scouring of the ravine. The headwall rises above the rocks in a curve of cliffs and gullies. Its jagged rim is 1,600 feet above you and ½ mile distant. To the left atop the east wall hikers on Air Line are moving specks. An about-face will show you northern skies, distant clouds, and far mountains.

Here the King Ravine Trail meets a branch trail, on the left, from the east wall. Named Chemin des Dames, it connects with Air Line up on Durand Ridge above treeline. (It will be your exit from the ravine when you return from the ice caves.)

Just beyond Chemin des Dames the

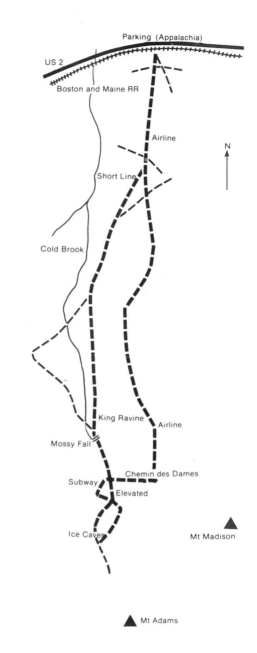

King Ravine Trail divides into easy and difficult routes. To the right the Subway's orange blazes on the rocks lead through a tortuous passage of about 200 yards among rocks as large as summer cottages. To the left the Elevated stays on higher open ground east of the rocks.

Turn right if you want to discover what it's like to scramble and crawl between and beneath untold tons of rock. At the end of the Subway you climb out into stunted woods, where the Elevated comes in from your left.

If you've taken the Subway turn right up the reunited King Ravine Trail. It soon passes the Great Gully Trail forking right up the southwest wall. Keep left as the King Ravine Trail winds among more tremendous boulders. Soon the trail forks. You are at the lower junction of a bypass trail to the ice caves on your right. Keep to the left along the King Ravine Trail. After about fifteen minutes you meet the bypass trail joining from the right. (The King Ravine Trail continues ahead to treeline and ascends the steep, difficult headwall.) Now turn onto the bypass trail to your right. Follow the blazes down to three or four different ice caves formed by the tumbled boulders. A flashlight helps locate the ice in the darker caves. Some of it is clearly visible by simple daylight.

Chill air is a good clue to the ice. Look carefully down into caves, because the ice has melted into the deepest recesses. It's gray and speckled with dirt and spruce needles. Lower yourself down to an irregular patch and stand on it. You are surrounded by the pervading cold. As you emerge from the cave you feel a rush of warm air.

After the last cave, continue on the bypass trail to the King Ravine Trail. Turn left. At the fork of Subway and Elevated, keep right and enjoy the openness of the Elevated. A few steps beyond the junction where Subway rejoins from the left, you come to your exit route, Chemin des Dames.

Turn right and begin the climb up the east wall. Orange blazes lead you over the massed blocks of rock. Then you climb among the dwarf spruces and birches, which help you pull yourself up. Boulders form a narrow passage that opens to a gully and a high rock face on your left. The trail angles steeply toward an upper crag outlined against the sky. You leave the trees, climb on, and step out beside the crag to a sudden view of Mount Madison's distant summit. You're atop Durand Ridge on the Knife-edge at 4,400 feet. Chemin des Dames ends here as it meets Air Line far above the ravine.

To your right Mount Adams, second highest of the Presidentials, a solid peak stacked with fractured gray slabs, backs up the deep gouge of the ravine. Northward the view is down to Israel River, flowing west, and across its valley to Mounts Starr King, Waumbek, and Cabot. To your right you can see as far east as Berlin, Gorham, the Androscoggin River, and the Mahoosuc Range.

Northern views stay with you as you start down Air Line. Soon you enter a corridor between spruces. The evergreens grow taller and taller along the rapidly descending trail. They give way to leafy forest on the lower slopes. You pass Short Line on your left for the completion of the loop and proceed to Appalachia, your car, and the highway's traffic.

41

North Twin Mountain

Distance: 8¾ miles
Walking time: 7 hours
Vertical rise: 2,910 feet
Maps: USGS 7½' South Twin Mountain;
  USGS 15' Whitefield

The controlling natural element in this hike is Little River. The North Twin Trail crosses it three times. During spring runoff or after prolonged rainfall this trail can be impossible. But I like it because its approach to the mountain is along a forested valley. The stream adds motion and sound. Then the steep climb to the 4,769-foot summit (1,000 feet per mile for the upper 2⅓ miles) establishes North Twin in your mind as an individual mountain in its own right, which it is. Many hikers treat it as a shoulder of South Twin. They combine North and South Twin, usually climbing South Twin first from AMC's Galehead Hut, continuing on the North Twin Spur, and returning to South Twin. That's peak bagging and I'm against it. North Twin is its own mountain and deserves special attention.

For this respectful treatment you must first find a U.S. Forest Service road branching southward from US 3, west of Twin Mountain village. There's no sign. Starting at the junction of US 3 and US 302 drive west 2.5 miles on US 3. You pass motels, restaurants, and amusements. You cross Little River. Watch for a big sign, on the right, announcing that you are about to enter the White Mountain National Forest. A few yards beyond turn left off US 3 onto the forest service road.

This narrow gravel strip, one car wide with turnouts, ends at a parking space 2.5 miles from US 3 on the east bank of Little River. Now you should walk back to the bridge and assess the depth and force of the stream. Remember there are three trail crossings above and no more bridges. If you're sure you can cross here get your pack and take the trail beyond the sign east of your car.

The North Twin Trail follows an old logging railroad grade of the Little River Railroad, built by George Van Dyke before he became the famous lumber baron of the upper Connecticut River. Of course the standard gauge tracks are gone and the depressions from the rotted ties are hardly noticeable. This good walking takes you through a leafy forest grown up since 1900, when the virgin timber had been leveled and hauled out to sawmills.

Beside the North Twin Trail the river dwindles to a brook as you ascend the valley, leaving behind various tributaries. The water alternates between wide pools and miniature rapids, and the charm of fluid motion and sound are with you constantly. At the crossings both are all around you. If balancing on damp rocks bothers you, try using a staff.

The last crossing begins at a little clearing on the east bank and angles upstream to the west bank where the trail continues on the railroad grade. For the last few hundred yards that the trail follows the grade the 2,400-foot elevation becomes apparent in the change to birch trees mingled with spruce and fir. The valley's precipitous slopes have closed in. A sign on a tree marks the right turn off the grade. The summit is 2⅓ miles ahead.

It's uphill in earnest. Two hours will get you to the top but patience is the watchword. Climbing is like sawing a log with an old-fashioned bucksaw. If you think ahead to the sawed pieces, the job becomes sweating drudgery. Don't think of the top. Enjoy the climb.

A small branch of Little River borders the trail on your left. You step across, move away from it, and climb parallel to it up the first steep pitch for about ½ mile.

The trail here was once a logging road that must have given more than one teamster a wild icy ride on his sled behind leaping horses. The instant horses slipped coming down ahead of a ton of logs, their one thought was to escape. The teamster might jump but, if he valued his horses and took pride in his skill, he'd try to guide them down the mountainside. Many a team went off into the woods with the logs and sled on top of them — "sluiced" the loggers called it. Particularly steep descents, such as this you're climbing, were covered with brush and hay. The sleds were eased down by a heavy rope. Still, accidents happened.

Now you cross the little brook again as the trail swings right. This is your last chance for a fresh drink from the forest floor. The trail passes through the site of a vanished logging camp. Investigation under the leaves reveals junk iron from the inevitable blacksmith shop — sled runners, peavey ferrules, hooks, and chain links.

After a wide swing northward, climbing steadily, you begin to appreciate

Little River

North Twin as its own mountain. The trail becomes rougher and curves southwest over a sharp rise. You negotiate a short section of muck and a ledge that requires a handhold or two. Treeline spruce scrub begins; then you surmount bare ledges to a lookoff.

Here a striking view opens toward Mount Hale, to the east, with Mount Washington stark and clear beyond. You look down into Little River valley and realize you have indeed been coming up in the world.

A five-minute walk along the ridge takes you to the wooded summit and the junction with the North Twin Spur from South Twin. Keep right at this fork and you emerge after a few yards on the west outlook toward South Twin and down on the roof of AMC's Galehead Hut. Beyond that rises Mount Garfield's rock cone, Garfield Ridge leading to Mount Lafayette, and the Franconia Range. The stretch of valley to the north beyond Twin Mountain village and the landing field centers along the Ammonoosuc River, which flows west to Littleton and south to join the Connecticut River at Woodsville. Its source is in Ammonoosuc Ravine, 5,000 feet up on Mount Washington. North Twin, rising above this wide valley, opens unequalled views across into Vermont.

The return is by the same route you

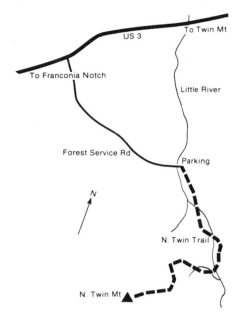

came up, North Twin Trail. Turn left at the junction with North Twin Spur, proceed across to the east lookoff, and then hike down and down to Little River. On a long summer afternoon, if you had an early morning start, the clearing beyond this upper crossing is a good supper spot.

But don't linger too long. Save an hour of daylight for the walk down the old railroad grade while you listen to the evening songs of thrushes and the sound of running water.

Mount Moriah

Distance: 9¾ miles
Walking time: 6½ hours
Vertical rise: 3,100 feet
Map: USGS 7½' Carter Dome

A nineteenth-century writer, with the charming and verbose anthropomorphism of the time, might describe Mount Moriah's summit rock as "the lonely sentinel guarding steadfastly the northeastern ramparts of grim Pinkham Notch."

Mount Moriah *does* stand out there. From an open crag you look across the notch to Mount Washington. Its Great Gulf is open for your inspection but hedged in by spectacular peaks to the north: Jefferson, Adams, and Madison. To the northeast you see the rugged summits terminating the Carter-Moriah Range. Then, beyond the Androscoggin River, the Mahoosuc Range extends all the way into Maine. North up the river, which makes a right angle turn at Gorham, you can see Berlin and the paper mills. Turning around to nearer views at the southeastern base of the mountain you'll be attracted by the forested sweep of the Wild River valley. It stretches to North and South Baldface in Chatham and to the summits forming Evans Notch on the Maine border. To the south you get a skyline view of the Carter-Moriah Range.

Although the mountain may be climbed from Gorham by the Carter-Moriah Trail, I favor the approach up Stony Brook, which is not to be confused with the Stony Brook near Mount Tremont. This way you avoid first climbing Mount Surprise and several tough little knolls.

Drive south from Gorham on NH 16 for 2 miles. You cross the Peabody River just before the Stony Brook Trail on your left. It begins as a road for two camps and a house. You'll take this trail for 3½ miles up to its junction with the Carter-Moriah Trail south of the summit, and then you'll follow the Carter-Moriah Trail 1¼ miles north. You return by the same route. Park your car off the highway, being careful to avoid the driveway to a house on the west side.

Walk past the Forest Service sign. You'll find that the gravel road bears right past two camps, and enters the front yard of a house as a turn-around. Beyond and left of the house, a logging road leads uphill at a chain gate. Here you begin your first climb of the day. The rough road curves to the ridge's shoulder, where a bulldozed opening has grown up to bushes. Here in 1972 and 1973 a "skidder" hauled logs from the cutting areas. This high-wheeled tractor with front blade and rear hoist has taken the place of the woods horse. There has been recent logging, so watch for blazes and arrows on trees.

The road swings left up easy slopes in the leafy forest. About a half hour from the highway the Stony Brook Trail keeps straight at a left fork. Soon it keeps straight again to pass between logging roads branching left and right. From here the trail follows a more ancient road. It has seen no lumberjacks since the days of horse teams and double-bitted axes. Leading steadily up the mountainside above Stony Brook, it is reinforced by numerous waterbars of logs which divert eroding water into adjacent forest duff.

About 2 miles from NH 16, walking in this hardwood forest, you enter a clearing. Grass in the sunny center and alders and raspberry bushes bordering the woods at once identify the site of a former logging camp. Bottle collectors have dug over the dump leaving broken glass, tin cans, and scattered leaf mold. On the opposite side of the trail, to the north, you can find the customary remains of the blacksmith shop: sled runners, horseshoes, and soft coal. The worn runners, broken shoes, and few chunks of coal weren't worth hauling out when the camp was dismantled.

Now the trail goes up a steep slope. It crosses a branch of Stony Brook. You are about 1½ miles from the Carter-Moriah Trail on top of the ridge. You'll need an hour to get there.

The Stony Brook Trail climbs steeply. It bears left and then curves right into upper spruce woods and across another source of Stony Brook. Here in wet weather the little cascade over the mossy ledge can be slippery. The spruces change to white birches, probably grown into an old burn. The trail becomes steeper for the final climb to the Carter-Moriah Trail, which is part of the Appalachian Trail.

This junction in a little col has four plank walkways across the sphagnum bog. Opposite Stony Brook Trail there's Moriah Brook Trail starting down the eastern side of the Carter-Moriah Range. (Moriah Brook Trail descends 5½ miles to the Wild River Trail ½ mile from the Wild River Campground.) To

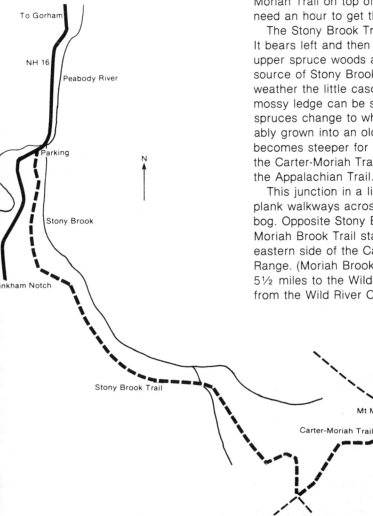

your left and right the Carter-Moriah Trail leads north to Mount Moriah and south to North Carter Mountain. (The Carter-Moriah Trail, to the south, ends at AMC's Carter Notch Hut, 8 miles and several summits away.)

Turn left onto the Carter-Moriah Trail. Beside the plank walkway, Indian poke plants grow tall and green. Also named false hellebore, the plant yields a toxic alkaloid and has a long history as a poison and drug. It appears early, just after snow melts, beginning with pointed, green cones. On lowland meadows if cattle are turned out before other pasturage tempts them with greenery, they sometimes eat the Indian poke and die. It's deadly for humans, too, of course.

You'll climb about a thousand feet in this 1¼ miles along the Carter-Moriah Trail. It begins innocently enough with a knoll, a slight descent, and a slabbing along a contour. But prepare yourself. It abruptly climbs from white birches into spruces along a rock-strewn gully. A left turn takes you through nearly level walking to another rough ascent. Then plank walkways over boggy ground feel good under your boots.

In a little notch you approach the summit ledges on your left. The trail surmounts them by a slot in the rocks, after which you scramble up hand and foot. Scrub spruces line the trail. Turn left onto a short path to the summit rock above you. (The Carter-Moriah Trail continues ahead for its descent of 4½ miles to a street in Gorham.)

The summit's flat, rectangular ledge—about ten by fifteen feet—contains three brass plugs recording government surveys. Elevation is 4,047 feet.

Your arrival at the summit puts you facing Carter Dome, five miles south. Perhaps the precipitous rise of North

Southwest from Moriah

Carter first catches your eyes. The mountain in between you and North Carter is Imp; the one beyond North Carter is Middle Carter. To the east Mount Hight (sic) shows as a jagged crest of rocks. Certainly, however, you'll turn to the Presidential Range before studying the Carter summits for long.

Mount Washington to the southwest seems far away, ethereal and inaccessible, although it's only ten miles distant. Clouds and glowing sun above the peak create the illusion. Sometimes haze on Jefferson, Adams, and Madison softens the harsh slabs of rock overlying the peaks.

If you have hiked the Mahoosucs — or even if you haven't, for that matter — turn about and look north and east for memories or with anticipation. Look for Mount Hayes at the west end above Gorham, Cascade Mountain, and the silvery glimmer of Page Pond. Farther away, beyond Mount Success and Goose Eye Mountain, the summits blend toward a far silhouette: a pyramid with western shoulder, which is Old Speck Mountain in Maine. It is eighteen miles away.

To the southeast, barren twin summits, North and South Baldface, still display the glaciated bedrock opened to the sky after the 1903 fire and subsequent erosion. That's the Wild River valley you're looking across.

The return down the route of ascent begins with the decision whether to face the rocks and lower yourself, or whether to gain some adherence from the seat of your pants, thus helping your hands and boots. Below the rocks turn right, to the south, along the Carter-Moriah Trail. (Avoid the Kenduskeag Trail to the left, which has the white blazes for the AT. It links to Rattle River Trail and US 2 east of Gorham.) Proceed down to Stony Brook Trail for the right turn, to the west, from the boggy col.

Champney Falls/Mount Chocorua

Distance: 9¾ miles
Walking time: 7½ hours
Vertical rise: 3,250 feet
Map: USGS 15' Mt. Chocorua

If you mark the passing of days, as I do, on one of those scenic New England calendars that arrive in the mail each year, courtesy of your friendly bank or insurance company, you will on the first of some month find yourself gazing at the image of Mount Chocorua. It is one of the most photographed mountains in the East because it combines a spectacular rock pinnacle with a foreground of blue lakes framed by white birches.

In real life the scene has a predictable effect on hikers. As they drive down the hill north of Chocorua village on NH 16 and see the peak, their immediate reaction is to start for the summit on the nearest trail. This they discover three miles farther north. It's the Piper Trail and many hikers use it because it's available.

I prefer a northern trail from the Kancamagus highway. This route gives you Champney Falls along with the interesting upper ledges of the Piper Trail. Mount Chocorua rewards you with rocky challenges that make up for its deficiency in elevation, which is only 3,475 feet.

To reach the beginning and end of this loop hike, drive on the Kancamagus Highway 11.5 miles from Conway and

NH 16. The Champney Falls Trail starts at the east corner of a large parking area south of the highway. The Bolles Trail, which will be your return route over a little-known pass west of Chocorua, comes out 100 feet farther west beyond this parking area.

The Champney Falls Trail, a graded path, at once crosses a bridge over Twin Brook. You walk through a hardwood forest for ten minutes to Champney Brook. This is a pleasant little stream named for the nineteenth-century White Mountain artist Benjamin Champney. The wide trail stays on the west bank. You gain altitude gradually until you climb more steeply above the brook. At 1¼ miles from your car you reach the Champney Falls bypass trail on your left. The main trail rises straight ahead, and you will return to it after passing the cascades.

Turn left and descend the bypass into the valley, which is a U.S. Forest Service Scenic Area — no camping or fires. At the brook turn upstream to your right. About ¼ mile from the main trail you come to the base of the cascades. You can step across the brook, on the left, to the short canyon where Pitcher Falls, a tributary, pours from a giant spout (if rain has been plentiful). Returning to the bypass you mount stone steps to the right of the cascades. The clear water slides and splashes down smooth chutes. (Stay away from them. The slippery ledges could become a watery ski jump leading to a smashup on the rocks below.) The bypass, a woods trail again, rises to the right and takes you back to the main trail.

A steeper grade now continues up through the forest until you're on a rocky trail high above the brook. You pass an unreliable spring on your right. Switchbacks take you up the steep mountainside and across slanting bedrock. On the left in spruces a cutoff trail branches to Middle Sister Trail, which you soon reach, also on your left. (The Middle Sister Trail crosses over the central summit of a

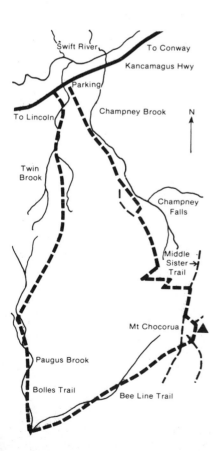

ridge called the Three Sisters and descends to White Ledge Campground on NH 16.)

The Champney Falls Trail swings to the right across a broad ledge well marked with yellow blazes. Ahead over the treetops rises craggy Chocorua. You enter the spruce and fir woods again and come to an elongated hut on posts to your right. It contains a rescue litter for carrying out victims of the summit rocks — and the litter has been used. The Champney Falls Trail ends here three miles from your car. (To the left the Piper Trail drops past a shelter and out to NH 16.)

Turn right onto the Piper Trail. After passing through a little hollow you climb again and pass the Liberty Trail on your right. (The Liberty Trail crosses below the summit and joins coinciding west slope trails, where you'll meet it early in your descent.) The spruces open to bare ledges and cliffs, which extend the remaining half mile to the summit. If a storm threatens this is the place to turn back. Also, in spring and fall Chocorua can be sheathed in dangerous ice and snow.

Yellow blazes mark the way. You climb the first slanting ledge and then angle left with the bulk of the rock on your right. The trail squeezes around a narrow corner. This shelf may trouble you if you're unaccustomed to open air below your left side. (You can retreat to an unmarked westerly route around and over the rock. Rejoin the trail on the south side by keeping left to the base of the narrow corner.)

The yellow blazes and arrows lead you up to the east rocks and to the right until you're on the west side of the peak. Shrubs and plants grow in the scanty soil: labrador tea, three-toothed cinquefoil, mountain cranberry, rhodora, and crowberry.

Climbing below the summit's west

Atop Chocorua

rock face you come to a trail sign at a broken ledge. Here coinciding trails from the south and west join the Piper Trail. (Returning from the summit you'll pick up this route for the next section of your loop hike.)

Turn left up the rock. Steep but simple in dry weather, the final climb is 50 yards up to the crags south of the summit. Turn left for this rock platform where a steel pedestal once supported a steel table remaining from a vanished lookout. The summit is a sky-high perch ten feet square with a lower ledge extending east another twelve feet or so. You are on a natural rock tower.

Directly ahead to the north the great view centers on Mount Washington and the Presidential Range. Mount Carrigain's outline shows the tiny block of its lookout tower. To the west, across the treetops far below, the Sandwich Range extends over Mounts Paugus, Passaconaway, and Whiteface. Farther west Tripyramid and Osceola surround the hidden Waterville Valley. Far to the northwest the Franconia Range cuts the horizon.

Turning southwest you look down to the green meadow at Wonalancet and beyond to Squam Lake and parts of Lake Winnipesaukee. You can face east toward Pleasant Mountain in Maine (it looks like a whale's outline) and then northeast for Carter Dome, Carter Notch, and Mount Wildcat.

According to legend these views were the last to be seen by the Indian Chocorua before he met his death at the hands of a one-time friend, Cornelius Campbell. The Pequawket chief's son had died while staying at Campbell's cabin. Retaliating, Chocorua massacred Campbell's wife and children. Campbell pursued Chocorua to this summit. Before he died the Indian is said to have proclaimed a curse on the white men, beginning doubtless with Campbell. The sickness and death of many cattle followed. Not until shortly before the Civil War was the ailment traced to muriate of lime occurring naturally in the water the cattle drank.

The return hike begins as you retrace your steps down to the junction sign at the broken ledge. Your trail descends to the left. Don't worry that your route into the valley, Bee Line, doesn't show on the sign, which lists Weetamoo Trail and others. Bee Line is down there twenty-five minutes away. (For this return to your car allow four hours. It's 6 miles away and includes 900 feet of vertical rise to the pass on the Bolles Trail.)

So turn left at the sign and make your way down into a corridor through scrub spruce. It takes you to a smooth, open ledge and yellow blazes. Near the bottom, joining from the woods on the right, the Liberty Trail coincides with your descent for about 100 feet to Bee Line on the right. The Liberty Trail bears left across open rock clearly marked with yellow blazes.

Turn right onto Bee Line. You again enter the spruce and fir woods, but soon descend to open rock once more. Arrows there show the right turn above the dropoff, which is dangerous when wet. Keep right and descend where ledges separate and provide holds for feet and hands. You reach the top of a slide that also requires caution. There's gravel on smooth rock, as well as slabs to climb over. Then you are down to woods again.

Evergreens surround you as you head down steeply over roots and stones. About a half hour from the start of Bee Line the trail becomes more level and you're walking in leafy woods. Hobblebush thrives in the valley of the brook on your right. You cross to the west bank and take up an old logging road. After another crossing of the brook you come to the Bolles Trail and Paugus Brook. (Bee Line continues west toward Mount Paugus and a junction with the Old Paugus Trail.)

Turn right, to the north, on the Bolles Trail. At once you cross the tributary you'd been following along Bee Line. The Bolles Trail, a wide old logging road, has an easy upward grade. It briefly takes to the woods on your right before crossing Paugus Brook and rejoining the logging road. You enter the clearing of a former camp, walk through the grass and bushes, and enter the forest again. Bearing left away from Paugus Brook past a seasonal, sandy tributary on your left, the trail traverses a fine growth of white birches that have grown into an old burn. Beyond a rock-strewn gully you begin the steep climb to the pass. This is a constant, thirty-minute test of your legs late in the day.

At the height-of-land in the pass, rocks among the beech woods are burned black, and an occasional stub or stump black with charcoal still stands. After about 250 yards walking beside a rugged, wooded knoll on your left, you begin the descent of the north slope. There a mucky area is the source of Twin Brook. Keep to the left as the trail leads along the accumulating water and down the west bank. The Bolles Trail follows with many crossings (ten, I think) until the ravine opens to the valley. Twin Brook swings away toward the parking area on your right, and at the highway you also turn right for your car.

44

South Twin Mountain

Distance: 11 miles
Walking time: 8 hours
Vertical rise: 3,330 feet
Maps: USGS 7½' South Twin Mountain;
    USGS 7½' Franconia

Which way to look first? That's the problem on this open, 4,926-foot summit. South Twin Mountain, located between the two major ranges of the White Mountains, exposes a great view of both. Actually, South Twin is much closer to the Franconias than to the Presidentials. Mount Lafayette is five miles away to the southwest, Mount Washington, fourteen miles to the northeast.

I think South Twin is best saved for the clear days and blue skies of early October. From the summit rocks you look south over the forested East Branch watershed. The Pemigewasset Wilderness flames no more with the lumberman's forest fires, but annually burns symbolically with the red leaves of swamp maples in the lowlands. The mountainsides display the yellow of birches, the tan of beeches, the orange of sugar maples, and the lemon of poplars.

To reach the trail for this hike, drive on US 3 from Franconia Notch toward Twin Mountain village. Go 7.5 miles from the Tramway in the notch to an intersection known as "Five Corners." It's .2 mile east of the bridge over the Gale River. Several roads branch from US 3. Opposite the road north to Bethlehem, a U.S. Forest Service road begins at a sign for the Gale River Trail.

Turn right, to the southeast, onto this gravel road. Keep left at the fork .7 mile into the woods. After another .7 mile turn right over the Gale River's North Branch. In .2 mile you come to parking at the trail head, on the left.

The Gale River Trail leaves from the northeast corner of the parking area. On an October day, having arrived early, you'll face into the low sun. It shines through branches dropping yellow leaves. They rustle underfoot. The trail winds to an old logging road, crosses a small brook, and then heads into a steady, gradual approach to the North Branch. Meeting this water supply for Littleton, the trail stays on the west bank to a crossing on a footbridge.

The way becomes steeper along the east bank, past clear pools and little cascades. The water is so clear I once took a picture of trout on a gravel bar. The trail is rough in places to the next stream crossing (over stones this time). Then, once again on the west bank, it climbs to another logging road. You follow this easy route to the rocks and earth at the base of two slides. The

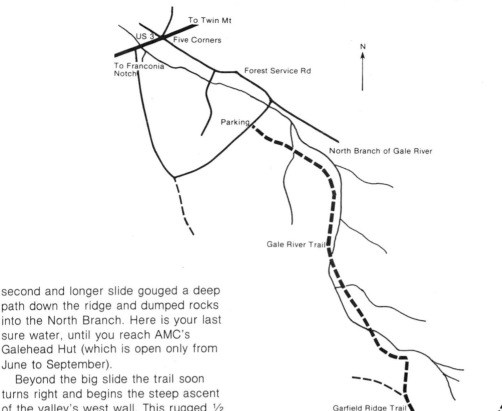

second and longer slide gouged a deep path down the ridge and dumped rocks into the North Branch. Here is your last sure water, until you reach AMC's Galehead Hut (which is open only from June to September).

Beyond the big slide the trail soon turns right and begins the steep ascent of the valley's west wall. This rugged ½ mile may suggest the stamina required of the Galehead hutmen and women who pack in supplies. You can rest in thick evergreens at the end of the Gale River Trail, where it joins the Garfield Ridge Trail.

Then turn left on the Garfield Ridge Trail. (To the right the Garfield Ridge Trail extends 6 miles over Mount Garfield to Mount Lafayette.) You continue in the spruce and fir woods as the trail slabs toward the head of the last valley, descends slightly, and climbs sharply for the last of this ½ mile on the Garfield Ridge Trail.

You pass a flat rock tipped at an angle in the middle of the trail. It's about the area of a kitchen table and knee-high. The gullied trail did not always divide around the rock. Dr. Claud Sharps, D.V.M., a hutman for six summers in the 1930s, told me he used to climb across the rock's surface

knowing, he said, that he would soon make the hut and unload his packboard. (You can see one of those packboards hanging on the wall of AMC's Pinkham Notch Camp. They were made by Roddy Woodward of North Conway. Hutmen are now called "hutboys." There are hutgirls, too. Both carry pack frames of wood and canvas.)

The Garfield Ridge Trail ends just east of the hut at a junction with the Twinway, which will be your hike's final section, on the left, to the summit of South Twin. But first turn right and walk the few yards to the hut.

It perches on a small wooded plateau, elevation 3,800 feet. Built of logs in 1932, now remodeled and shingled, its two porches give you views up a thousand feet of South Twin's spruce-grown dome. The west porch opens to a vista extending twelve miles southward across the Pemigewasset Wilderness to Mount Osceola and Scar Ridge. From the helicopter pad west of the hut you look at nearby Galehead Mountain. On your right, north of Mount Galehead, Mount Garfield shows its summit rock. To the left and also against the sky the Franconias form a jagged horizon.

In season the hut is a busy place. Two bunk rooms, dining room, kitchen, and the summertime crew — usually college students — can accommodate up to thirty-eight guests. Reservations must be made through AMC's Pinkham Notch Camp. Thousands of other hikers pass by, including those trekking the Appalachian Trail, which follows Garfield Ridge Trail and Twinway. In June and September the hut may be open only on a "caretaker basis," meaning no meals or blankets.

The final climb to South Twin begins from the junction of the Garfield Ridge Trail and the Twinway. Keep straight through onto Twinway. You pass a spur trail, on your left, to a lookoff ledge among spruces. The Twinway descends into a little hollow where a pool on your right supplies the hut with water.

Then upward for those thousand final feet of vertical rise. Although the scant mile is not devastating to your legs, you may be glad for a brief pause at an opening in the woods halfway along; you can admire Mount Lafayette, Lincoln, Liberty, and Flume. Climbing on, you notice the spruces getting smaller. When they are only head-high, you emerge on the summit rocks.

Two hundred feet of glacier-scoured ledges and rocks give you the panorama I spoke of earlier. In addition, off to the west on this clear October day you can see into Vermont as far as Mount Mansfield and Jay Peak.

South and east from the summit curves the ridge connecting to Mount Guyot. South of bare and rounded Guyot the horizon is dominated by its neighbor Mount Bond and the pinnacle of West Bond. But looking again eastward along the ridge followed by Twinway you can see the scarred hump of Whitewall Mountain forming the cliffs above Zealand Notch. Evergreens are slowly coming back after the searing forest fire of 1886.

Continuing around to your left you see the horizon outlined by Mounts Willey, Field, and Tom, all connected, and in the distance, Mounts Washington, Jefferson, and more, far more. Mountains too numerous to mention (as old auction notices used to describe "other items").

Let's not forget North Twin. It lives up to its name by being directly north only a mile away, as ravens fly. (Actually they don't fly that straight. They're always looping and sailing in fancy curves.)

If you are on South Twin during a busy weekend such as Columbus Day, you'll have the company of at least forty or fifty people. The summit presents a gala scene in the bright sun as hikers come and go in groups, in couples, in marching files.

Turning to the descent, you find it steep. Now facing into treetops you catch glimpses of boreal chickadees.

From Galehead Hut take the Garfield Ridge Trail back the way you came; turn right onto the Gale River Trail, and so back to your car.

The Presidentials: Southern Peaks

Distance: 12 miles
Walking time: 10½ hours
Vertical rise: 3,600 feet
Maps: USGS 15' Mt. Washington;
　　　USGS 15' Crawford Notch

This hike traverses one of the most spectacular routes in the White Mountains. It starts on the western side of Mount Washington and soon encounters the pools and waterfalls in rugged Ammonoosuc Ravine. It goes up to the AMC Lakes of the Clouds Hut (5,050-foot elevation) under Mount Washington's peak, turns south for four miles above treeline, and passes over Mounts Monroe, Franklin, Eisenhower, and Clinton. Then from the AMC Mizpah Spring Hut it concludes the Southern Peaks with Mount Jackson and provides a great lookoff back the way you've come. Finally it descends to Crawford Notch by the Webster-Jackson Trail.

Two cars are required. Park one off US 302 at the northern end of Crawford Notch, either at the parking area for the Crawford Path or west of Saco Lake near the AMC Crawford Depot information center. You should be there by 6:30 A.M. or earlier.

Perfect weather is an absolute necessity. Dangerous exposure in sudden storms above treeline on the Crawford Path can overcome unwary, overconfident, or unfit hikers.

In the second car drive north a few yards past the Crawford Path parking area and turn right onto the Mount Clin-

ton Road. Drive 4 miles to the Base Road. Turn right and drive 1 mile to hiker parking for Ammonoosuc Ravine Trail on the right.

This is the place to check equipment. Every hiker in the party should have sturdy clothing including boots, wool socks, shirt, pants, warm caps, gloves, and parkas. In your rucksack carry lunch, extra food, water, and survival gear to preserve life in a subarctic environment. That's what you'll be climbing to.

This new parking in the woods restricts views that formerly, at the Base Station and trailhead, made you take stock of your fitness and equipment. Those rocky heights are still in place although you start without their enticement--or warning.

From the east side of the parking, take the Ammonoosuc Ravine Trail. It leads up an easy slope into a forest of spruce, fir, and hardwoods. You cross Franklin Brook after ¼ mile. The trail leads southeast away from the noises of engines, and descends to the former route from the Base Station. Here, ¾ mile from your car, keep right and begin this worn old path along the Ammonoosuc River.

The Ammonoosuc River Trail is a popular approach to Mount Washington; yet it gives the effect of lifting you into a lonely, forested, mountain fastness. An hour's hiking steadily upward through spruce and fir woods along the brook brings you to the first waterfall and pool. The trail crosses the stream.

Log steps hold the path on the mountainside. After ten or fifteen minutes of serious climbing, watch for a side trail, on the right, and a sign "Gorge" on a tree. Here you will find a lookoff up the ravine toward two rock sluices shooting white cascades at you.

Returning to your climb, you find other spectacular falls and views as the trail emerges into smaller evergreens. The brook divides. In rock crevices an alpine plant, mountain avens, blooms during July like an exotic buttercup. You are climbing into a gloriously barren world of sky and rock bathed in either mist or bright sunlight. Cairns lead upward. The gray cone on your left is Mount Washington and, beyond it, Mount Jefferson. The ravine falls away behind you, clear to the diminutive base station.

Three hours and three miles from the parking, at the col between Mount Washington and Mount Monroe, the AMC Lakes of the Clouds Hut is a shingled haven and, for you, the point of no return. Examine the peaks for signs of storm. Go inside and check the weather report posted on the bulletin board.

Unless clear weather blesses you, go back down the Ammonoosuc Trail and try again another day. Aside from the exposure dangers of chilling rain, blinding clouds, sleet, or snow, the scenic values and joys are wasted during a slogging trek above treeline. If the skies are fair and the forecast stable, take the Crawford Path south.

It leads toward craggy Mount Monroe. *Please* stay on the path. The alpine mosses, lichens, and plants such as diapensia, mountain cranberry, sandwort, three-toothed cinquefoil, crowberry, bilberry, and Labrador tea are rare and delicately balanced in their survival arrangements. Boots damage them easily and irreparably. Follow the trail's cairns.

Approaching Mount Monroe the Crawford Path bears left around the base. To reach the summit turn right onto the Mount Monroe loop. The vertical rise from the hut to Mount Monroe is only 335 feet. You'll be rewarded by a tremendous view of the Lakes of the Clouds, the upper Crawford Path, tiny hikers, and Mount Washington's buildings and broadcasting towers.

The Mount Monroe Loop continues to the western summit, from which it descends south to rejoin the Crawford Path.

The crossing of Mount Franklin, 5,004 feet, is a nearly level section above the cliffs that drop into Oakes Gulf and the misnamed Dry River. Beyond the gulf, extending south from the minor peak called Boott Spur, a long ridge includes Mount Isolation and Mount Davis.

Along the Crawford Path here are relics of the past. Two pairs of iron rods, imbedded in a ledge and bent to hold oak timbers years ago, gave hoofholds to horses scrambling up and down the rock. In the mid-1800s visitors rode horses up the Crawford Path. Winslow Homer painted and sketched along here.

Not far beyond these rods, as you descend rapidly and, before approaching Mount Eisenhower's barren dome, you arrive at a ledge for lunching and sunning. A spring trickles across the path. Sandwiches and a brief rest prepare you for the Mount Eisenhower Loop over the summit, ¼ mile farther along.

As at Mount Monroe, the Crawford

Cog Railway

Ammonoosuc River

Base Road   Parking

Ammonoosuc
Ravine Trail

To Bretton Woods

Mt Clinton Rd

Lakes-of-the-Clouds Hut

Edmands Path

Mt Monroe

Mt Eisenhower

N

To Bretton
Woods

Crawford Path

Crawford Path

Mt Clinton

Crawford
House
Site

Webster Cliff Trail

Saco Lake

Mizpah Hut

Parking

Webster-Jackson
Trail

US 302

Crawford
Notch

Mt Jackson

To Bartlett

Path swings east around the base of
Mount Eisenhower from a junction near
a little pool named Red Pond. (Here
also is an escape route in bad weather:
the Edmands Path, which runs 3 miles
down through sheltering woods to the
Mount Clinton Road.) The Mount
Eisenhower Loop, to the right, takes you
up to another exhilarating summit of
4,761 feet. A giant cairn protects you
from the steady west wind while you appreciate the miraculous adaptation of
alpine plants around you.

The Mount Eisenhower Loop returns
via cairns south to the Crawford Path in
scrub spruce. This is your last mile on
the famous old trail. Mount Clinton is
ahead. At its northern base turn left onto the Webster Cliff Trail. (The less har-
dy members of the party may continue
on the Crawford Path the easy 3 miles
to US 302 just north of Saco Lake and
your car.)

Mount Clinton (known officially as
Mount Pierce in honor of New Hampshire's only United States president) is
a flattened, spruce-grown, 4,312-foot
knob 150 yards beyond the Crawford
Path junction. Your route drops away
steeply for the ¾ mile along the
Webster Cliff Trail to the AMC Mizpah
Spring Hut, the club's newest (1965).
Situated in a clearing at 3,800 feet, it's
near the unfailing spring, now boxed in

with concrete and a cover but still pouring from a pipe its cold, sweet water.

Keep to the right of the hut; don't linger, for the afternoon is waning. From Mizpah Cutoff's beginning turn left. Take up again the Webster Cliff Trail. You climb through spruce woods and walk along sawed half logs laid on stringers resting on the boggy ground. You come out of the woods into a mountain meadow before the trail rises to the open ledges and Mount Jackson's summit at 4,052 feet.

There's a magnificent exposure of the valleys and a ridges extending north to Mount Washington. The Southern Peaks are all displayed.

Continuing from the summit to the southwest past scrub spruce, you come to a junction with the Mount Jackson section of the Webster-Jackson Trail. This is your return to Crawford Notch. (The Webster Cliff Trail descends

Southern Peaks from Mount Hale

southeast.) On a northerly bearing, from which you may look across Crawford Notch to Mount Willey, keep to the cairns and paint marks until the trail descends the rocks to your left and dips into spruce woods. Then the way is clear, past Tisdale Spring on your right.

Forested for the remainder of the 2¾ miles to US 302, the Webster-Jackson Trail crosses several streams and passes a junction where a south fork leads to Mount Webster. Keep to the right. Bugle Cliff, reached by a short spur trail, on the left, is a worthwhile lookoff into the notch from the thick forest.

The same cannot be said of the next spur trail, on the left, to Elephant Head. The view is anticlimatic. Walk on down to a woods road. Turn left to busy US 302, then turn right past Saco Lake to your car.

The highway is a *real* anticlimax after the everlasting mountains. But isn't it good for rolling along on those four wheels while you rest your legs?

Gordon Pond

Backpacking Hikes

Gordon Pond

Overnight
Distance: 8½ miles
Walking time: 8 hours
Vertical rise: 2,300 feet
Maps: USGS 7½' Lincoln;
USGS 7½' Mt. Moosilauke

The last time I hiked to Gordon Pond I saw a red fox carrying a limp hare in her jaws. Evidently she was taking dinner to her cubs. This rare sight appeared along one of the old logging roads that make backpacking so pleasant in the middle sections of the Gordon Pond Trail. The pond, 2,560 feet above sea level at the north end of an interesting, swampy plateau, lies under Mount Wolf and below a rugged section of the Appalachian Trail, the southerly 3½ miles of the Kinsman Ridge Trail.

Two cars are necessary unless you hitchhike. Park one at the Appalachian Trail's crossing of NH 112 in Kinsman Notch. With the second car, drive 4½ miles east to the Forest Service sign for the Gordon Pond Trail. It's on the north side of NH 112 opposite Govoni's Restaurant, which is 2 miles from North Woodstock's traffic lights. Park on the highway shoulder west of the restaurant to avoid the area reserved for customers.

The Gordon Pond Trail — 4½ miles to the pond with 1,800 feet of climbing — first follows a driveway between cottages uphill and then 100 yards farther in the woods makes a right turn onto the old logging railroad grade last used in October 1916. Although unmarked, this wide grade is unmistakable. After ¼ mile it passes under a power line and crosses a development road.

Continuing along the railroad grade, past a house among the trees to the right, the trail begins a wide curve to the left, northward from its easterly bearing, and is joined by a branch road coming in from the right along Gordon Pond Brook. Signs inform you that the brook is the water supply for Woodstock. The fine for pollution is $500. No swimming or bathing.

Midway in this sweeping northerly curve past dark hemlocks among the beeches and birches, you pass a service road, on the right, leading across the brook to the power line. Keep left. Rose-breasted grosbeaks sing in the sunny treetops. Soon you cross under the high cables through open brush and return to deep woods again. A few minutes later you swing right to the bank of Gordon Pond Brook. Smooth stones take the place of a washed-out bridge.

The angle of incline increases. You have left the railroad grade behind and

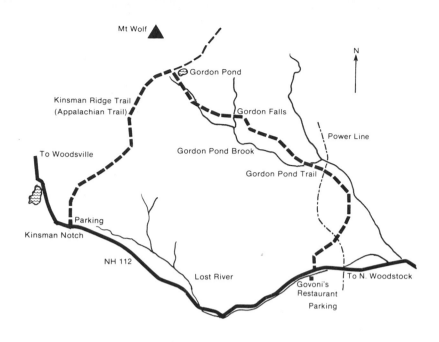

Mt Wolf

Gordon Pond

Kinsman Ridge Trail
(Appalachian Trail)

Gordon Falls

N

Power Line

To Woodsville

Gordon Pond Brook

Gordon Pond Trail

Parking

Kinsman Notch

NH 112

Lost River

Govoni's
Restaurant
Parking

To N. Woodstock

are on a logging road dug out of the slope years ago for sleds. It takes you high above the brook on your left. Here's where I saw the red fox.

The trail, making for the head of the valley, turns left across Gordon Pond Brook, and begins the sharp ascent to Gordon Falls, which is on a tributary brook. During times of high water, you can hear the splashing as you reach the spruce woods. Gordon Falls is really a cascade down a cleft in solid rock. The V-shaped trough, after rains, contains sparkling water for fifty feet until it escapes as white spray at the rocks in the pool.

Above the falls the brook becomes darker, or seems to, where the trail crosses to the west bank. Beware of a crude pole bridge and slippery ledges. They are directly above the cascade.

The brook flows through boggy, spruce-shadowed flats. You cross this tributary again as it dwindles away west, and you walk into birches high above Gordon Pond Brook on your right.

One shallow crossing of this stream puts it on your left for the final fifteen minutes to the pond.

To reach these three or four acres of clear water and the view of Mount Wolf, continue straight beyond the trail's turn left across the outlet. Several paths wind among dead trees drowned from a higher water level when beavers constructed a dam to plug the outlet and raised the water to protect their big lodge on the north shore. Beavers no longer occupy the pond.

A rock-and-sand beach is an ideal lunch spot. Breezes blow across the water. You face the forest on Mount Wolf. It sweeps to the steep east face — a blend of spruce green and birch green. To the right of Mount Wolf a low gap rises slightly to a wooded ridge. As in all impounded water habitats, birds enliven the scene.

But remember this is Woodstock's water supply. Locate your campsite far back from the shore on the ridge to the right. The inlet to the pond, clear and cool, opposite your lunch-time beach, curves from the woods through an open meadow that was once flooded before the outlet's neglected beaver dam opened.

For the next day's hike, retrace the route past the pond and among the stubs along the south shore to the Gordon Pond Trail where it turns west across the outlet. Fifteen minutes up through spruce woods takes you to the junction with the Kinsman Ridge Trail, which along here is part of the Appalachian Trail. Turn left, to the south. (The Kinsman Ridge Trail extends north for 13 difficult miles over two summits of Mount Kinsman and over Cannon Mountain, with assorted minor summits in between, to Franconia Notch Parkway near the Tramway.)

At once the Kinsman Ridge Trail leads south down into a hollow and then up and over the first of six wooded knolls, which present you with something like 500 feet of climbing in the next 3 miles. This is no former logging road. The trail is rough and trampled into mud in many places. It twists over ledges, rocks, and roots. Along this evergreen ridge the boggy hollows beside the trail are often green with carpets of sphagnum moss, showing how bogs look when not churned by hikers' boots. Now you walk mostly on sawed balsam fir logs which the trail crews have flattened with chain saws. In places the old wet trail has been bypassed. Lookoff rocks eastward occasionally show the Pemigewasset River's East Branch valley all the way to Mount Carrigain.

You may think that the uphill is over when you leave the evergreens and descend into leafy woods. Ahead, however, are two more knolls to climb over. At the first you climb past a rock face deeply spread with a tapestry of green moss. The last knoll grows from a deep hollow and descends as abruptly.

Kinsman Notch seems much lower than when you parked your car there the previous day. Your descent to it is partly on rock steps laid slab over slab down to the asphalt of NH 112 and the noise of cars. They appear first through the treetops. The trail is so steep that you see gleaming hoods and tops but no wheels.

The Kinsman Ridge Trail ends at NH 112. Now you know one rough section of the route between Maine and Georgia.

Cheney Brook

Two nights
Distance: 3 miles
Walking time: 3 hours
Vertical rise: 580 feet
Map: USGS 7½' Mt. Osceola

To spend nights camped near a boggy beaver pond is to place yourself in direct relationship to the life of the wilds. Bogs are active both day and night but their effect in darkness is downright other-worldly. Your eyes, the principle sense in daytime, are replaced at night by your ears. Instead of seeing a bullfrog's green arc into the water you hear his deep basso sound out as night descends. Birds sing twilight notes and go to sleep. The chorus is taken over by trilling tree frogs. Maybe an owl hoots from a dead stub in the bog. Or a sudden puff of wind above your tent rubs a tree branch along a smaller tree and you immediately think that a bobcat has screeched. You turn on your flashlight and play its beam up into the branches. No bobcat, of course. But on the ground the light may reveal a deer mouse hopping lightly away or it may catch the twitching ears of a curious hare. If you move too quickly you'll startle him and he'll demonstrate his alarm by a thump with his hind foot.

There are other more mysterious sounds. Is that splashing caused by a coon foraging after frogs? Or a beaver mending his dam? A mink swimming after trout? A deer feeding on water plants? At Cheney Brook the slow sloshing of heavy hoofs and body might be a moose. The last time I was there we followed moose tracks up the steep bank beside this tributary to Pine Brook.

A primary problem in bog camping is finding a high and dry campsite. Another is insect life: mosquitoes, blackflies, deer flies. At Cheney Brook the campsite can be on rising ground north of the bog and far enough away to avoid some of the insects gathered along the water. But a bug-proof tent is a must.

Another problem in bog camping is water of another kind — drinking water. As a kid I got sick on bog water, although it appeared clear enough. At Cheney Brook's boggy beaver pond there's a source of good water in the spring holes that contribute to the western inlet. I regret to say they are densely protected by tangles of withe rod and mountain holly.

Because there is no trail to the bog on Cheney Brook, you'll be more than ever dependent on a map. Travel by streams eliminates the need for a compass, but of course you'll have one with you if you should need it. The map to use is USGS Mount Osceola Quadrangle.

First Day

Kancamagus Highway to Cheney Brook's beaver pond

Distance: 1½ miles
Walking time: 1¾ hours
Vertical rise: 580 feet

The Kancamagus Highway is the access road to this bushwhack. Drive east from Lincoln. At 4.7 miles you cross the Pemigewasset River's East Branch and pass the Wilderness Trail on your left. Another 3 miles brings you to a parking area on your right bordering Hancock Branch. A sign identifies it as "Otter Rocks Rest Area, White Mountain National Forest."

Now you'll be wise to check the water level in Hancock Branch. Walk down through the wooded rest area. Across the stream you'll see Pine Brook cascading in from spruces below the smooth ledges called Otter Rocks. Your aim is to reach the east bank of Pine Brook. Crossing at low water can be merely careful long steps across the channels in the ledges, or stepping from rock to rock below Pine Brook, where the stream is broader but usually shallow. For medium-high water a solution is to drive another .7 mile to the East Pond Trail and follow it until you hear the sound of Pine Brook on your right; then cut down through the woods. In time of real freshets, I suggest you backpack elsewhere.

Following up Pine Brook on its east bank, you'll pass bivouac sites no longer allowed along the Kancamagus Highway, where the Forest Service's Restricted Use Area extends ¼ mile from either side.

Your progress through the spruces,

both around the trunks of large trees and through the young and clinging thickets, must be made slowly to avoid aggravation of body and nerves. At times you move faster in open woods. Generally, the route should be maintained forty or fifty yards from Pine Brook, bypassing some of the steep bank.

But keep returning to the brook and watching for the tributary running down from the west. That's Cheney Brook. The obvious remedy for missing it is to cross to the west bank of Pine Brook, but the walking there is more difficult. You can be alerted by your watch if you've noted the time you started. I use up most of an hour contesting the way with hobblebush and admiring the falls and pools under magnificent pines, which now and then tower above the spruces.

Another indication that you should cross to Cheney Brook may be voices of hikers on the East Pond Trail, to the left, which follows an old railroad grade here and approaches Pine Brook.

Watch for a change in the brook bed from stones and boulders to ledges and sluices of yellowish rock. Then look for a big sheltering rock on the left, whose overhang could protect you from a rainstorm. It's the size of a small garage. Keep past it and climb a ten-foot bank. From the edge of Pine Brook you look for a large boulder on the west side. About fifty yards upstream and also on the west side is another imposing boulder. Cheney Brook joins Pine Brook between these. A massive log partially blocks the flow from Cheney Brook. Some years, depending on debris washed down in the spring, Cheney Brook may split into three trickles to join Pine Brook. The tributary shows the dark cast of water that has been impounded behind a beaver dam.

Cross here and head up the north

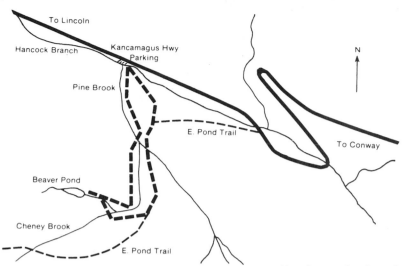

To Lincoln

Hancock Branch

Kancamagus Hwy
Parking

Pine Brook

E. Pond Trail

To Conway

N

Beaver Pond

Cheney Brook

E. Pond Trail

bank; it's easier than the south side. Almost at once you may notice an ancient windfall with exposed roots that suggest a giant tarantula, according to one of my companions who dislikes spiders. A few minutes later, as you approach the steeper climb, you come to a great prostrate pine which was sawed from its stump and abandoned by early loggers. Why?, one wonders. It looks sound enough, without the hollow that sometimes explains left-behind logs.

Now you begin the steep climb. Spruce woods are mixed with maple and beech on which you can haul yourself up. Slow and steady does it. Keep above the brook and its ravine. A half hour should bring you to the little plateau and bog on the side of the mountain. You no longer look *up* to daylight, but ahead at it. Mountain? Yes, you're climbing the approach to Scar Ridge and Mount Osceola's West Peak.

Swing right, along the north side of the bog, before you reach the nearly impenetrable bushes growing from wet sphagnum moss where several outlets drain from the beaver pond. This curve should take you across an old logging road through damp, semiopen ground.

Here's a safe place for a campfire. I suggest you drop your pack and look around for a tent site. There's a little bank and a higher location for the tent, although a growth of spruce and fir obstructed by many fallen young trees adds nothing to the ease of selecting a space. Persevere, however, and note how the crisscross tangle demonstrates an interesting example of natural forest thinning.

Your next move should be to acquaint yourself with the pond and bog before you pitch your tent. (You may find a better place for it.) Go west a short distance through the spruce woods. The bog is on your left. Then you see the old beaver dam and an acre or so of water, along with its dead stubs, water brush, sunlight, and bird life. A breeze usually comes from up on Scar Ridge across the pond. Over there, a dominant summit, Mount Osceola, tops the range that includes its East and West Peaks.

For drinking water, keep on through the woods to the west end of the pond. Or you may walk along the shore, wet with sphagnum moss and thick with leatherleaf to your waist. Mountain holly grows higher at the end of the pond and hides the little spring holes. You'll need a cup to fill your kettle.

After you've made camp there's probably not enough time for further exploration and enjoyment of the pond. Soon after the light fades on Osceola, night descends with its frog chorus. If *you* quiet down you begin to hear the animal splashings at the water's edge. High on the ridge night winds rush through the trees. In the pond an alert beaver may get a sniff of your campfire — or of you — and slap his tail to warn of the intrusion. The sound is like that of a canoe paddle brought down flat and hard.

Second Day

Spent at the pond

Next day can be devoted to the bog and the pond, to pastimes like admiring the tree swallows nesting in the dead stubs. Study of the bog shows many of the unusual plants that thrive in the cold, acid habitat created by sphagnum moss. Leatherleaf, the most common of the water bushes, provides a nest place a foot above the pond for red-winged blackbirds. Pitcher plant grows near a hummock under a great pine stub that hulks over tiny twinflowers. (Before visiting Cheney Brook a reading about bogs is rewarding. The *Audubon Nature Encyclopedia* contains a good, concise account.)

The second night you'll feel more at home. Your camp arrangements will come naturally. Familiarity with a woodland environment makes living there easier and pleasanter.

Third Day

Cheney Brook's beaver pond to Kancamagus Highway

Distance: 1½ miles
Walking time: 1¼ hours
Vertical rise: 5 feet

Return on the third day need not be back down the brook. You may cross the bog outlet, where the various seepages and drainings join to pitch over the steep slope you climbed. On the south side bear left downstream. Watch carefully for a faint trail east along the bank. There are ancient blazes grown almost over with bark. The trail seems to be kept open (if that's the adjective) by rabbits, deer, and moose, more than by men. It follows a logging road grown to young trees.You should look ahead for that indefinable appearance of lesser growth along the suggestion of a sled road's eight-foot width. It leads away from the brook in an easterly direction to the East Pond Trail.

Turn left on the East Pond Trail. You soon descend to Pine Brook and a crossing that puts you on the old railroad grade. If you've had enough bushwhacking, follow the grade out to the Kancamagus Highway. But remember there'll be ¾ mile (west) of asphalt marching, gravel shoulder crunching, and zooming cars. I'd rather cut through the woods when I hear the traffic noise and pick up Pine Brook, to the left and west, for the return to the car.

Smarts Mountain

Overnight
Distance: 14 miles
Walking time: 11 hours
Vertical rise: 2,860 feet
Map: USGS 7½' Smarts Mountain

This was the second mountain I climbed as a boy, after nearby Mount Cube. I'm a former Orford resident, so I naturally recommend the approach from that side, where the north slope rises from a valley of deserted farms known as Quinttown. But this loop hike will show you both sides of the mountain and return you to Quinttown along a woods road that once linked Orford and Lyme.

The Appalachian Trail (AT) swings over the mountain, so you'll be following its rectangular white blazes as well as the Dartmouth Outing Club's (DOC's) black and orange blazes. The DOC maintains the Appalachian Trail in this area.

Note: Trail relocation for summer 1988 may alter one or two of the links in this loop backpack. Before undertaking it check with the Dartmouth Outing Club, Robinson Hall, Hanover, N.H.

Although only 3,240 feet in elevation, Smarts Mountain provides excellent views from its now disused steel fire tower. You look up and down the Connecticut River valley and over into Vermont. Northern mountains extend all the way to the Presidential Range.

I advise a tent for your night on the summit. The empty DOC cabin and the DOC's open log shelter may be crowded. There's a spring northeast of the cabin, ¼ mile from the summit. Don't drink from the pool water 150 yards west of the tower. It's near the south-branching spur trail to the DOC shelter and is polluted. When I was a kid we drank there and it was a clear, mossy bowl of cold water, but times have changed.

The unimproved Quinttown road leaves NH 25A 1.5 miles east of Orford-ville. It climbs southeast 2 miles along the north bank of Jacob's Brook. This narrow, gravel-dirt road has hardly changed since horse and buggy days. There's no village at Quinttown now and the old farmland — some of it first cleared by Benjamin Quint who served during the Revolution as a sailor for John Paul Jones—has largely returned to forest. What once was Quinttown is now just a deserted intersection. Your mountain, Smarts, appears as a long ridge to the southeast culminating in a wooded summit and the fire tower.

At this intersection turn right, cross the bridge over Jacob's Brook, and drive about 200 yards to a T-shaped fork in the road. (You are facing the site of the former schoolhouse.) Turn right over the bridge spanning Mousley Brook. The road twists up steeply through a hairpin turn, to the left, and continues uphill through woods. Then it levels through open fields and pastures with a great view of the mountain from the only open land left in Quinttown.

The possibly passable road ends about ¾ mile from the Quinttown corners. Don't drive down the logging road to Mousley Brook. Park far enough off the road to let a logging truck by. Even after two hundred years of logging in Quinttown there still are trees to be hauled out.

The Smarts Mountain Trail is marked with AT and DOC signs. (Refer to the USGS Smarts Mountain quad.) Below your parked car you descend the logging road and soon cross the brook. At a fork beyond bear left. (The right fork is the route of the DOC Quinttown Trail and will be the final section of your return route.)

For most of the first 2 miles the trail ascends gradually. This is an early farm road, as indicated by old apple trees and stone walls. Except for the small camps on the left, only a cellar hole and the walls remain as vestiges of human habitation and agriculture. These woods were open fields grown with brush when I first explored them. About 20 minutes from your car, keep straight at a left fork.

Leaving this area for higher valley forests along Mousley Brook, you pass on your left several yarding and loading spaces used for logs taken from the eastern ridges. This operation apparently does not disturb the black bears, who probably now outnumber the people in Quinttown. During the time of ripe shadbush berries, about the first week in August, bears leave tracks in the mud of the trail and break off branches from the small trees in greedy attempts to reach the berries. Don't worry about meeting a bear. He'll be long gone before you come anywhere near him . . . except perhaps after rain, when the combination of quiet footing and a wind in your face might prevent your sounds and scent from preceding you.

The logging road keeps to the north of Mousley Brook as far as the base of the mountain. There it crosses to the south bank and begins the real ascent for the 1¼ miles to the summit. The climb alternates between short, steep sections and older, contour-following sled roads, which the trail uses. Among tall beeches and maples you pass stumps of huge yellow birches.

Finally you are climbing on a mountain trail over rocks and roots. White birches give way to spruce and fir. Leveling, the trail swings right. It passes on split logs over a boggy area draining from Murphy Spring, which you pass on

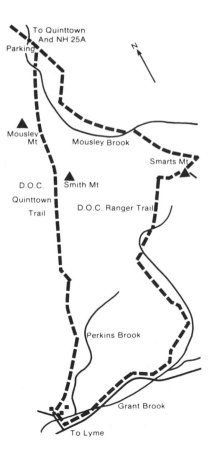

Smarts Mountain from Dame Hill

your left. Boreal chickadees have a liking for these evergreen woods. You climb out of the spruces into a small clearing around the former fire lookout's cabin, now maintained by the D.O.C. You can see ahead to the summit and the tower partially hidden by spruces.

From the unused tower you look across the Connecticut River valley to Vermont where you see Mount Ascutney southward, Killington and Pico southwest, and Camel's Hump and Mount Mansfield northwest. Turning to New Hampshire you look north and east over nearby Mount Cube's quartzite-frosted summit. Then there are Mounts Carr, Stinson, Kineo, Moosilauke, the Franconia Range, and finally

Washington.

I always look northwest into Orford. I select a domed hill called Sunday Mountain. (I once thought it so named because it was shaped like the scoop of ice cream in a sundae.) Then I pick out the house on its shoulder, called Dame Hill, where I once lived for a year.

To the south from the tower, under the steep brow of the mountain, Reservoir Pond gleams. Cummins Pond lies to the east along the Lyme-Dorchester road. To the southwest there's the Dartmouth Skiway's open slopes and lifts near Holt's Ledge, and farther south, Moose Mountain in Hanover.

Much of this southern view can be seen from the DOC shelter. It's west from the tower a short distance along the Ranger Trail, at the end of a spur trail branching left. An open log structure, it is exposed to high winds. Cables hold the roof on. I prefer a tent back in the spruces.

After shouldering your pack the next morning, set out west down the Ranger Trail. It crosses through grassy openings. Then it descends steeply in a northerly direction. An abrupt turn south leads you to a section of switchbacks from which you look into the valley and across into Vermont. Bushes about head-high with crimson branches are red osier dogwood. You'll see cairns in the woods. They once supported telephone poles for the line to the summit. That was after the forest fire, when no trees remained to which the wire could be attached.

Continuing steadily downward you cross an upper branch of Grant Brook and soon cross it again to the west bank near a shingled shed formerly used as a garage by the fire warden. You are 1½ miles from the summit, with 2 miles of eroded jeep track ahead. As you walk along the west bank of the brook, the water sparkles in the sun or runs darkly in the shade of spruces and hemlocks. Deer or moose tracks sometimes indent the sandy mud of the jeep road.

The Ranger Trail ends near a bridge on the Lyme-Dorchester road. Like the Quinttown road it is a relic of the past. Turn right and walk west along it for 1⅓ miles to a branch road, on the right. A DOC sign to your left on a tree informs you that the Quinttown Trail is 5.1 miles long. Turn right onto this side road, walk past a house, and continue ¼ mile to a fork just beyond a bridge over Grant Brook. You face a house in the "vee" of the fork. Turn right and walk about 150 yards past a mobile home with wooden additions; it's on your right. Then the auto road ends.

The Quinttown Trail begins along a woods road marked with orange and black blazes straight ahead. Soon you cross a stream on an old stone culvert. The trail and woods road bear left uphill and are well marked with blazes.

The grade is a steady upward slant as you reach Perkins Brook and follow its west bank. You curve up much more steeply over a 1,700-foot hill named Lambert Ridge. The general direction of the trail is northeast. You cross a tributary of Smith Mountain Brook and in less than ½ mile cross the main brook itself. Climbing up again for the last time, to about the 1,820-foot elevation, you slab along the northwest shoulder of Smith Mountain and dip past Mousley Mountain on the left, to the west. You can relax. You're heading into Quinttown and the end of your loop 1 mile away.

Redrock Brook

Two nights
Distance: 19 miles
Walking time: 12 hours
Vertical rise: 2,200 feet
Maps: USGS 7½' Mt. Osceola; USGS 7½'
     South Twin Mountain

During this backpack to a nameless pond in a glacial cirque without trails, the approach is along one of the most heavily used routes in the White Mountains. From peopled trails and campsites you take off into solitude. The Wilderness Trail north of the Kancamagus Highway leads to the Franconia Brook Trail. On both you can pass a multitude of hikers, but when you turn into the bushes from Franconia Brook Trail you're on your own in a different world, although the USGS South Twin Mountain quadrangle map will help.

This valley leading to the upper cirque is a bushwhacker's dream of variety. It includes most of the forest growths you'll encounter in the mountains. Leafy bushes and open hardwoods change to nearly impenetrable scrub spruce. The cirque's headwall rises toward Mount Guyot and South Twin. To the southeast the cirque is enclosed by the ridge curving from Mount Bond and culminating in the crags known as West Bond.

I wonder how many hikers on West Bond notice the little pond. An old friend, Doc Sharps, pointed it out to me. He had heard of it years before as a hutman at Galehead Hut, when West

Bond had no trail. Of course we had to go see the pond.

First Day

Kancamagus Highway to Redrock Brook

Distance: 7¼ miles
Walking time: 4 hours
Vertical rise: 1,035 feet

Drive the Kancamagus Highway 4.7 miles east from Lincoln. Just after the bridge over the Pemigewasset River's East Branch there is a parking area on the left for the Wilderness Trail. Before you cross the footbridge from the north corner of the parking area, you should read the notices and rules on the U.S. Forest Service bulletin board. The Wilderness Trail passes through a Restricted Use Area.

Now settle your shoulders into your pack straps and enjoy the steady slogging walk along the railroad grade built by a cantankerous old lumber baron, John Everell Henry. He rose from barefoot boy to millionaire and also made sure his men built a good grade for the fifty miles of his logging railroad, which he extended all through the East Branch valley as he cut down the virgin spruce, starting in 1892.

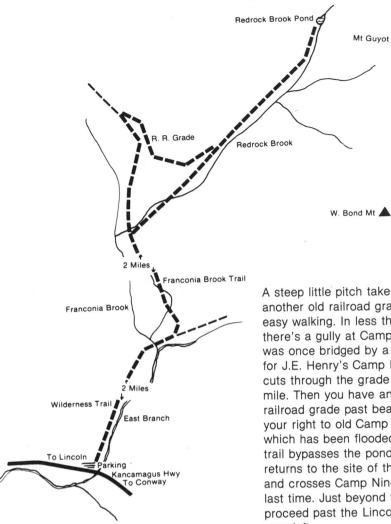

Redrock Brook Pond

Mt Guyot ▲

R. R. Grade

Redrock Brook

N

W. Bond Mt ▲

2 Miles

Franconia Brook Trail

Franconia Brook

2 Miles

Wilderness Trail

East Branch

To Lincoln

Parking
Kancamagus Hwy
To Conway

A steep little pitch takes you up to another old railroad grade. Here's more easy walking. In less than ½ mile there's a gully at Camp Nine Brook. It was once bridged by a trestle. Named for J.E. Henry's Camp Nine, it again cuts through the grade and trail in ¼ mile. Then you have another ½ mile of railroad grade past beaver ponds on your right to old Camp Nine clearing, which has been flooded by beavers. The trail bypasses the pond to the right, but returns to the site of the lumber camp and crosses Camp Nine Brook for the last time. Just beyond the footbridge, proceed past the Lincoln Brook Trail on your left.

You regain the railroad grade and continue on it for a mile to where Hellgate Brook breaks through with a choice of stones for crossing. Another mile brings you to Redrock Brook. This makes a total of 3 miles from the Wilderness Trail. Here you have two approaches to the valley.

A dyed-in-the-wool bushwhacker may push east up beside the brook. If, however, you've never carried a pack frame in a thicket before, you'll learn that pack frames were never designed for bushwhacking. When my friend Doc

The Wilderness Trail follows the East Branch. After 2¾ miles you come to the spruce woods around the Franconia Brook Shelter and sixteen tent platforms on your left. Keep straight across the footbridge. You are entering the Pemigewasset Wilderness, long so-known, but since 1984 a Federal Wilderness Area under Wilderness Act protection.

About 50 yards beyond the bridge turn left onto the Franconia Brook Trail.

and I once found ourselves tangled there in the puckerbrush, we agreed that we should have carried our old Duluth packs. These square canvas bags, with shoulder straps and head-band or tumpline, ride on your butt the way a woodsman's pack ought to, out of reach of overhead branches. With a pack frame you'll just have to look for taller holes in the bushes.

You may avoid much of the brush by searching ahead along the Franconia Brook Trail and finding a railroad spur leading into the valley toward the site of Camp Fourteen. It will take you far up the brook, for about a mile of extra walking. For me the extra distance is worthwhile, and I've included it in the first day's mileage.

To find the spur, cross Redrock Brook to your right, where a short track leads to stepping stones and a return to the Franconia Brook Trail on the same grade you've been walking. Check your watch and march straight ahead steadily for fifteen minutes, then begin to look on your right for the spur joining at an angle ahead. It's visible as a little slanting bank for about a hundred feet along the grade you're on, but it must be watched for. It joins at a wide left turn; if you pass that left curve and come to a small brook, you've gone too far.

This Camp Fourteen spur takes you back almost exactly in the direction you've come, slanting up a grade dug from the mountainside. You make your way among a few young spruces and deciduous saplings such as white birch and yellow birch. You see depressions where the ties once supported rails, and there are two cuts through ledge. Then the trail bears left on a curve as it levels and approaches the high bank above Redrock Brook.

About ¾ hour from the Franconia Brook Trail you come to the end of the grade, which seems to vanish into the steep bank and open hardwoods. Down to the right there's a large island in the brook. Here you turn to your left and climb up for fifty feet to an old logging road. It follows the slope's contour until it deteriorates, after about fifteen minutes, into a rough trail. A distant view of mountains opens through the trees surrounding the glacial cirque you'll climb into the next day. Below you to the right are flats and openings for your tent. It's best to camp here, for beyond this the mountainsides close in so abruptly that you'll find no level, smooth space for a tent until you climb into the cirque.

Depending on the season and the rainfall, you may discover at the brook only a dry bed of boulders above a gusher coming from the south bank. My theory is that a landslide buried Redrock Brook, and though spring freshets later opened the present course for high-water flow, in summer the water is accommodated by an underground passage that reappears as a gushing spring on the south bank.

What might have caused the land-slide? Perhaps you have seen on the island or beside the brook various parts of stoves, barrel hoops, sled runners, or other hardware. Lumberjacks for J.E. Henry lived in a camp and chopped down the spruce forest in this area. But a fire finished it. In August of 1907, the valley of Franconia Brook and its tributary valleys went up in flames. More than 25,000 acres of slash — stumps, logs, branches, and tops — caught fire, probably from a lightning strike on the side of Owl's Head. Along this great whale-backed ridge between Franconia Brook and Lincoln Brook the fire blazed out of control. It was a freaky holocaust. Windy days drove it back and forth. It created its own rushing drafts as it swept eastward up

Mount Bond and Mount Guyot, west up Mount Lafayette, and north to Garfield's summit.

Now the valley and mountainsides are green again. The scorched earth renewed itself and was preserved because the Society for the Protection of New Hampshire Forests and other conservationists pushed the 1911 Weeks Bill through Congress. The law created national forests to protect the watersheds of navigable rivers, and the White Mountain National Forest came into being.

Second Day

Redrock Brook to pond

Distance: 2¼ miles
Walking time: 2¼ hours
Vertical rise: 1,155 feet

In the morning, if you hesitate to carry all your gear into the cirque, you may wish to leave your present campsite set up. If so, carry a small pack containing lunch, a warm sweater or shirt, a parka, and emergency equipment, as you would for a day hike. This will eliminate the pack frame which might catch on bushes and scrub evergreens. If the day has turned wet, you'll welcome a pitched tent and dry firewood when you return.

But if you *must* spend a night in the cirque, pack up and obliterate your campsite. Climb back to the old logging road and take up the rough trail where, perhaps, a landslide filled the dug grade. It's a steep slope, and as you climb — or even crawl — you find yourself clinging to spruces. About ¾ hour from your campsite you arrive at a fork in the brook (or brook bed, if the season has been dry). Rocks lie scattered about in the woods nearby.

Take to the woods between the forks. In spite of appearances on the USGS map, you cannot assume that either fork will lead to the pond. Although the northwest branch leads in the direction, the climb is difficult and confusing. Besides, scrambling up brookbeds is dangerous. I advise the woods route, and I've used both. So proceed into the woods on a compass bearing of sixty degrees east of magnetic north.

There's some steep climbing just after you leave the fork, then easier slopes open under handsome white birches and luxuriant ferns. Farther along you begin to climb again into thick spruce/fir growth mixed with twisted birch and mountain ash. This is the dropoff from the basin ahead, and is typical of glacial cirques. As you fight your way through the branches, you'll see the outline of Mount Guyot and the slides of the real headwall.

The pond lies in the northwest area of the cirque. You'll step through dense evergreens into a wide swale. Indian poke and tall grasses sprout from the shore beside the shallow water. Directly below the headwall along the pond's northwest shore, a rockslide merges with the water. The few trees are dwarf spruce and fir. Beside you, deep down in the cirque, the dark water somehow shines from the light in the sky. Barren Mount Guyot is overpowering. The isolation seems aeons old. The pond, because of its location, exposure, and 3,350-foot elevation, is set in alpine surroundings among plants such as Labrador tea and mountain cranberry.

Yet myrtle warblers seem to delight in this cold climate, where the little birds, now designated yellow-rumped warblers, dart after flying insects emerging from the pond.

The pond's seclusion can be broken from the sky by a jet plane leaving its white trail and following thunder. But you don't see the hikers beyond the headwall: hikers striding along a busy trail, Twinway, between AMC's

Spruce tree and sheep laurel

Galehead Hut and Zealand Falls Hut.

If you have backpacked into the cirque instead of planning to return to your first night's campsite, retreat down into the woods where spruces protect you from the sudden storms that seem to shake the mountains with real thunder. Unlike the jets that pass in moments, the storms sometimes rumble around and around for half the night. The rain drums on the tent, and the brook rises until in the morning it has become a splashing cascade down the headwall.

Third Day

Pond to Kancamagus Highway

Distance: 9½ miles

Walking time: 5¾ hours
Vertical rise: 10 feet

Probably you know from experience or hearsay that travel in treeline evergreen scrub is either impossible or pure hell. Therefore, don't try to climb out of the cirque; return the way you came.

Watch for the "spring" gushing from the south bank, and for the island a little farther along. From here you descend a few yards and pick up the railroad grade. Follow it out to the Franconia Brook Trail, where you turn left. I'll bet that you meet some hikers before long, and many more on the Wilderness Trail. They seek their "backpacking" experience along a beaten path. You are allowed a certain smugness.

Wild River
Time allowed: 5 days, 4 nights
Distance: 21¼ miles
Walking time: 17½ hours
Vertical rise: 5,310 feet
Maps: USGS 7½' Wild River;
      USGS 15' North Conway
      USGS 7½' Carter Dome

The forested Wild River valley extends southwest from the Maine border to Carter Dome. The river is well named. In the 1890s it specialized in washing away the grade and bridges of the Wild River Railroad. Begun in 1891 by the Wild River Lumber Company, the railroad eventually transported logs from far up the valley out to Hastings, Maine. This now vanished lumber town has grown to woods but still shows on maps. From Hasting's sawmills the railroad carried lumber to Gilead, Maine, and the Grand Trunk Railroad, running from Portland to Montreal.

The Wild River Railroad crews were tough. For twelve years they kept the trains going despite the washouts. The line was also noted for runaway trains that hurtled down the steep grades and for one boiler explosion. But the camp-fire of trout fishermen did what the river and its valley couldn't do. Logging ended with the disastrous forest fire of 1903.

Nine years later the remaining forest and the devastated land, known as Bean's Purchase and comprising about 34,000 acres, became one of the first three properties to be bought by the federal government for the White Mountain National Forest.

The first day of this backpack, and a short climb, place you for the night on the south ridge of the Wild River valley. The second day you climb over two rocky peaks and descend to make camp near the Wild River. The third night you spend beside the bogs and beaver ponds at the source of the river. On the fourth day the high point of the backpack at 4,843 feet, Carter Dome, shows you both the Wild River valley and the Presidential Range to the west. After the fourth night, camped at a tributary on the north ridge, you descend to the river once more and complete the loop.

First Day

Wild River Campground to
Blue Brook Shelter

Distance: 2¼ miles
Walking time: 2 hours
Vertical rise: 580 feet

Your first day's hike is on the Basin Trail to Blue Brook Shelter. This is an ideal beginning for a backpack. It's a woods trail and provides just enough distance and effort on a backpack's first day, which often shrinks to an afternoon or less for actual hiking. Late companions, loading the car, driving, and last minute stops always seem to accompany the beginning of a week-long outing like this.

The Wild River Campground is the jumping off place for this backpack. The U.S. Forest Service maintains eleven campsites on the river's south bank 5¾ wooded miles from NH 113 at the end of the gravel Wild River Road. The turn west from NH 113 is north of Evans Notch and 3 miles south of Gilead, Maine. The junction where you turn shows on maps as Hastings, Maine— that former lumber town.

At this corner you'll notice a bronze plaque on a boulder. Shaded now by pines, it commemorates the completion of the Evans Notch Road (NH 113) in 1936 by the Civilian Conservation Corps. Here you turn west onto the Wild River Road to the campground.

Before long you drive back into New Hampshire. The road follows the route of the Wild River Railroad with the river northwest to your right. It ends in the campground's parking area from which the Basin Trail and the Wild River Trail enter the woods. (You'll return on the Wild River Trail.)

The Basin Trail begins as a crushed stone path leading south up to a former railroad spur. It passes campsites and proceeds into deeper woods. The trail crosses wet ground on a plank walkway. Your boots plunk along until you're on solid ground again and are ascending beside Blue Brook to a crossing at pools and cascades. The trail curves right to follow the stream. Cliffs form the opposite bank and at their base the rock slants into the clear water, through which you see a pale band bisecting the smooth ledge.

Now comes a section of trail whose easy steepness stretches your leg muscles. Big yellow birches give you shade and beeches are joined by increasing growths of spruce and fir. You climb upward to a fork in the trail. Turn right for Blue Brook Shelter. It's ¼ mile away and you reach it by slabbing around the slope. (The Basin Trail leads ahead ¼ mile to Rim Junction, which you'll learn about the next day.)

The shelter, built of logs and stained brown, faces a good fireplace and grill. The water supply is Blue Brook, which you reach by a short path north from the shelter. The stream glides down a nearly vertical ledge. The shelter's popularity may cause you to seek a tent site off in the woods.

The trail through the clearing is the Black Angel Trail. (The Black Angel Trail to the west climbs over the next ridge and then descends to the Wild River Trail at Spider Bridge and continues up Carter Dome. It will be your descent route from the Dome on the fourth and fifth days.)

Second Day

Blue Brook Shelter to Mount Meader, Eagle Crag, and Wild River

Distance: 6 miles
Walking time: 5 hours
Vertical rise: 1,800 feet

In the morning the first destination is Rim Junction. Take the Black Angel Trail uphill from the shelter. An easy pace will best prepare you for scaling the summits south of Rim Junction. During the first twenty minutes on this trail eager anticipation often conflicts with a protesting body.

About ½ mile from the shelter open hardwoods surround Rim Junction. You're on the col between Royce Mountain to your left and Mount Meader to your right. Five trails intersect here and the Black Angel Trail ends. These five prongs at the junction warrant careful study of trail signs and your map.

Turn right, to the south, from Rim Junction onto the Basin Rim Trail to Mount Meader.

The Basin Rim Trail leads down through spruces and across ledges, which open to wide views east into the basin, a perfect little glacial cirque. You can look beyond the basin to the Cold River valley along the Maine-New Hampshire boundary. Behind you to the northeast are the cliffs of West Royce Mountain, East Royce Mountain, and Evans Notch. Ahead Mount Meader looms more and more rugged as you approach along the rim of the basin.

Formidable little Mount Meader! Well, formidable enough for ordinary folks. There's a rock face where I, with three companions, took off packs and handed them up to the agile leader. At another vertical pitch we scrambled among spruce roots and rotten rock, wondering which set of boot scrapings led to the next paint blaze. We chose correctly and the blaze finally appeared. The trail wasn't really obscure; it just reflected the various choices of individual hikers.

The trail does level out for a bit through open woods that shade thriving hobblebushes. Then you climb steeply again into spruces along the very edge of the Basin. Views to the east are toward Speckled Mountain in Maine, identified by its long ridge and fire tower. The woods close in again and you come to a seasonal brook. Beyond it begins the final stiff climb of a half hour to Mount Meader's ledges. There you reach a good lunch lookoff, although not the true summit. The green valley of Cold River spreads out its deltalike meadows and forests from the crags of Evans Notch. Away to the north the summits are in the Mahoosuc Range.

The Basin Rim Trail ends among scrub spruce and open rock at a junction near these lookoff ledges. From the junction turn right onto the Meader Ridge Trail heading for Eagle Crag. (To the left (southeast) the Mount Meader Trail descends to NH 113 near North Chatham.)

The Meader Ridge Trail takes you to the true summit, 2,783 feet. It's in the woods and you could easily walk over it without noticing. This is 933 feet above the col that initiated the Mount Meader ascent. You may wonder at the sweat and puffing it caused.

The Meader Ridge Trail, winding up and down, passes some east lookoffs and a spur trail to a western vantage point. You descend in spruces to a rocky ravine and brook. Keep left across the brook and up a ledge and knoll. You pass along a narrow ridge where the trees are so sparse you can see the Carter Range off to the west.

Next you climb to a minor summit only to step down again so you can climb once more, this time to treeline. Eagle Crag rises above you, 3,060 feet high.

As you emerge on Eagle Crag you first look to North Baldface's barren bulk and peak. Like South Baldface, it was burned over in the 1903 forest fire. You look at it across a glacial cirque. On the mountain's east shoulder a curiously contorted rock formation shows the unimaginable pressures that formed North Baldface. Turning from this toward the west you see into the Wild River valley and beyond to the Carter Range, the Dome (appropriately named), and Mount Washington.

The Meader Ridge Trail continues a short distance across ledges marked by cairns to a junction and its end at the Baldface Circle Trail. Your route to the Wild River and to your night's tent site is Eagle Link, branching west off the ridge.

Turn right onto Eagle Link. It may seem tedious after those exhilarating

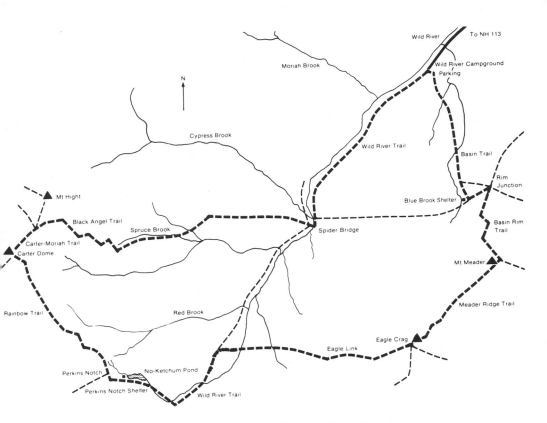

Map labels: To NH 113, Wild River, Moriah Brook, Wild River Campground, Parking, N, Cypress Brook, Wild River Trail, Basin Trail, Rim Junction, Mt Hight, Black Angel Trail, Spruce Brook, Blue Brook Shelter, Spider Bridge, Basin Rim Trail, Carter-Moriah Trail, Carter Dome, Mt Meader, Rainbow Trail, Red Brook, Meader Ridge Trail, Eagle Crag, Eagle Link, Perkins Notch, No-Ketchum Pond, Perkins Notch Shelter, Wild River Trail

views. It's a boggy trail at first as it leads into the spruces. It's also a rough trail. At least it's downhill. Then you climb briefly over a shoulder of North Baldface. The lower section of the trail improves when it begins to follow an old logging road. You walk down through a white birch forest. The first crossing of an unnamed brook's tributary and the brook itself should not deceive you into assuming you've reached Wild River. You still have about ¾ mile to go. The trail descends by an easy grade.

The trail turns left and presents you with Wild River, which you'll recognize by its dark bed of mossy rocks. There is no bridge. When you have made your way across, pause and consider camping for the night. Eagle Link Trail continues ahead about ¼ mile to its junction with

the Wild River Trail. That's for tomorrow.

The likeliest site for your tent in this area is to the left upstream. If you follow indications of an old trail and explore off it to the right and toward a low ridge you can locate a flat, dry spot in open woods, but keep it at least 200 feet away from the stream. Even that far, the soothing sound of the current should suggest early sleep after this day of good exercise and fresh air.

Third Day

Eagle Link campsite to Perkins Notch Shelter

Distance: 2 miles
Walking time: 1¾ hours
Vertical rise: 550 feet

This is an easy day. Use it for settling into the forest, for rest, for observation near the source of the Wild River, for exploration.

After striking camp return downstream to Eagle Link Trail at the crossing of Wild River. Turn left and proceed to the junction with the Wild River Trail. You are 5 miles southwest of the Wild River Campground. A left turn puts you onto the Wild River Trail as it follows up the stream, out of sight of the water. The woods have grown up since the 1903 fire. About ¾ mile of walking brings you to a crossing of the river. Then curving south with level going, the trail swings uphill and westerly as it passes, on the left, the East Branch Trail, which leads to the East Branch of the Saco River.

Another crossing to the north bank heads you abruptly northwest, where the stream comes down through a gap in the ridge. One final crossing to the south bank precedes your arrival at the bog country that distinguishes Perkins Notch. Glimpses through the spruce and fir show you the east slopes of Carter Dome. You are above and walking parallel to No-Ketchum Pond. The name must refer to one of those days when bog-channel trout refuse to take either bait or flies.

The pond existed in 1880 and it was then long and narrow as at present. Appalachian Mountain Club hikers exploring Perkins Notch estimated its length at five hundred feet and its width at sixty feet. I'd say it's narrower now due to growth of the quaking bog that borders it. This floating mass of roots and humus contributed by sphagnum moss, pitcher plant, leatherleaf, and sheep laurel (to mention only a few) extends back from the water's edge several yards to solid though wet ground.

This long channel and source of the Wild River gathers the flowage from another ½ mile of bog to the west.

Beavers in No-Ketchum Pond were noted as early as 1927. (Of course beavers were here earlier before they were trapped out.) This date coincides with the return of beavers to New Hampshire from the north after their virtual extinction in the state. They add greatly to the interest of this bog country, which preserves its wild and desolate expanse all the way to the foot of Carter Dome and to the shoulder that ends at Perkins Notch. There are no cliffs or crags in this notch; it's an imperceptible height-of-land.

Just beyond No-Ketchum Pond you come to the Perkins Notch Shelter. It is built of peeled spruce logs, which formerly rose as trees in front of the old cabin used by beaver trappers in the winter and by trout fishermen in the summer. The logs, stained brown inside and out, partially close the front under the overhanging eaves. There's a stone fireplace and grate. The board bunk accommodates six people. Here again as at Blue Brook you may want to camp outside the shelter.

Water can be a problem. A spring, southeast of the shelter, is unreliable, and probably polluted. Northwest of the shelter a cleared swath opens toward the bog and Carter Dome, offering a wet approach to the channel of Wild River. The water is very organic, and I avoid it except for boiling to wash dishes. Instead, carrying water bottles or canteens, and a cup, walk about fifty yards up the Wild River Trail west beyond the shelter and clearing. Turn right into open woods. There's a trace of a path, but if you don't locate it, keep to the slope's contour until you see, after a few minutes, a line of dark evergreens. The trees hide a spring draining through sphagnum moss to the bog.

If you arrive early at the shelter, with the afternoon ahead of you, take advantage of a unique opportunity to study the plants, animals, and birds of the bog. (Also, take plenty of fly dope.) The bog country extends north to Red Brook, whose upper reaches are a series of beaver ponds plentifully supplied by water draining from Carter Dome. Bog-trotting enthusiasts and avid trout fishermen can make their way to Red Brook by crossing a beaver dam between No-Ketchum Pond and the next pond west and heading north with compass and map. The distance in only about ¾ mile, but very difficult. For a landmark beyond Red Brook, watch for a rocky knob bared by the forest fire—if you can see over the bushes in which you thrash around most of the way.

Fourth Day

Perkins Notch Shelter to Carter Dome and Spruce Brook on the Black Angel Trail

Distance: 6 miles
Walking time: 5½ hours
Vertical rise: 2,340 feet

The Wild River Trail continues to be your route for the first section of today's hike. It leads southwest from the shelter and up the ridge a short distance. Then you slab around the contour above the bog. This forest trail goes for ¾ mile before a brief descent to Perkins Notch at 2,586 feet. On your left water flows into the Saco River system; on your right, into the Androscoggin. The actual dividing point, the height-of-land, lies to your right at a patch of sphagnum moss.

Here the Wild River Trail bears left, to the west. You take the Rainbow Trail, on the right, for Carter Dome.

You may find no trail sign. Bears have thoroughly clawed the fir trees to which the sign has been attached. Sometimes the sign lies in splinters on the ground. You'll recognize the Rainbow Trail, however, by its northerly direction and by its soon-to-be encountered sharp ascent. After a steady northwest climb from leafy forest into evergreens, the trail bends more to the west and then heads north for the approach to the top of the barren shoulder at 4,274 feet. The views prove that you've been climbing. You're almost 1,700 feet above Perkins Notch. The Wild River valley extends eastward beyond the bogs, a wide forest rising left to massive Carter Dome, and on the right, to Mount Meader and the Baldfaces.

Now the trail takes you down 75 feet in elevation to the spruce/fir col before you start up the Dome's rounded green cap. You're climbing again for the final ¾ mile of the total 2½ miles from Perkins Notch.

There's one last shoulder and the scrub spruces open to the summit's clearing, which is rapidly returning to evergreen woods. Mount Washington pierces the horizon ahead of you beyond the Wildcat Range. The ledge around you once supported a fire tower where a lookout was killed by lightning. The elevation is 4,832 feet.

The Rainbow Trail ends at the Dome's summit. Now you take the Carter-Moriah Trail in a northeasterly direction. (Left, to the southwest, the Carter-Moriah Trail descends to its terminus in Carter Notch near the AMC hut.)

About ½ mile from the Dome you come to the Black Angel Trail, on the right. Here, at 4,600 feet, begins your route back to the Wild River valley. You may feel disappointed about the views from the Dome. If so, you can think about leaving your pack in the spruces for a side trip to Mount Hight. This

Footbridge over Wild River

rocky pinnacle is one of the great lookoffs in the mountains. It rises ¾ mile farther along the Carter-Moriah Trail.

Time and energy will be factors in your decision. The round trip will take an hour—not counting the time you spend on the crags of Mount Hight. You'll need at least another 1½ hours to reach the night's camping place along Spruce Brook down the Black Angel Trail. You'll need enough energy for an extra 200 feet of vertical rise, because Mount Hight peaks beyond a col. If you decide in favor of Mount Hight, avoid the left-forking Carter Dome Trail down to Zeta Pass. Stay on the Carter-Moriah Trail and return on it.

As for the Black Angel Trail, the walk down it is at first gradual for ¼ mile, dropping only about 100 feet in elevation. You have then a rugged climb downward. Certain sections are rough with ledges and roots. The trail angles down more gradually, and at times seepage wets the trail into mucky walking. The spruces become taller and older.

Before the 1903 fire, loggers never reached this high forest and somehow neither did the flames. So you walk through aisles of spruces, with mossy carpets on either side and wood sorrel spreading across alternating shadow and sunlight. Axe and saw *almost* did slash the virgin evergreens. A camp existed on the middle fork of Spruce Brook. Lumberjacks had cut sled roads up the slopes from the spur track off the main railroad.

The trail enters birch woods. They change to spruces, and back to birches again. The trail jogs left off a long ridge, bears right, and then left again as it heads down abruptly. You descend to the upper branch of Spruce Brook, which trickles between steep, moss-grown rocks. Although camping is possible here the forest floor pitches down at a sharp angle. Across the brook 50 yards and up to the left there's a site for one small tent.

You're better off to descend for another half hour to the middle fork of Spruce Brook. This mossy stream crosses the trail through ground more nearly level. You may choose your campsite, limited only by the U.S. Forest Service rule that requires you to be two hundred feet from water and trails.

Maybe you should think of the careless fishermen who neglected their campfire and started the 1903 blaze. Campfires, as Ben Franklin (I think) said of freedom, require eternal vigilance. The holocaust caused by the fishermen ironically killed thousands of trout, as ashes fell into the streams. Years passed before trout once more appeared in any numbers.

Fifth Day

Spruce Brook campsite to Wild River Campground

Distance: 5 miles
Walking time: 3¼ hours
Vertical rise: 40 feet

Walking the Black Angel Trail in the morning—after erasing all signs of your camp—can be a letdown after the mountaintops and the strange environment of Perkins Notch; yet it's pleasant and relaxing for the 2¼ miles to the Wild River Trail. You soon cross the lower fork of Spruce Brook (usually dry) and descend to damp areas where one or two springs cross the trail.

Then you are off the ridges and enter the valley. A backpack's end, like its start, should be simple. You swing along easily, your pack lightened by all the good meals you've eaten out of it. Watch on your left for a curiously grown yellow birch. The big stump that nursed the one-time seedling has rotted away and left a massive tangle of roots five feet off the ground but supporting the main trunk. You walk on through more woods of young deciduous trees.

The Black Angel Trail joins the Wild River Trail as the latter comes downstream on the old railroad grade. Turn left onto the Wild River Trail. The Black Angel Trail coincides with it for a short distance until after the river crossing on Spider Bridge. Just before this footbridge the Highwater Trail leaves left for its route on the north bank to Hastings and NH 113.

Your dryshod crossing of the river takes you in a few yards to Black Angel's branching, on the right, toward Blue Brook Shelter. The Wild River Trail, which you follow, is now a wide way above blue pools and sparkling rapids. Beyond a mudslide grown to bushes the trail becomes a jeep road at an earth roadblock.

There are more lovely pools in the river. They are tempting on a hot day if you have time for a dip before lunch. From Spider Bridge to your car is only 2¾ miles, and requires only 1¾ hours to reach it. The rushing river and the calm pools, hot sun to dry you, a good lunch from your quickie supplies—what a way to end a backpack.

Guidebooks from The Countryman Press and Backcountry Publications

Written for people of all ages and experience, these popular and carefully prepared books feature detailed trail and tour directions, notes on points of interest and natural phenomena, maps and photographs.

Walks and Rambles Series

Walks and Rambles on the Delmarva
  Peninsula $8.95
Walks and Rambles in Westchester (NY)
  and Fairfield (CT) Counties $7.95
Walks and Rambles in Rhode Island
  $8.95

Biking Series

25 Bicycle Tours in New Jersey $8.95
25 Bicycle Tours on Delmarva $8.95
25 Bicycle Tours in Maine $8.95
25 Bicycle Tours in Vermont $7.95
25 Bicycle Tours in New Hampshire
  $6.95
20 Bicycle Tours in the Finger Lakes
  $7.95
20 Bicycle Tours in and around New
  York City $6.95
25 Bicycle Tours in Eastern Pennsylvania
  $7.95

Canoeing Series

Canoe Camping Vermont and New
  Hampshire Rivers $6.95
Canoeing Central New York $9.95
Canoeing Massachusetts, Rhode Island
  and Connecticut $7.95

Hiking Series

50 Hikes in New Jersey $10.95
50 Hikes in the Adirondacks $9.95
50 Hikes in Central New York $8.95
50 Hikes in the Hudson Valley $9.95
50 Hikes in Central Pennsylvania $9.95
50 Hikes in Eastern Pennsylvania $9.95
50 Hikes in Western Pennsylvania $9.95
50 Hikes in Maine $8.95
50 Hikes in Vermont, 3rd edition $9.95

50 Hikes in Massachusetts $9.95
50 Hikes in Connecticut $8.95
50 Hikes in West Virginia $9.95
50 Hikes in the White Mountains $9.95
50 More Hikes in New Hampshire $9.95

Adirondack Series

Discover the Southern Adirondacks $9.95
Discover the South Central Adirondacks
  $8.95
Discover the Southeastern Adirondacks
  $8.95
Discover the Central Adirondacks $8.95
Discover the Southwestern Adirondacks
  $9.95
Discover the Northeastern Adirondacks
  $9.95
Discover the Eastern Adirondacks $9.95
Discover the West Central Adirondacks
  $13.95

Ski-Touring Series

25 Ski Tours in Central New York $7.95
25 Ski Tours in Maine $5.95
25 Ski Tours in the Adirondacks $5.95
25 Ski Tours in the White Mountains
  (revised edition available fall 1988)

Other Guides

State Parks and Campgrounds in North-
  ern New York $9.95
The Other Massachusetts: An Explorer's
  Guide $12.95
Maine: An Explorer's Guide $13.95
Vermont: An Explorer's Guide, 3rd edition
  $14.95
New England's Special Places $10.95
New York's Special Places $12.95

The above titles are available at bookstores and at certain sporting goods stores or may be ordered directly from the publisher. For complete descriptions of these and other guides, write: The Countryman Press, P.O. Box 175, Woodstock, VT 05091.